CW00801151

THE TREE *of* LIFE

THE TREE *of* LIFE

FROM EDEN TO ETERNITY

EDITED BY
JOHN W. WELCH AND DONALD W. PARRY

PROVO, UTAH

SALT LAKE CITY, UTAH

Visit us at DeseretBook.com

Library of Congress Cataloging-in-Publication Data

ISBN: 978-1-60908-674-9
[CIP information on file]

Printed in the United States of America
Publishers Printing, Salt Lake City, UT

10 9 8 7 6 5 4 3 2 1

Contents

Illustrations

Figures

Color Plates

Introduction

The tree of life is a richly evocative symbol seen in sacred art, architecture, houses of worship, and literature throughout the ages and around the world. With its roots reaching downward and its branches extending upward, this tree signifies a mystical, primordial linkage between heaven and earth that is the locus of manifold blessings reflective of a culture's deepest yearnings—be it unity with the gods, wisdom, wholeness, renewal, peace, or everlasting life in God's presence. The tree's precious fruit carries similar connotations, such as the pure love of God, eternal joy, and triumphal entry into the eternal realms. Perhaps no other religious motif is so rich in allegorical potential or so accommodating of spiritual meanings for so many religious traditions.

The concept of the sacred tree is widely diffused. Rooted in the world's oldest cultures, tree imagery crops up in the myths, symbols, and rites of ancient and modern religious institutions throughout the world. It is found among the Assyrians, Babylonians, and others of the Levant (greater Eastern Mediterranean area); various groups in Egypt, sub-Saharan Africa, and Greece; the Aborigines and Warramunga of Australia; the Coorgs and Khasiyas of India; and several other Asian religions (especially Buddhism, Taoism, and Hinduism). Furthermore, sacred trees serve to characterize North American native religions, including the Kwakiutl of the Pacific, the Karok in the Northwest, and the Seneca of the Northeast, as well as the Haida, the Salish, the Kiowa, the Zuni, the Navaho, the Mandan, the Lakota, and the Oglala Sioux. South American and Mesoamerican sacred tree mythologies are also prominent and include the Uyurucares of Bolivia, the Maya, the Aztecs, and the Warao.

The tree of life is prominent in the Old Testament, most strikingly in Genesis, with its reverberations extending figuratively into Sinai's burning bush and Aaron's budding rod, and literarily into passages in scriptural books such as Proverbs, Psalms, and Isaiah. In the New Testament, the tree is a significant part of the temple in heaven: "And he shewed me a pure river of water of life, clear as crystal, proceeding out of the throne of God and of the Lamb. In the midst of the street of it, and on either side of the river, was there the tree of life, which bare twelve manner of fruits, and yielded her fruit every month: and the leaves of the tree were for the healing of the nations" (Revelation 22:1–2).

Ancient Jewish lore features the tree of life, as do the teachings of Jewish Kabbalah, which seeks to explore ontological relationships and the mysterious Creator. The tree also burgeons in Christian tradition, especially in medieval art and architecture, where the cross and the tree of life are intertwined.

The deep religious meaning of the tree of life intrigues Latter-day Saints as much as, if not more than, any other people on earth. Latter-day Saints encounter this image in the Old and New Testaments, the books of Abraham and Moses, and the Book of Mormon, where it figures prominently in the visions of Lehi (1 Nephi 8) and Nephi (1 Nephi 11; 15:22–36), in the words of Alma the Younger (Alma 12:21–26; 32:40–42), and elsewhere.

Indeed, it is difficult to conceive of a more vibrant, enduring, accommodating, powerful, and universally meaningful religious symbol than the tree of life. In Jewish thought and Christian art, architecture, and literature, this potent symbol embraces many religious ideas and represents an elusive and curious complexity regarding its historical interpretation and development. Beyond its roles in the Judeo-Christian tradition, questions regarding its development only multiply, making this subject all the more fitting as an object for scholarly inquiry in the field of religious studies.

The contents of this volume explore many of the roots and branches of this persistent and expansive religious symbol. These published papers derive from the Tree of Life Symposium held at Brigham Young University on September 28–29, 2006. Sponsored by the Neal A. Maxwell Institute for Religious Scholarship, this event brought together specialists from various disciplines and institutions who shared the fruits of their research on the religious, cultural, scriptural, and artistic aspects of the tree of life motif.

Our survey begins in the Garden of Eden with Donald Parry's analysis of Hebrew meanings underlying the description in Genesis 3:24 of the path leading to the tree of life. Parry discusses this path in terms of sacred space, identifies the critical "gestures of approach" needed to safely reach the tree of life, and thereby likens temple ritual to a return to Eden and its temple. Andrew Skinner finds tree of life symbolism persisting throughout Israelite and Jewish history while it acquired added meanings, such as wisdom and wholeness, in keeping with prominent religious issues of the day. By decoding complex theological symbolism in biblical and extrabiblical texts, Margaret Barker shares valuable insights on the role of Wisdom in the Garden of Eden and in the temple tradition that passed into Christianity.

From there our survey moves into the New Testament and early Christian traditions, where the cross of Christ's death is transformed into the verdant, victorious tree of resurrection and life. John Welch pursues the tree of life as a vibrant, multifaceted metaphor in early Christian textual and artistic traditions; and Wilfred Griggs focuses on the Gospel of John as fertile ground for the development of several images derived from the tree of life motif. Picking up where the fruitful boughs spread abroad to the New World is Charles Swift, who finds in Lehi's vision of the tree of life the perfect archetype for conveying the Book of Mormon's theme of coming unto Christ. Also in the New World, we find the World Tree of the ancient Maya cosmically connecting the earth with the heavens as Allen Christenson describes how that tree was the ultimate expression of how the Maya could escape the harrowing of the underworld by tapping the tree's sacred power. Jaime Lara discusses the tree of life in the Catholic religious imagination and how the friars used it in the New World to establish common ground for converting the Aztecs to Christianity.

Back in the Old World, the tree of life is seen to have influenced Islamic thought as well through its appearance in the Qurʾan. Daniel Peterson explains significant differences between the biblical and Qurʾanic versions of the Garden of Eden narrative and its mystical trees. John Lundquist finds the Cosmic Tree in the far reaches of Southeast Asia, where it is an integral part of the "primordial landscape" that is reproduced architecturally and artistically in ancient temple traditions, such as in images of the Buddha attaining enlightenment under the sacred Bodhi tree.

Our survey ends with a multicultural array of depictions of the tree of life in Mormon art around the world. Richard Oman shows how Latter-day Saints everywhere have expressed their yearnings and testimonies as they celebrate the joyous thought of pressing forward through the mists of adversity and finally partaking of the sweet and delicious fruit of this tree in the garden of God's love and abundance.

The pages of this volume turn over only a few of the many leaves of this vast subject. Much earlier work has been done on this topic, as is evidenced by the bibliography assembled by Daniel McKinlay at the end of this book, and much work remains to be done to further illuminate the origins and development of this nourishing and nurturing symbol.

We especially thank Andrew S. Skinner and M. Gerald Bradford, former executive director and associate executive director of the Maxwell Institute, respectively, for their overall support and encouragement, and S. Kent Brown, former director of FARMS, for organizing the symposium. We owe a deep debt of thanks to Don L. Brugger for masterfully editing the manuscripts and overseeing the production process, Alison V. P. Coutts for skillfully typesetting this volume and for producing the indexes, Jacob D. Rawlins for creatively laying out its pages, Paula W. Hicken for obtaining permission for all the images, and Shirley Ricks, Charlotte Wood, Rebekah Atkin, and Julie Davis for essential help with proofreading, copyediting, and indexing.

John W. Welch
Donald W. Parry

The Cherubim, the Flaming Sword, the Path, and the Tree of Life

Donald W. Parry

Before Adam and Eve were driven out of the garden, they experienced an environment that had qualities and symbols that were later reflected in the design and functions of the Mosaic tabernacle and the Jerusalem temple.[1] This experience included God's presence and open communication with them (e.g., Genesis 2:16–18; 3:8–19). However, after Adam and Eve partook of the tree of knowledge of good and evil (Genesis 2–3), the Lord expelled them from the temple-like setting of the Garden of Eden. According to Genesis 3:24, the Lord God "drove out the man." The English translation correctly represents the Hebrew root *grsh*, for Adam and Eve were not simply invited to leave the garden but were forcibly thrust out of it.[2] In fact, the same Hebrew root is used in the Mosaic law with the meaning "to divorce" (Leviticus 21:7, 14; 22:13). God drove them out of the garden in the same manner that a married couple divorces—they are physically separated from each other. To punctuate this expulsion and to

---

1. According to Gordon J. Wenham, *Word Biblical Commentary, Genesis 1–15* (Waco, TX: Word Books, 1987), 1:86, in the Garden of Eden "there is a remarkable concentration of powerful symbols that can be interpreted in the light of later sanctuary design." These symbols collectively combine "to suggest that the garden of Eden was a type of archetypal sanctuary." See also Gordon J. Wenham, "Sanctuary Symbolism in the Garden of Eden Story," in *Proceedings of the Ninth World Congress of Jewish Studies* (Jerusalem: World Union of Jewish Studies/Jerusalem Academic Press, 1986), 19–25; and Donald W. Parry, "Garden of Eden: Prototype Sanctuary," in *Temples of the Ancient World: Ritual and Symbolism*, ed. Donald W. Parry (Salt Lake City: Deseret Book and FARMS, 1994), 126–51.

2. Francis Brown, S. R. Driver, and Charles A. Briggs, *A Hebrew and English Lexicon of the Old Testament*, trans. Edward Robinson (Oxford: Clarendon Press, 1977), 176.

protect against the couple's return, God set up a number of safeguards to guard the path to the tree of life.

This chapter considers the *path* leading to the tree of life in the context of Genesis 3:24: the Lord God "drove out the man; and he stationed at the east of the garden of Eden cherubim, and a flaming, revolving sword, to guard the path of the tree of life." In order to establish the proper setting for the path, I will examine the expressions in this verse that relate to protecting that path, with a particular focus on the words *garden; cherubim; flaming, revolving sword;* and *to guard.* Then I will address the question of the nature of the path. Lastly, I will investigate how one may journey past the cherubim and the flaming, revolving sword in order to return to the path leading to the tree of life.

Part 1: Protecting the Path

The Lord "stationed at the east of the garden of Eden . . ."[3] The Hebrew root underlying the English *stationed* (*shkn*) ties the Garden of Eden to sacred space because it is the same root used to refer to the Mosaic tabernacle (*mshkn*) and the temple of Jerusalem.[4] According to a prominent Hebrew lexicon, this root often signifies the "abode of Yahweh."[5] Biblical scholar Gordon Wenham has written that *shkn* in this verse means, "literally, 'caused to camp'" and "is particularly associated with God's camping in the tabernacle among his people (e.g., Exod. 25:8). . . . The word's cultic overtones are further reinforced by the presence of the cherubim."[6]

The Hebrew root underlying the English word *garden* is *gnn*, signifying to "cover, surround, defend."[7] By way of illustration, the root is used in the Old Testament as follows: "For I will defend (*gnn*) his city to save it for mine own sake" (Isaiah 37:35); "I will defend (*gnn*)

3. Unless otherwise noted, the translation of Genesis 3:24 is mine and the translations of other Bible passages are from the King James Version.

4. Ludwig Koehler and Walter Baumgartner, *The Hebrew and Aramaic Lexicon of the Old Testament* (Leiden: Brill, 1994), 2:647; see also Brown, Driver, and Briggs, *Lexicon of the Old Testament*, 1015.

5. Koehler and Baumgartner, *Hebrew and Aramaic Lexicon*, 2:647.

6. Wenham, *Genesis 1–15*, 86.

7. Brown, Driver, and Briggs, *Lexicon of the Old Testament*, 170.

this city" (38:6); "As birds flying, so will the Lord of hosts defend (*gnn*) Jerusalem; defending (*gnn*) also he will deliver it" (31:5); "The Lord of hosts shall defend (*gnn*) them" (Zechariah 9:15); and "In that day shall the Lord defend (*gnn*) the inhabitants of Jerusalem" (12:8). From the same root comes the word *shield* (*magen*),[8] denoting an instrument of armor used by warriors to defend themselves from the enemy. The word *garden* in Hebrew (*gan*) therefore denotes "enclosure"[9] and gives the sense that a garden is an enclosed space (with a wall, thickets, or another protective covering) that is protected and defended against outside intruders (animals, thieves, and so on).

Further evidence of an enclosed garden is suggested by the fact that God stationed cherubim and the flaming sword at the east. Why would he station the cherubim at the east if the garden were open territory and an intruder could approach the tree of life from other cardinal directions?

This brings us to the narrative's threefold reference to "east," which is *the* direction of significance in Eden: (1) The detail about God's planting the garden in the east section of Eden (Genesis 2:8) suggests a primacy for the direction. (2) East is mentioned in connection with the four rivers of Eden (2:10–14; compare Enoch 18:19; 19:4). Eden is depicted as being established at the center of those rivers, perhaps providing the source of the water. Of special note in the narrative is that all four rivers are mentioned by name—Pison, Gihon, Hiddekel, and Euphrates—yet only one of the four directions is mentioned. The third river flowed eastward, but the directional flow of the other three rivers is unknown, although these rivers probably flowed outward toward the remaining cardinal directions—north, south, and west. (3) After Adam and Eve were expelled from the garden, God stationed cherubim and the flaming sword "at the east of the garden of Eden" (Genesis 3:24; Alma 12:21). Why at the east? Because the entrance to the garden was located there.[10] By placing cherubim and the

8. Brown, Driver, and Briggs, *Lexicon of the Old Testament*, 171.

9. Brown, Driver, and Briggs, *Lexicon of the Old Testament*, 171.

10. Victor P. Hamilton, *The Book of Genesis: Chapters 1–17* (Grand Rapids, MI: Eerdmans, 1990), 210.

flaming sword at the east of the garden, God was blocking the path to the tree of life from an unauthorized return.

The Lord "stationed . . . cherubim."[11] The etymology of *cherubim* (from the root *krb)* is uncertain, and most or all translations of the Bible transliterate rather than translate the word *cherubim.*[12] Beyond its use in *cherub* or its plural, *cherubim, krb* is not attested in the Hebrew Bible. Scholars have likened *cherub* to the Akkadian *karābu,* which has the meaning of "pray, bless, greet (persons), worship (deities and persons), promise or offer a sacrifice."[13] Others relate *cherub* (*krb*) to the Hebrew *rkb* ("ride") or *brk* ("bless").[14] None of these attempts to determine the etymology of *cherub* are satisfactory. As Menahem Haran has observed, "Now it appears that the name *kuribu* has so far been found only in Assyrian sources, which do not, however, describe the creature to which this name is assigned. Its identity in Assyrian examples seems therefore to be at present a matter of conjecture."[15]

The primary mission of the cherubim, together with the flaming sword, was to serve as guardians of the path to the tree of life.[16] For example, Victor Hamilton writes that "God stations the cherubim and the fiery whirling sword east of the garden of Eden to prevent reentry

---

11. For various approaches to the status and nature of the cherubim, see Robert H. Pfeiffer, "Cherubim," *Journal of Biblical Literature* 41/3–4 (1922): 249–50; Édouard (Paul) Dhorme, "Les Cherubins," *Revue biblique* 35 (1926): 328–39; and William F. Albright, "What Were the Cherubim?" *Biblical Archaeologist* (1938): 1–3.

12. Referring to the Hebrew *ha-kerubim*, John W. Wevers, in *Notes on the Greek Text of Genesis* (Atlanta, GA: Scholars Press, 1993), 50, writes, "The concept was foreign to the Greek, and the translator took over the Hebrew word into Greek. . . . In due course the word was adopted into Latin as *cherubim* (Vulg)."

13. D. N. Freedman and M. P. O'Connor, "k^erûb," *Theological Dictionary of the Old Testament*, ed. G. Johannes Botterweck, Helmer Ringgren, and Heinz-Josef Fabry (Grand Rapids, MI: Eerdmans, 1995), 7:308; also Koehler and Baumgartner, *Hebrew and Aramaic Lexicon*, 2:497.

14. Freedman and O'Connor, "k^erûb," 308.

15. M. Haran, "The Ark and the Cherubim: Their Symbolic Significance in Biblical Ritual," *Israel Exploration Journal* 9 (1959): 93.

16. The cherubim were guardian creatures, a function shared by winged creatures of other ancient Near Eastern religions. See James B. Pritchard, ed., *The Ancient Near East in Pictures Relating to the Old Testament* (Princeton, NJ: Princeton University Press, 1969), 163–65.

to the garden, as if reentry into the garden is only through an opening on its east side, much as the entrance into the tabernacle/temple complex was by a gate on the eastern side. In such a capacity the cherubim function much like the later Levites who are posted as guards around the tabernacle, and who are to strike down any person who encroaches upon the forbidden sancta (Num. 1:51, 53)."[17] Gerhard von Rad describes the cherubim as protectors[18] that "had the duty, above all, of protecting sacred regions (1 Kings 6:23 ff; 8:6)."[19]

Functioning as divine sentinels, the cherubim protect the tree of life so that humankind in its unworthy state cannot partake of the fruit of the tree (compare Alma 42:2–3). The cherubim's location in the temple was significant—placed on either side of the throne of God (mercy seat), embroidered into the veil, and situated along the path leading to God's presence.

The "door-gods" of ancient Sumer correspond to the biblical cherubim. One such door-god was Ig-alima, the son of Ningirsu, who was "but a personification of the sacred door to Nin-Girsu(k)'s holy of holies, Gir-nun, in the temple E-ninnu in Lagash."[20] According to the Gudea Cylinder, Ig-alima's duties "as great door" of the temple were "to admit the righteous, to keep away the wrong-doer, to strengthen the houses, to embellish the houses, to give to his city (and) to his sanctuary in Girsu firmness (?), to establish the throne of destiny."[21] In sum, it was Ig-alima's "function . . . to decide who should be admitted to the temple, i.e. to the god."[22]

Kapelrud compares the duties of Sumerian door-gods to those of the biblical cherubim. He writes that "among Ig-alima's tasks as a

---

17. Hamilton, *Book of Genesis*, 210. See also Bruce K. Waltke, *Genesis: A Commentary* (Grand Rapids, MI: Zondervan, 2001), 96, emphasis removed.

18. Gerhard von Rad, "The Tent and the Ark," in *The Problem of the Hexateuch* (New York: McGraw-Hill, 1984), 108.

19. Gerhard von Rad, *Genesis: A Commentary* (Philadelphia: Westminster Press, 1961), 95.

20. A. S. Kapelrud, "The Gates of Hell and the Guardian Angels of Paradise," *Journal of the American Oriental Society* 70/13 (1950): 152.

21. Kapelrud, "Gates of Hell," 152 (the question mark is in the original).

22. Kapelrud, "Gates of Hell," 155.

doorkeeper was that of admitting the just and excluding the evil. This point may give us the clue to an O. T. figure of a similar character. After man's trespassing in Paradise, God placed guardians to keep him out of the garden (Gen. 3:24)."[23] Beyond the biblical cherubim and Sumerian door-gods, there are parallels between cherubim and protectors from other nonbiblical religious systems (e.g., Hittite, Egyptian, Assyrian, and Babylonian).[24]

The Lord "placed . . . a flaming sword which turned every way." Three features in this phrase perform together to cause fear in potential garden intruders. The first is the sword itself. With rare exceptions,[25] the sword (*hereb*) in the Hebrew Bible refers to a weapon of war or an instrument of destruction (Numbers 19:16; Joshua 10:11; 13:22; 1 Samuel 17:51).[26] Some swords were two-edged (Judges 3:16), an innovation that made their destructive quality even more potent. Perhaps the flaming sword of the Genesis account anticipated the "sword of the Lord," which is God's weapon that delivers judgment upon the wicked (Judges 7:20; Isaiah 34:6; Jeremiah 12:12; 47:6–7; compare Deuteronomy 28:22). Deuteronomy 32:39–42, written in poetic form, parallels *judgment* and the Lord's *sword*: "See now that I, even I, am he, and there is no god with me: I kill, and I make alive; I wound, and I heal: neither is there any that can deliver out of my hand. For I lift up my hand to heaven, and say, I live for ever. *If I whet my glittering sword, and mine hand take hold on*

23. Kapelrud, "Gates of Hell," 153; see 154–55.

24. For guardianlike creatures associated with sacred trees in various ancient Near Eastern religions, see Kapelrud, "Gates of Hell," 154–55; T. Stordalen, *Echoes of Eden: Genesis 2–3 and Symbolism of the Eden Garden in Biblical Hebrew Literature* (Leuven: Peeters, 2000), 293; Roger Cook, *The Tree of Life: Image for the Cosmos* (New York: Avon, 1974), plates 2, 3, 19, 47 and figures 18, 23, 24, 25. Depictions of the Assyrian tree of life generally show either animals (generally ibexes, gazelles, goats, and stags), supernatural characters, or humans flanking the tree. See Simo Parpola, "The Assyrian Tree of Life: Tracing the Origins of Jewish Monotheism and Greek Philosophy," *Journal of Near Eastern Studies* 52/3 (July 1993): 164–65.

25. Exceptions include Exodus 20:25 and Ezekiel 26:9, which refer to an iron tool or chisel.

26. The Hebrew verbal root *hrb*, with its meaning "to slay," is the same root used to formulate the Hebrew word for *sword* (*hereb*). The connection, therefore, between "to slay" and "sword" emphasizes the fact that the sword is an instrument of destruction.

judgment; I will render vengeance to mine enemies, and will reward them that hate me. I will make mine arrows drunk with blood, and my sword shall devour flesh" (emphasis added). Truly, the Lord wields his sword to deliver judgment on the disobedient (Exodus 22:24; Leviticus 26:25, 33; Isaiah 1:20; Amos 9:10).

The second feature in the phrase "placed . . . a flaming sword which turned every way" that causes fear is the flame of fire. Only here in Genesis is the Hebrew *lahat* ("flame") attested as a noun; in all other places the root is verbal and translates as "to blaze, burn" or "to scorch, devour."[27] This indicates that the sword under discussion was exceptional; in addition to the danger of the blade itself, this sword burned or scorched its victims as it slashed and cut. A verse from Isaiah also connects *fire* and *sword*: "For by fire and by his sword will the Lord plead with all flesh: and the slain of the Lord shall be many" (Isaiah 66:16; see vv. 15, 17).

The third feature that may cause dread is expressed by the Hebrew verb *hamithapeket*, which translates into the English phrase "turned every way" (Authorized Version). This verb makes it clear that the sword is continuously whirling or revolving "round and round,"[28] perhaps in a zigzagging manner, to protect the path. Such a revolving sword would make it impossible for unauthorized individuals to proceed along the path.

The three features—the sword, the blazing fire, and the whirling or zigzagging motion—present a frightening prospect to those who are not qualified to approach the tree of life. Combine this with Ezekiel's description of the cherubim, the living creatures who held the flaming sword: "This was their appearance; they had the likeness of a man. And every one had four faces, and every one had four wings. . . . As for the likeness of their faces, they four had the face of a man, and the face of a lion, on the right side: and they four had the face of an ox on the left side; they four also had the face of an eagle." Ezekiel continues his description by describing the lightning speed of the creatures:

27. Koehler and Baumgartner, *Hebrew and Aramaic Lexicon*, 2:521.
28. Koehler and Baumgartner, *Hebrew and Aramaic Lexicon*, 1:254.

"And the living creatures ran and returned as the appearance of a flash of lightning" (Ezekiel 1:14; see vv. 5–6, 10, 13). This lightning-speed would make it impossible for unauthorized intruders to make it past the cherubim and flaming sword.

Perhaps a vague connection to the cherubim with the flaming sword is located in the Balaam narrative, where the Lord's angel has a drawn sword in his hand: "And the ass saw the angel of the Lord standing in the way, and his sword drawn in his hand. . . . Then the Lord opened the eyes of Balaam, and he saw the angel of the Lord standing in the way, and his sword drawn in his hand: and he bowed down his head, and fell flat on his face. And the angel of the Lord said unto him, . . . the ass saw me, and turned from me these three times: unless she had turned from me, surely now also I had slain thee, and saved her alive" (Numbers 22:23, 31–33).[29]

"*. . . to guard the path of the tree of life.*" The Hebrew verb *shmr*, translated here as "to guard," has the sense of "to take care of, preserve, protect" or "to perform guard duty."[30] God established the cherubim and the flaming sword to serve as guards. Their function would anticipate the priests and Levites who served as guards of the tabernacle and temple (1 Kings 14:27; Jeremiah 35:4). *Shmr* is also used in connection with guarding captives (Joshua 10:18; 1 Kings 20:39).[31]

"*. . . the path.*" The Hebrew *drk* may be translated "way, road, path."[32] In the context of Genesis 3:24, *drk* denotes a path or road leading to the tree of life. Elsewhere in the Hebrew Bible, *drk* may also refer to a road or path—for example, Genesis 16:7, a "spring that is beside the road to Shur" (NIV); Genesis 38:14 (also v. 21), "the road

29. "The idea is clear: a revolving or zigzagging sword, especially one wielded by angels, is one that is sure to hit and bring death (cf. Num 22:23, 31, 33)." Wenham, *Genesis 1–15*, 86.

30. Koehler and Baumgartner, *Hebrew and Aramaic Lexicon*, 4:1582–83.

31. Brown, Driver, and Briggs, *Lexicon of the Old Testament*, 1036.

32. Koehler and Baumgartner, *Hebrew and Aramaic Lexicon*, 1:231; Brown, Driver, and Briggs, *Lexicon of the Old Testament*, 202.

to Timnah" (NIV); and Deuteronomy 2:27, "we will stay on the main road" (NIV).[33]

"*. . . the tree of life.*" Sacred trees or plants figure prominently in ancient Near Eastern cultures. Not only are they mentioned or described in texts, such as the Epic of Gilgamesh,[34] but there exist numerous art motifs of sacred trees that are displayed on jewelry, seals, sculptures, wall paintings, stelae, cylinder seals, monuments,[35] and garments.[36] The concept of sacred trees also belongs to the ancient Mediterranean communities and Far Eastern cultures.[37] According to Amihai Mazar, these trees "have been and continue to be one of the most basic features of human religion in many cultures and periods."[38] These trees have supernatural or healing powers.[39] The trees may represent a deity, a king, or a queen.[40] Scholars have also associated the tree of life with the menorah, Jesus's cross, or Jesus Christ himself.[41]

---

33. For other examples of *drk* as a way, road, or path, see Genesis 35:3; 48:7; Deuteronomy 19:3.

34. The epic focuses on Gilgamesh, who obtains a plant that restores his "life's breath." Pritchard, *Ancient Near Eastern Texts*, 96.

35. See Parpola, "Assyrian Tree of Life," 161–63; see also Parpola's accompanying notes and bibliography. According to Parpola, there are "hundreds of available specimens of the Late Assyrian Tree" (p. 163).

36. For the tree of life displayed on royal garments, see Austen H. Layard, *The Monuments of Nineveh, from Drawings Made on the Spot* (London: J. Murray, 1849), plates 5 and 6b (garment of Ashurnasirpal II); Jeanny V. Canby, "Decorated Garments in Ashurnasirpal's Sculpture," *Iraq* 33 (Spring 1971): 31–33, plate XVIII; and Eva Strommenger and Max Hirmer, *5,000 Years of the Art of Mesopotamia* (London: H. N. Abrams, 1964), plates 251 and 254.

37. Amihai Mazar, "A Sacred Tree in the Chalcolithic Shrine at En Gedi: A Suggestion," *Bulletin of the Anglo-Israel Archaeological Society* 18 (2000): 31; and Cook, *Tree of Life: Image for the Cosmos*.

38. Mazar, "Sacred Tree in the Chalcolithic Shrine," 31.

39. Howard N. Wallace, "Tree of Knowledge and Tree of Life," in *The Anchor Bible Dictionary*, ed. David Noel Freedman (New York: Doubleday, 1992), 6:658.

40. Parpola, "Assyrian Tree of Life," 167; Geo Widengren, *The King and the Tree of Life in Ancient Near Eastern Religion* (Uppsala, Sweden: A. B. Lundequistska, 1951), 42–58.

41. On the association of the tree of life to Jesus's cross or to Jesus himself, see the chapters herein by Margaret Barker, "The Fragrant Tree" (pp. 64–65, 75–76); John W. Welch, "The Tree of Life in the New Testament and Christian Tradition" (pp. 82–83, 86, 88–91, 95–99); C. Wilfred Griggs, "The Tree of Life in John's Gospel" (pp. 112, 115, 122, 125–27); Jaime Lara, "The Tree of Life in the Catholic Religious and Liturgical Imagination" (pp.

The author of Genesis 2–3 refers explicitly to the tree of life on three occasions. Genesis 2:9 states that God planted "the tree of life in the middle of the garden" (my translation). In this account the tree is a definite tree (*tree* is preceded by the definite article *the*) and is located at the center of Eden's garden. The tree stands opposite the "tree of knowledge of good and evil," or the tree of death.[42] The second and third references to the tree of life are mentioned in connection with God's desire to protect the tree (Genesis 3:22–24). Had Adam and Eve been permitted to partake of the fruit of the tree of life, they would have lived forever in an imperfect state of transgression. To prevent premature access to the tree, God established cherubim and a flaming sword at the east entrance of the garden.

Rabbinic commentators argue that the tree of life was not simply in the midst of the garden but that it was in the center of the garden. For example, A. J. Rosenberg writes that "since Scripture is discussing the Garden of Eden, it was unnecessary to state that the Tree of Life was within the Garden. It could only mean that it was in the very center of the Garden."[43] Similarly, *Targum Onkelos* argues on the basis of the sentence syntax of Genesis 2:9 (translated in the King James Version as "the tree of life also in the midst of the garden, and the tree of knowledge of good and evil") that "the positioning of [the phrase] 'in the midst of the garden' after 'the tree of life' and before 'the tree of knowledge of good and evil' indicates that it describes a quality peculiar to the tree of life; thus, it is understood as 'in the center of the garden.'"[44] One archaeological study regarding an actual sacred tree

---

175, 176, 178–81); and Charles Swift, "'I Have Dreamed a Dream': Lehi's Archetypal Vision of the Tree of Life" (pp. 139–42). See also Rivka Nir, "The Aromatic Fragrances of Paradise in the *Greek Life of Adam and Eve* and the Christian Origin of the Composition," *Novum Testamentum* 46/1 (2004): 30; Max Wilcox, "'Upon the Tree'—Deut 21:22–23 in the New Testament," *Journal of Biblical Literature* 96/1 (1977): 85; and Erwin R. Goodenough, *Jewish Symbols in the Greco-Roman Period* (New York: Pantheon, 1958), 7:110–21.

42. On the tree of knowledge of good and evil as the tree of death, see Ingvild Saelid Gilhus, "The Tree of Life and the Tree of Death: A Study of Gnostic Symbols," *Religion: A Journal of Religion and Religions* 17/4 (1987): 337–53.

43. A. J. Rosenberg, *Genesis: A New Translation* (New York: Judaica Press, 1993), 1:40.

44. Yisrael I. Z. Herczeg, trans., *Rashi: The Torah, with Rashi's Commentary* (Brooklyn, NY: Mesorah Publications, 1994), 25. See Ramban Nachmanides, *Commentary on the*

located at the center of the Chalcolithic sanctuary of En Gedi supports the idea of the tree at the center.[45] Modern biblical commentators, however, are divided on the idea of the tree of life being in the center of the garden.[46]

Having the tree of life at the garden's center enriches its symbolic significance as the focal point in the Eden narrative. This significance is enhanced even more by the fact that God was the divine planter of the garden (Genesis 2:9). "The fact that [Genesis 2:9] emphasizes not the tree of life but the tree's planter reinforces the idea that life is from God, not from the tree."[47] God retains complete power over the garden and its trees, for he can grant or deny access to the tree of life according to his divine purposes.

Part 2: The Nature of the Path

The Garden of Eden and the Israelite temple systems (the Mosaic tabernacle, Solomon's temple, Ezekiel's temple) that followed appropriately paid close regard to the "four fundamental modes of monumental architecture."[48] (1) Sacred space must have a precinct, which implies location and spatial demarcation. Whether or not a man-made edifice or structure is attached to the site is ultimately irrelevant. (2) It includes the "cairn, which makes the site visible from afar and indicates its importance." The writers of the scriptures have consistently associated the temple with a mountain. (3) Necessarily attached to sacred space is "the path that signals a direction." The path represents

Torah: Genesis, trans. Charles Chavel (Brooklyn, NY: Shilo Publishing House, 1999), 71.

45. Mazar, "Sacred Tree in the Chalcolithic Shrine," 31–36. Mazar argues that this sanctuary had a sacred tree at its center and a stone platform built around the tree.

46. In his translation of Genesis 2:9, for example, Wenham places "the tree of life in the middle of the garden." Wenham, *Genesis 1–15*, 44. Compare Esther C. Quinn, *The Penitence of Adam* (University, MS: Romance Monographs, 1980), 113, and Mircea Eliade, "The Yearning for Paradise in Primitive Tradition," *Daedalus: Journal of the American Academy of Arts and Sciences* 88 (Spring 1959): 257–60; but contrast Hamilton, in *Book of Genesis*, 162, who places the tree in the midst of the garden rather than in the center.

47. Hamilton, *Book of Genesis*, 163. See Paul Watson, "The Tree of Life," *Restoration Quarterly* 23/4 (1980): 235.

48. As identified by J. G. Davies, "Architecture," in *The Encyclopedia of Religion*, ed. Mircea Eliade (New York: Macmillan, 1987), 1:386–87. The quotations immediately following are from this source.

the way to approach the center of the precinct. (4) "There is the hut that acts as a sacred shelter." The hut may be represented by a sacred tree, a cloud, or in more developed forms, an edifice. In many of the Hebrew Bible's models the hut was represented by an edifice.

Item number 3, "the path that signals a direction," calls for our attention. According to J. G. Davies, "for a path to be identifiable, it must have (1) strong edges, (2) continuity, (3) directionality, (4) recognizable landmarks, (5) a sharp terminal, and (6) end-from-end distinction."[49] The Garden of Eden's path to the tree of life was clearly identifiable. Although the text does not mention the path's edges, the path was well defined and demonstrated continuity from point A (the eastward entrance) to point B (the tree of life). Its directionality likely was westward, as suggested by the garden's eastward orientation. The path's most recognizable landmarks were the cherubim and the flaming sword at one end and the tree of life at the other. The path abruptly terminated at the tree of life, the garden's center. The path's end-from-end distinction is also present in the garden narrative.

Besides the Garden of Eden narrative, three other scriptural texts identify a path that is associated with the tree of life, sacred waters, cherubim, or a combination of all four: Lehi's tree of life dream, John's vision of the celestial city, and the tabernacle and temple texts of the Old Testament.

Lehi's dream of the tree of life (1 Nephi 8; compare 1 Nephi 11; 15) refers explicitly to the path that leads to the tree of life. Lehi wrote, "And I beheld a rod of iron, and it extended along the bank of the river, and led to the tree by which I stood. And I also beheld *a strait and narrow path*, which came along by the rod of iron, even to the tree by which I stood; and it also led by the head of the fountain, unto a large and spacious field, as if it had been a world. And I saw numberless concourses of people, many of whom were pressing forward, that they might obtain the *path* which led unto the tree by which I stood. And it came to pass that they did come forth, and commence in the *path* which led to the tree" (1 Nephi 8:19–22).

49. Davies, "Architecture," 391.

This "strait and narrow path" was not the only path or road envisioned by Lehi. He also refers to "forbidden paths" (1 Nephi 8:28) and "strange roads" (v. 32) that were traveled by those who were lost. Nephi, who also saw the tree of life in vision, similarly wrote that lost persons were traveling on "broad roads" (1 Nephi 12:17).

John's account of the celestial city, similar to Lehi's dream, explicitly refers to a path or road in connection with the tree of life: "Then the angel showed me the river of the water of life, as clear as crystal, flowing from the throne of God and of the Lamb down the middle of the *great street* of the city. On each side of the river stood the tree of life, bearing twelve crops of fruit, yielding its fruit every month. And the leaves of the tree are for the healing of the nations" (Revelation 22:1–2 NIV, emphasis added; see Ezekiel 47:7–12).[50] Note that the path in this passage is not a simple footpath but a "great street" or a "main street."[51]

The celestial city's landscape is reminiscent of the Garden of Eden's. Both feature a tree or trees of life, a river of water, and a path. Although cherubim are not mentioned in the immediate context (Revelation 21–22) of the celestial city, some scholars maintain that "the 'living creatures' of Revelation 4 and 5 and Isaiah 6 are similar if not identical beings" to the cherubim.[52] If this is the case, then cherublike creatures do exist in the celestial city.

Similar to Lehi's dream of the tree of life and John's account of the celestial city, the tabernacle and temple texts also draw upon themes from the Garden of Eden. For example, symbolic representations of the cherubim were embroidered into the walls and veil of the tabernacle (Exodus 26:1, 31; 36:8, 35) and carved into the walls, doors, and

50. It is probable that Ezekiel saw the same tree and received the same understanding as John; compare Ezekiel 47:1, 8, 12.

51. David E. Aune, *Word Biblical Commentary, Revelation 17–22* (Nashville: Thomas Nelson Publishers, 1998), 52c:1136.

52. James M. Boice, *Genesis: An Expositional Commentary* (Grand Rapids, MI: Zondervan, 1998), 1:243. "It is probable that the [seraphim] of Is 6:2–6 are another form of the cherubim. The [Apocalypse] of the seals Rev 4–6 combines them in four [creatures]." Brown, Driver, and Briggs, *Lexicon of the Old Testament*, 501.

panels of Solomon's temple (1 Kings 6:29–35; 7:29–36).[53] In addition, two large cherubim were placed on either side of God's throne[54] in the holy of holies (Exodus 25:18–22; 37:7–9; 1 Samuel 4:4; 2 Samuel 6:2; 1 Kings 6:23–28; 8:6–7). The cherubim were identical in size and possessed great wings, and each was made of olive wood and overlaid with gold. Ezekiel also refers to cherubim in his description of Jerusalem's future temple (Ezekiel 41:18–25).

The tree of life of the Mosaic tabernacle and subsequent Israelite temples is represented by the seven-branched lamp stand, or menorah.[55] Exodus 25:31–40 describes the menorah as a tree. The menorah had the appearance of an almond tree, with its trunklike base, seven branches, and blossoms or flowers. The menorah, as an important religious symbol for the Israelite community, is given due consideration in the Pentateuch. The scriptures set forth its construction (Exodus 25:31–40; 37:17–24), consecration (30:26–27; 40:9), placement in the tabernacle (25:37; Numbers 8:2–3), and the manner of transporting it (Numbers 3:31; 4:9). This sacred object was also located in Solomon's temple (1 Kings 7:49), wherein ten pure gold menorahs were used: five stood on the north and five on the south of the holy place of the temple. The second temple (the one that bore Herod's name) also boasted a lamp stand, although the sources regarding this are unclear and contradictory.[56]

As a physical, inanimate object, the menorah was not the tree of life itself but a representation of it. Located in the holy place in both the tabernacle and temple, it was overlooked or guarded by the cherubim that were featured on the walls.

---

53. Ancient Assyrian religion had the equivalent of the Israelite cherubim according to Menahem Haran, "The Ark and the Cherubim: Their Symbolic Significance in Biblical Ritual," *Israel Exploration Journal* 9 (1959): 30–38, 89–94.

54. For a discussion of the ark of the covenant as God's throne, see Gerhard Von Rad, "The Tent and the Ark," in *The Problem of the Hexateuch and Other Essays* (New York: McGraw-Hill, 1984), 103–24.

55. For the menorah as a representation of the tree of life, see Carol Meyers, *The Tabernacle Menorah: A Synthetic Study of a Symbol from the Biblical Cult* (Missoula, MT: Scholars Press, 1976).

56. Meyers, *Tabernacle Menorah*, 36–38.

The large basin of water that belonged to the courtyard of both the tabernacle and Solomon's temple parallels the waters of Eden, and the eastward orientation[57] of the garden parallels similar motifs belonging to the tabernacle and temples of Jerusalem.[58] Many temples were situated so that the entrance faced eastward. The Garden of Eden, with its templelike qualities, produced the prototypical pattern for subsequent Israelite temple orientation.

Within the tabernacle and Solomon's and Ezekiel's temples (and spoken of in the Temple Scroll), a path was established that led the entire distance from the courtyard's outside walls to the holy of holies. Often the path consisted of a straight-line axis and possessed vertical aspects, an ascension, and an eastward orientation.[59] The scriptural texts set forth the path's form, its approachability, and various architectural safeguards that protected the precinct from impurity and desecration and discouraged unqualified persons from approaching too close to the center. These architectural safeguards included horizontal zones, walls, and gates or veils.

For example, the wall as an architectural component formed one of the most basic and important elements in sacred dwellings. Each wall served to demarcate space between the sacred center and the profane

---

57. "Eastward orientation" is in point of fact a redundancy because *orient* has etymological ties to the term *east*. Landsberger explains that "etymologically, 'orientation' signifies a turning toward the east." Franz Landsberger, "The Sacred Direction in Synagogue and Church," *Hebrew Union College Annual* 28 (1957): 181.

58. Wenham, *Genesis 1–15*, 86. On the subject of spatial orientation, see John Wilkinson, "Orientation, Jewish and Christian," *Palestine Exploration Quarterly* 116 (January–June 1984): 16–30; L. A. Snijders, "L'orientation du temple de Jérusalem," *Oudtestamentische Studiën* 14 (1965): 214–34; Hans-J. Klimkeit, "Spatial Orientation in Mythical Thinking as Exemplified in Ancient Egypt: Considerations toward a Geography of Religions," *History of Religions* 14/4 (1975): 266–81; B. Diebner, "Die Orientierung des Jerusalemer Tempels und die 'Sacred Direction' der frühchristlichen Kirchen," *Zeitschrift des Deutschen Palästina-Vereins* 87/2 (1971): 153–66; and Bezalel Porten, "The Structure and Orientation of the Jewish Temple at Elephantine—A Revised Plan of the Jewish District," *Journal of the American Oriental Society* 81/1 (1961): 38–42.

59. See, for instance, B. L. Gordon, "Sacred Directions, Orientation, and the Top of the Map," *History of Religions* 10/3 (1971): 212.

field.[60] "The wall in combination with the terrace can provide horizontal definition," suggests Martienssen.[61] The wall creates a frame around a designated spot, a pronounced border that all can see and that no one can misapprehend. Jonathan Z. Smith's vision of the experience within the temple is instructive. He sees the architectural components functioning together to produce a centripetal apparatus. That is to say, the people were held in their place between the four walls of a single court or sphere, pushing toward their God while at the same time having their approach arrested by the walls, gates, and stairs.[62]

Notwithstanding these architectural safeguards, the path provided passage for ritually qualified individuals (i.e., those who had participated in the rites or gestures of approach). The path traversed through three chief horizontal zones—the courtyard(s), the holy place, and the holy of holies. Each zone was demarcated with walls, but gates[63] and veils[64] allowed ingress and egress from zone to zone. Raglan writes that "gates and doors mark the division between the sacred and the profane world."[65] Eliade proposed that the threshold and

60. Mircea Eliade, *The Sacred and the Profane: The Nature of Religion*, trans. Willard R. Trask (New York: Harcourt, Brace and World, 1959), 25.

61. Rex D. Martienssen, *The Idea of Space in Greek Architecture* (Johannesburg: Witwatersrand University Press, 1956), 8; see Rudolf Arnheim, *The Power of the Center* (Berkeley: University of California Press, 1988), 51.

62. Jonathan Z. Smith, *To Take Place: Toward Theory in Ritual* (Chicago: University of Chicago Press, 1987), 65. Arnheim utilizes similar imagery when he writes that a tall wall or tower arising from the center "will be seen essentially as a centrifugal vector emanating from the massive center of the building." Arnheim, *Power of the Center*, 22.

63. The meaning of the Hebrew verbal root of *gate* (*sha'ar*) during the biblical period was to "break . . . through," to create a "gap" or "opening," to "split, divide." Brown, Driver, and Briggs, *Lexicon of the Old Testament*, 1044–45; compare Ludwig Koehler and Walter Baumgartner, *Lexicon in Veteris Testamenti Libros* (Leiden: Brill, 1953), 1001–2.

64. Umberto Cassuto, in *A Commentary on the Book of Exodus*, trans. Israel Abrahams (Jerusalem: Magnes, 1967), 359, points out that the Hebrew word for *veil* (*parokhet*) is derived from a verb stem that is unattested in the Hebrew Bible—*prkh*, which means to "close" or "to shut." *Prkh* can also mean "to separate" or "to divide." Walter C. Kaiser Jr., "Exodus," in *The Expositor's Bible Commentary*, ed. Frank E. Gaebelein (Grand Rapids, MI: Zondervan, 1990), 2:461–62. These definitions conform to the scriptural usage of *veil*, for according to Exodus 26:33, the function of the veil is to divide the holy place from the holy of holies.

65. Fitzroy R. S. Raglan, *The Temple and the House* (New York: Norton, 1964), 26.

the door "are symbols and at the same time vehicles of passage from the one space to the other."[66]

Part 3: Safely Returning to the Tree

Although the Garden of Eden narrative sets forth aspects about the tree of life, the cherubim, the flaming sword, and the path, the narrative provides no information about how Adam or Eve or any individual could safely return to the tree via the path, past the guardians and the flaming, revolving sword. In fact, Genesis 3:24 ("and he stationed . . . cherubim, and a flaming, revolving sword") concludes the Garden of Eden narrative. The next passage begins with "And Adam knew Eve his wife; and she conceived, and bare Cain" (Genesis 4:1) and continues with the story of Cain's fallen countenance and the subsequent murder of his brother Abel. There is no explanation of how one may return to the tree; the author of Genesis abruptly discontinues one story and moves to the next. None of the remaining narratives in the book of Genesis unambiguously return to the topic of the tree of life.

The other three scriptural texts—Lehi's dream of the tree of life, John's vision of the celestial city, and the tabernacle and temple texts—do indeed provide information about how one may journey past the guardians to the path that leads to the tree of life. Lehi's dream plainly sets forth the manner by which a person travels the path to this tree—one must hold on to a rod of iron that extends along the path to the tree (1 Nephi 8:19–20). The rod of iron symbolizes God's word (11:25). Nephi's brothers inquired, "What meaneth the rod of iron which our father saw, that led to the tree?" Nephi responded, "It was the word of God; and whoso would hearken unto the word of God, and would hold fast unto it, they would never perish; neither could the temptations and the fiery darts of the adversary overpower them unto blindness, to lead them away to destruction" (15:23–24).

John's revelation explains what one must do to eat of the tree of life: "To him that overcometh will I give to eat of the tree of life, which

66. Eliade, *The Sacred and Profane*, 25. See Martienssen, *Space in Greek Architecture*, 4; and Ad de Vries, *Dictionary of Symbols and Imagery* (Amsterdam: North-Holland Publishing, 1974), 143.

is in the midst of the paradise of God" (Revelation 2:7). The phrase "to him that overcometh" is found seven times in the letters to the seven churches (vv. 11, 17, 26; 3:5, 12, 21) and is directed to each individual who overcomes the world. The word *overcometh*[67] refers to prevailing over Satan and the wicked world. This is accomplished through obedience to God's laws. In John's own words, "Blessed are they that do [God's] commandments, that they may have right to the tree of life, and may enter in through the gates into the city" (22:14). Presumably, when one enters the city's gates, he or she is on the main road that leads to the tree of life.

The texts pertaining to the Mosaic tabernacle or to the Israelite temple systems set forth how one may approach the symbolic representation of the tree of life—the menorah—that was located in the holy place of the tabernacle. Gestures of approach[68] are rituals[69] or religious gestures[70] conducted by those who occupy the path that leads from the profane to the sacred. Those who wish to leave profane space and approach the sacred center must participate in these gestures. Inasmuch as the concepts of sacred and profane have reference to two antithetical powers—the profane contaminates, the sacred sancti-

67. *Overcome* is also used in association with those who are faithful (Doctrine and Covenants 61:9; 63:20), those who believe that "Jesus is the Son of God" (1 John 5:5), those who obey the commandments (D&C 50:35), and those who are "born of God" (1 John 5:4).

68. It is difficult to ascertain who first coined the phrase "gestures of approach." Certainly it is now a common expression. See, for example, Mircea Eliade, *Patterns in Comparative Religion*, trans. Rosemary Sheed (New York: Sheed and Ward, 1958), 370–71; and Baruch M. Bokser, "Approaching Sacred Space," *The Harvard Theological Review* 78/3–4 (1985): 279–80, 299.

69. This accords with the standard dictionary definition, which defines *rite* (from the Latin *ritus*) as "a formal procedure or act in a religious or other solemn observance." *The Oxford English Dictionary*, prepared by J. A. Simpson and E. S. C. Weiner, 2nd ed. (Oxford: Clarendon Press, 1989), 13:990. See James C. Livingston, *Anatomy of the Sacred: An Introduction to Religion* (New York: Macmillan, 1989), 98, where the author defines a religious ritual as "an agreed-on and formalized pattern of ceremonial movements and verbal expressions carried out in a sacred context" (emphasis removed).

70. According to Raglan, the rite of transition is common to many religions. He further observes, "This ritual gradually dwindles, but people still mark their transition from the profane to the sacred sphere by removing their hats—or their boots." Raglan, *The Temple and the House*, 31.

fies—the two must be strictly separated,[71] and gestures of approach serve to separate the two. "Any attempt, outside the prescribed limits, to unite sacred and profane brings confusion and disaster."[72] The entry into the sacred is potentially dangerous. Those who enter or serve in the sacred arena when unprepared are subject to death by the hands of man or by the power of God.[73]

The gestures of approach are as follows:

1. The removal of profane items. Moses was commanded by God to remove his shoes—"put off thy shoes from off thy feet, for the place whereon thou standest is holy ground" (Exodus 3:5). Joshua, Moses's successor, had a similar experience (Joshua 5:15).[74]
2. Ritual ablutions—for example, immersion (Hebrew *tevilah*) and the cleansing of hands and feet. It was incumbent upon a priest to ritually wash his hands and feet lest he incur the death penalty by the hand of heaven: "For Aaron and his sons shall wash their hands and their feet thereat: When they go into the tabernacle of

71. Speaking of sacred and profane space, Davies writes, "The one is potent, full of power, while the other is powerless. They cannot therefore approach one another without losing their proper nature: either the sacred will consume the profane or the profane will contaminate and enfeeble the sacred." Davies, "Architecture," 384.

72. Davies, "Architecture," 385.

73. The laws regarding trespass into sacred space are well defined in the rabbinic literature. The Mishnah asserts that one of the thirty-six most punishable transgressions of the Torah is entering the temple while unclean (M. *Kerithot* 1:1); also, when a ritually impure priest ministered, he was not taken to a court of law, but "young priests" took him from the courtyard and with clubs broke his head (M. *Sanhedrin* 9:6; 10.1). Likewise, if a nonpriest served in the temple he was killed either by strangling or by "the hands of Heaven" (M. *Sanhedrin* 9:6, 10.1; see BT *Sanhedrin* 81b). Furthermore, if a priest lacked atonement and deliberately entered the temple court, he incurred the penalty of excommunication. According to a prescription based upon Leviticus 16:2, a priest who stepped across the prescribed boundaries of his zone (beyond the first eleven cubits of the entrance to the tripartite building, compare BT *Yoma* 16b) received forty lashes, or if he entered within the veil of the holy of holies he incurred death at the hands of heaven (BT *Menaḥot* 27b; compare T. *Kelim* 1:6), meaning no human punishment would be rendered. Foreigners who trespassed the temple precinct were also subject to death (BT *Sanhedrin* 83b).

74. Rabbinic literature sets forth the idea of removing profane items before entry into sacred space. Compare *Exodus Rabbah* II.6; BT *Yebamot* 6b, 102b; M. *Berakot* 9:5; BT *Berakot* 61b–62b; *Ecclesiastes Rabbah* IV.14.

the congregation, they shall wash with water, that they die not" (Exodus 30:19–20; see 29:4).

3. Anointing with olive oil, which was first poured upon the recipient's head and then smeared (Exodus 29:7). The rite followed the ritual ablutions with pure water but preceded the vesting rite. The locale where the anointing rite took place was significant. For the priests of the Mosaic law, the anointing rite took place at the door of the temple court. Hence the gestures involved in the anointing prepared the individual to approach the holinesses located within the walls of the temple. Those who received the anointing were sanctified and set apart from the profane world and were thus required to adhere to certain responsibilities (Leviticus 21:10–12), but they were also offered special privileges (6:20–22; 16:32–34; Numbers 4:16; 18:8). In connection with the anointing, priests were sprinkled with oil mixed with the blood of a sacrificial victim (Exodus 29:21; Leviticus 8:30).
4. Offering of a variety of sacrifices for various occasions. These included burnt offerings (Leviticus 1:3–17; 6:8–13), grain offerings (2:1–16), peace offerings (3:1–17), sin offerings (4:1–5:13), and trespass or guilt offerings (5:14–6:7).
5. Investiture of special vestments (Exodus 28) that were deemed to be holy (vv. 2–3). The ordinary priestly vestments consisted of four parts—breeches, a headpiece, a girdle, and a tunic. The high priestly vestments consisted of eight pieces, the four belonging to the priest plus an ephod, robe, breastplate, and frontplate (29:5–6). The high priest wore four vestments on the Day of Atonement. They were white in color and included a girdle, tunic, mitre, and breeches.

These gestures of approach sanctified and prepared the individual for entrance into the holy. Only after the gestures of approach were individuals permitted to approach Deity in his state of holiness.

Violating Sacred Space

The scriptures offer examples of individuals who violated sacred space. Isaiah 14 records an instance of one such transgressor who presumably encountered the flaming, revolving sword. The text in part reads:

> How art thou fallen from heaven, O Lucifer, son of the morning! how art thou *cut down to the ground*, which didst weaken the nations! For thou hast said in thine heart, I will ascend into heaven, I will exalt my throne above the stars of God: I will sit also upon the mount of the congregation, in the sides of the north: I will ascend above the heights of the clouds; I will be like the most High. Yet thou shalt be brought down to hell, to the sides of the pit. They that see thee shall narrowly look upon thee, and consider thee, saying, Is this the man that made the earth to tremble, that did shake kingdoms; that made the world as a wilderness, and destroyed the cities thereof; that opened not the house of his prisoners? All the kings of the nations, even all of them, lie in glory, every one in his own house. But thou art cast out of thy grave like an abominable branch, and as the raiment of those that are slain, *thrust through with a sword*, that go down to the stones of the pit; as a carcase trodden under feet. Thou shalt not be joined with them in burial, because thou hast destroyed thy land, and slain thy people: the seed of evildoers shall never be renowned. (Isaiah 14:12–20, emphasis added)

In this text, Lucifer makes five statements (each beginning with the personal pronoun *I*) that indicate his desire to encroach upon God's holy, heavenly sphere: "I will ascend into heaven, I will exalt my throne above the stars of God: I will sit also upon the mount of the congregation [or "in the Mountain Assembly" for the gods],[75] in the sides of the north: I will ascend above the heights of the clouds; I will be like the most High" (Isaiah 14:13–14). Nine words are associated with Lucifer's goal to elevate himself to God's exalted sphere: *ascend* (twice), *heaven*, *exalt*, *stars*, *mount*, *heights*, *clouds*, and *most High*. Lucifer, however, did

75. For this reading, see John D. W. Watts, *Word Biblical Commentary, Isaiah 1–33* (Waco, TX: Word Books, 1987), 24:207.

not succeed in his quest. Two phrases in the text suggest that he was halted by the flaming, revolving sword: "how art thou cut down to the ground" (v. 12). The verb *cut* conveys the idea that Lucifer was cut with a sword, an action explicitly referenced in verse 19: "thou art . . . thrust through with a sword."

A second text refers to the king of Tyre (perhaps a symbol of some unnamed person). The Lord commanded Ezekiel to

> raise a dirge over the king of Tyre, informing him that the message of the Lord Yahweh is as follows: You were once a seal of intricate design, full of wisdom, perfect in beauty. You used to live in Eden, God's garden. You wore precious stones of every kind—sard, topaz, moonstone(?), gold topaz, carnelian, jasper, lapis lazuli, garnet and emerald—and the mounts and settings you wore were made of gold and had been fashioned on the day you were created. With a winged(?) guardian cherub I set you. On God's sacred mountain you lived, and amidst blazing gems you walked about. Your conduct was blameless from the day you were created until wrongdoing was discovered in you. Your extensive trading filled your habitat with violence and you committed sin. So I removed you in your sullied state from the divine mountain, and the guardian cherub banished you from the habitat of the blazing gems. Your beauty gave you a proud attitude. With your splendor in mind, you used your wisdom perversely. So I threw you down to the ground and exposed you to the gloating gaze of other kings. Your serious wrongdoing involved in your wicked trading led you to sully your sacred places. So I made fire issue from your habitat and it consumed you. I turned you into ashes before the gaze of all who saw you. All who know you among the peoples are appalled at you. You have become a victim of terror and will be no more for ever. (Ezekiel 28:11–19)[76]

76. Translation by Leslie C. Allen, *Word Biblical Commentary, Ezekiel 20–48* (Dallas, TX: Word Books, 1990), 29:90. See also Allen's accompanying critical notes on pages 90–92.

This passage from Ezekiel makes straightforward references to the Garden of Eden with the expressions "Eden" and "God's garden."[77] Furthermore, the passage makes it clear that Eden represents sacred space with the phrases "God's garden," "God's sacred mountain," "divine mountain," "guardian cherub," and "sacred places." The king of Tyre, who inhabited the garden for a period of time, was once "full of wisdom" and "perfect in beauty" and "blameless." He wore precious stones, which were perhaps symbolically associated with the precious jewels located on the high priest's breastplate (Exodus 28:15–21). In time, however, the king became wicked. The text sets forth his state of wickedness: he became guilty of "wrongdoing," and he "committed sin"; the king's beauty gave him a "proud attitude," and he kept his "splendor in mind." He was guilty of "serious wrongdoing" involving his "wicked trading." This led the king to "sully," or pollute, the sacred place in which he lived.

It was because of the king's great wickedness that the Lord, together with the guardian cherub, cast him out of the Garden of Eden. "So I [the Lord] removed you in your sullied state from the divine mountain, and the guardian cherub banished you from the habitat of the blazing gems." The king's removal from the garden recalls Adam and Eve's banishment from the Garden of Eden. The Ezekiel text, however, has a different ending than the Genesis narrative does. Whereas Adam and Eve are allowed to live outside the sacred garden, the king is destroyed, presumably by the guardian cherub's flaming sword.[78] Two references communicate the idea of death by the flame from the sword. The first is found in the Lord's words to the king: "I made fire issue from your habitat and it consumed you." The second sets forth the end result of this fire and its consummation: "I turned you into ashes." The Lord concludes

77. Allen summarized the content of Ezekiel 28:11–19 by stating, "Basically it makes use of a version of the garden of Eden story that appears in Gen 2–3." *Word Biblical Commentary, Ezekiel 20–48*, 94. E. O. James, in *The Tree of Life: An Archaeological Study* (Brill: Leiden, 1966), 74, makes a similar statement when he writes that Ezekiel 28:11–19 is "the Phoenician counterpart of the Genesis myth."

78. With a variety of approaches, scholars associate the flaming sword of Genesis 3:24 with the fire that consumes the king of Tyre. See, for example, Leslie, *Word Biblical Commentary, Ezekiel 20–48*, 95.

with this promise to the king: "You have become a victim of terror and will be no more for ever."

Conclusion

Part 1 of this article examined expressions from Genesis 3:24 that reveal much regarding the nature of the cherubim, the sword, and the path and the manner in which the cherubim and the flaming, revolving sword serve to guard the path to the tree of life. Part 2 discussed the physical characteristics of the path. Part 3 drew on Lehi's tree of life dream, John's vision of the celestial city, and the tabernacle and temple texts of the Old Testament to explain how one journeys past the guardians and enters the path leading to the tree of life—namely, by holding on to the rod of iron (the word of God), overcoming the world, and participating in the gestures of approach. All three components are obligatory for those who wish to approach the tree of life and partake of its fruits. Anyone attempting to travel the path in order to enter the Lord's sacred temple must first obtain the authorization provided by those components. Those who fail to do so will be cut down by the sword, burned by the sword's flame, or both.

Donald W. Parry, professor of Hebrew Bible at Brigham Young University, has authored or edited more than a dozen books that are directed to the academic community. These include works on the Dead Sea Scrolls, Isaiah, and 1 and 2 Samuel. He has also authored books for nonspecialist readers, including Understanding Isaiah, Temples of the Ancient World, *and* Symbols and Shadows: Unlocking a Greater Understanding of the Atonement. *Since 1994, he has been a member of the international team of translators of the Dead Sea Scrolls. He was recently appointed to serve on the Biblia Hebraica Quinta team, which is producing the new edition of the Hebrew Bible for scholars and translators.*

The Tree of Life in the Hebrew Bible and Later Jewish Thought

Andrew C. Skinner

The images and symbolism of trees have long occupied an important place in the theological as well as geographical landscape of Judaism, including the history and religion of ancient Israel. The Hebrew Bible reminds us that from the earliest stages of Israel's existence trees were associated with, or represented the highly prized concepts of, judgment, wisdom, beauty, renewal, prosperity, longevity, and even eternal life. Consider just a few examples.

- The prophetess Deborah "judged Israel. . . . And she dwelt under the palm tree of Deborah between Ramah and Beth-el in mount Ephraim: and the children of Israel came up to her for judgment" (Judges 4:4–5).
- According to Moses, the symbol of the severest form of punishment in Israel was a tree: "And if a man have committed a sin worthy of death, and he be to be put to death, . . . thou hang him on a tree: . . . for he that is hanged [on a tree] is accursed of God" (Deuteronomy 21:22–23).
- Wise King Solomon "spake three thousand proverbs: and his songs were a thousand and five. And he spake of trees, from the cedar tree that is in Lebanon even unto the hyssop that springeth out of the wall. . . . And there came of all people to hear the wisdom of Solomon" (1 Kings 4:32–34).
- The author of the Song of Solomon compared his beloved to a tree: "thy stature is like to a palm tree" (Song of Solomon 7:7).
- The prophet of messianic anticipation, Isaiah, described a millennial age of renewal and peace, saying: "I will rejoice in Jerusalem,

and joy in my people. . . . And they shall build houses, and inhabit them. . . . They shall not build, and another inhabit; they shall not plant, and another eat: for as the days of a tree are the days of my people" (Isaiah 65:19, 21–22).

- Again from Isaiah: "Instead of the thorn shall come up the fir tree, and instead of the brier shall come up the myrtle tree: and it shall be to the Lord for a name, for an everlasting sign that shall not be cut off" (Isaiah 55:13).

Preeminent above all varieties of trees, as the author of Judges suggests in a parable of Jotham, is the olive tree. "The trees went forth on a time to anoint a king over them; and they said [first] unto the olive tree, Reign thou over us. But the olive tree said unto them, Should I leave my fatness, wherewith by me they honour God and man, and go to be promoted over the trees?" (Judges 9:8–9). This is a reference to the use of olive oil in a wide variety of activities that were part of Israel's religious system, particularly as they related to the tabernacle and temple and to the anointing of prophets and kings. Other texts also state or imply that the olive tree is first among others. Second Maccabees explicitly connects the olive tree with the most sacred spot on earth, mentioning the "festal olive boughs of the Temple" (2 Maccabees 14:4). The pseudepigraphic *Apocalypse of Sedrach* 8:2 states that God himself preferred the olive tree above others. And we know that certain strands of Jewish tradition from late antiquity identify the olive tree as the tree of life.[1] Thus the tree of life is given credence as the most important of all trees by its association with the olive tree.

As we examine the tree of life in the biblical, postbiblical, and medieval and early modern periods, we shall see how not only this symbol but also the meanings associated with it are a strong indicator of the values, mores, and practices that each era held in highest esteem.

---

1. See the Babylonian Talmud, *Hagigah* 12b; *Pirque Rabbi Eliezer* 35; Jerusalem Talmud, *Berakot* 1:9b; and *Book of the Secrets of Enoch* (*2 Enoch*) 9:1.

Biblical Period

The earliest biblical mention of the tree of life, *ētz-hayyim* in Hebrew, is found in Genesis and is referred to three times in the story of Adam and Eve in the Garden of Eden. The tree of life is first described as growing up among other trees in the midst of the garden and is coupled with the tree of knowledge of good and evil: "out of the ground made the Lord God to grow every tree that is pleasant to the sight, and good for food; the tree of life also in the midst of the garden, and the tree of knowledge of good and evil" (Genesis 2:9).

It has been suggested that one of the reasons the two trees are coupled is that they are complementary of one another, not opposites. Both are involved in the bringing of immortality to humankind. The result of eating of the tree of life is obvious, while eating of the tree of knowledge of good and evil brings not only a likeness to God by imparting knowledge he possesses, but also a "quasi-immortality through offspring"—achieved by the physical union of the man and the woman.[2]

After Adam's disobedience in the garden, the tree of life is mentioned twice more as God institutes protective measures by driving the man and woman out of the garden to prevent them from eating of the tree of life and imposes dramatic sanctions to bar their return.

> And the Lord God said, Behold, the man is become as one of us, to know good and evil: and now, lest he put forth his hand, and take also of the tree of life, and eat, and live for ever [in his new condition]: Therefore the Lord God sent him forth from the garden of Eden, to till the ground from whence he was taken. So he drove out the man; and he placed at the east of the garden of Eden Cherubims, and a flaming sword which turned every way, to keep the way of the tree of life. (Genesis 3:22–24)

Thus in the book of Genesis the tree of life bestows immortality on all those who eat from it. It is suitable for those in an unfallen,

---

2. Raymond E. Brown, Joseph A. Fitzmyer, and Roland E. Murphy, eds., *Jerome Biblical Commentary* (Englewood Cliffs, NJ: Prentice-Hall, 1968), 13.

uncorrupted state. But it brings dire consequences to those who are not fully gods and yet eat of it *after* eating from the tree of knowledge of good and evil. Notice that the Lord God is quick to drive the man and the woman out of the garden so that they do not eat of the tree of life and live forever in their new, corrupted, sinful state. Once the man and the woman have partaken of the tree of knowledge of good and evil, which brings about a corrupted condition, the effects of the tree of life are "turned upside down" and it becomes a tree of damnation, a "tree of death"—spiritual death.[3] The progress of the man and woman is damned. The tree of life is, therefore, bound up with the proper order of things as decreed by God.

Most modern scholars see a significant relationship between the tree of life in Genesis and similar trees or plants described in the literature of the ancient Near East. Though almost all cultures of the ancient world, especially the ancient Near East, possess some kind of reference to the tree of life and humankind's quest to enjoy its fruit, there seems to be more profound connections between the Bible and the tree of life motifs in the oldest cultures of Mesopotamia than anywhere else. From an old Babylonian seal impression, now in the British Museum, the biblical Garden of Eden scene appears to be clearly depicted, reflecting a "tradition [that] is no doubt of very ancient origin."[4] In this scene, a tree stands in the middle, its boughs stretched out. On either side of the tree, two human figures are seated, each with an arm stretched forth, presumably to take the fruit of the tree. A serpent stands erect behind the figure on the left. The tree of life and the tree of knowledge of good and evil are merged into one.[5] (See fig. 1.)

Other counterparts to the biblical tree of life appear in Babylonian culture, namely, the sacred cedar. It was "employed in magic rites to restore strength and life to the body [and] was also 'the revealer of the oracles of earth and heaven.' Upon its core the name of Ea, the god of

3. Benedikt Otzen, "The Paradise Trees in Jewish Apocalyptic," in *Apocryphon Severini* (Aarhus, Denmark: Aarhus University Press, 1993), 140.

4. J. H. Philpot, *The Sacred Tree or the Tree in Religion and Myth* (London: Macmillan and Co., 1897), 130.

5. Philpot, *Sacred Tree*, 131.

Fig. 1. Babylonian seal impression.

wisdom, was supposed to be written. . . . The tree of life also finds a parallel in the divine soma, the giver of eternal youth and immortality, a drink reserved only for the celestial gods or the souls of the blessed."[6]

In the famous Mesopotamian (Akkadian) tale entitled the Epic of Gilgamesh, the hero embarks on a quest to find the plant that bestows "new life," or immortality. As part of his epic ritual journey, he is washed, dressed in a new garment "to clothe his nakedness" after "cast[ing] off his [old] skins," and given a new headband—all in preparation to acquire the plant of new life. Tragically, as Gilgamesh goes down into a well of water to bathe after acquiring the plant, a serpent carries off the plant and Gilgamesh is left to weep.[7]

Nowhere were the tree of life and the paradisiacal garden in which it grew as important to the underpinnings of Mesopotamian society as they were at Eridu, in the ancient kingdom of Sumer, where, according to cuneiform texts, the "*Kiskanu*-tree grew in the sanctuary of Apsu near the sacred pool in the temple."[8]

6. Philpot, *Sacred Tree,* 131.

7. Epic of Gilgamesh, Tablet XI, lines 240–90, in James B. Pritchard, ed., *Ancient Near Eastern Texts Relating to the Old Testament*, 3rd ed. (Princeton: Princeton University Press, 1969), 96.

8. E. O. James, *The Tree of Life: An Archaeological Study* (Leiden: Brill, 1966), 69.

In a seminal study entitled *The King and the Tree of Life in Ancient Near Eastern Religion*, Professor Geo Widengren described the foundational role that the *kiškanu* tree, the tree of life, played in ancient Mesopotamian myth and ritual, and, significantly, also the close relationship between the tree of life and the "Water of Life" in that worldview. He states: "Already in the Sumerian literature provided with an Accadian interlinear translation the Tree of Life is said to be growing near the streams of Life flowing in paradise."[9] He then quotes the following well-known Sumerian text:

> In Eridu there is a black *kiškanu*-tree,
> growing in a pure place,
> its appearance is lapis-lazuli,
> erected on the *Apsū* [the primordial waters].
> Enki, when walking there, filleth Eridu with abundance.
> In the foundation thereof is the place of the underworld,
> in the restingplace is the chamber of Nammu.
> In its holy temple there is a grove, casting its shadow,
> therein no man goeth to enter.
> In the midst are the Sun-god and the Sovereign of heaven,
> in between the river with the two mouths.[10]

The *kiškanu* tree, the tree of life, is intricately associated with the temple in this text. It grows in a "pure place." It has a special appearance, and it is "erected" or planted on or over the primordial waters. As Widengren himself notes, we have a "temple grove with the Tree of Life growing in the sanctuary [temple] as in a fine garden."[11] Furthermore, "the garden is tended by a gardener, who is associated [or equated] with the King. The King is not only the guardian of the Tree of Life, but also [possesses] a twig from the Tree of Life which is his scepter. The person of the King becomes [bound] up with the image of

9. Geo Widengren, *The King and the Tree of Life in Ancient Near Eastern Religion* (Uppsala, Sweden: A.-B. Lundequistka Bokhandeln, 1951), 5.

10. Widengren, *The King and the Tree of Life*, 5–6.

11. Widengren, *The King and the Tree of Life*, 10.

the tree."[12] Professor Widengren summarizes his lengthy discussion in the following two paragraphs:

> The complex of ideas and customs treated by us . . . is obviously intimately bound up with the oldest strata of Sumerian culture and religion. All interest centres around the holy garden of the divinity. In this garden is found the Tree of Life, the fruits of which are eaten by man while its oil is used for the anointment of his body and especially his head. There the Water of Life is streaming from beneath the roots of this tree. Further we note the crown twined from the shoots of the tree, from its leaves and flowers, the branch cut from the trunk of the tree, a rod acting both as a sign of dignity and as an instrument for magical-medical purifications, the water drawn from the well with the Water of Life, serving for medical-religious purifications. In this garden too is erected the hut, built from branches and twigs taken from trees of this garden of paradise, the dwelling where the holy marriage is celebrated.
>
> The king in the cultic ceremonies represents the god. For this reason he in all rites acts as the representative of the deity. In his capacity of water-drawer and gardener he surveys the cultic equivalent of the paradise-garden, i.e. the temple-grove with the cult-tree that represents the Tree of Life. He wears as his crown the garland and the branch as his rod. In the hut he undergoes some purification ceremonies before his *hieros gamos* [sacred marriage]. He carries out libations over the life-tree, the divine symbol, and hence is styled *išib* = *ramku* [that is, "a priest who has passed through the *mis pī*-ritual"].[13] By using the Water of Life and the magical rod, the twig cut from the Tree of Life, he is the great *a-zu* = *āsū,* just in the

12. This summary is found in Brant Gardner, "Nephi's Tree of Life," 2, http://www.al-qiyamah.org/pdf_files/tree_of_life-nephi's_(highfiber.com).pdf (accessed March 15, 2011).

13. Widengren, *The King and the Tree of Life*, 14 n. 1.

> same manner as Marduk or Tammuz. Exactly like Tammuz himself he is the *gutug* = *pašīšu,* he who is anointed with the oil from the life-tree.[14]

In summary, then, the oldest tree of life text from Sumer describes, according to Professor Widengren, the tree of life as planted in a pure place, in the midst of the temple, in the middle of a garden, from which flows the Water of Life. It is significant that "a pond or stream of sacred water" also often lies under or near the tree of life in ancient Egyptian depictions, "with the god of writing, Thoth, inscribing the name of the king on the tree. . . . In all these examples, partaking of the fruit of the tree is a sacramental act, one that symbolizes unity with the gods."[15] (See figs. 2 and 3.) In the elaborately decorated and painted tomb of Thutmosis III (whose name means "child of the god Thoth"), located in the Valley of the Kings, Pharaoh Thutmosis III is shown being nourished from the tree of life (see fig. 4).[16]

In Widengren's Sumerian example, the temple is the house of the god and is where the king—who is the gardener—undergoes some purification ceremonies before the ritual of the sacred marriage whereupon he becomes like the gods. The king is equated with the tree of life. The king's scepter, his symbol of both authority and power, is cut from the tree of life, and his crown is made from leaves and flowers of that tree.

We see here that there are significant "touch points" between this Mesopotamian description of the tree of life and what is represented as well as implied in the Genesis story. We may also recognize a significant correspondence between these religious elements depicted in the oldest traditions of ancient Mesopotamia and some parallels found in the Book of Mormon (see 1 Nephi 8; 11). Regarding any ancient Israelite parallels to the Mesopotamian view of the tree of life being connected to the temple, it must be admitted up front that no Hebrew Bible (Old Testament) text, either in or out of Genesis, makes such an explicit connection. However, several scholars have proffered that

14. Widengren, *The King and the Tree of Life*, 59–60.
15. C. Wilfred Griggs, "The Tree of Life in Ancient Cultures," *Ensign*, June 1988, 29.
16. Mohammed Nasr, *Valley of the Kings* (Luxor: Tiba Artistic Production, 2003), 50.

Fig. 2 (top left). Egyptian illustration of a pharaoh kneeling under tree of life (palm tree).

Fig. 3 (bottom). Egyptian god Thoth inscribing king's name on leaves of ished tree.

Fig. 4 (top right). Thutmosis III taking nourishment from the life tree of Isis.

the biblical menorah was a symbolic or abstract representation of the tree of life. As used in the Hebrew Bible, *menorah* is a technical term for the seven-branched candelabra, or lampstand, found in the tabernacle and in the first temple (Solomon's) and also for the lampstand ("candlestick" in the KJV) in Zechariah's vision (Zechariah 4:2, 11). From Leon Yarden's interesting study *The Tree of Light*, we read: "In general it may be said that most scholars now seem to suppose that the menorah originated from a sacred tree, more specifically the Tree of Life mythology—a primal image which can be glimpsed as early as the third millennium B.C. . . . and which played a decisive role in the tree cult of the ancient world."[17]

Thus the tabernacle-temple menorah derives both its form and symbolism from the tree of life. Its origin is traced to Exodus 25:31–40, where Moses is instructed by God to make it according to the divine pattern shown him on Mount Sinai. The connection between the tree of life and the sanctity of the temple was therefore demonstrated. Moses was shown the pattern for the menorah while standing in God's presence—represented by a bush or small tree. The seven branches of the menorah surely reflect the symbolism attached to the number seven—wholeness, completeness, infinity, eternity, consummation, and perfection—in ancient times.[18]

From Genesis 3:8 it also appears that the Garden of Eden, in which the tree of life was placed, was something of a favorite resort of Jehovah and therefore served a similar function as the future tabernacle and later Jerusalem temple, both of which were the earthly abode of God, the repository of his divine presence. The Garden of Eden served this same purpose before physical structures were built, and, significantly, in the midst of the temple-paradise of Eden grew the tree of

17. Leon Yarden, *The Tree of Light: A Study of the Menorah, the Seven-Branched Lampstand* (Ithaca, NY: Cornell University Press, 1971), 35.

18. For the symbolism associated with the number seven, see Marvin H. Pope, "Seven, Seventh, Seventy," in *The Interpreter's Dictionary of the Bible*, ed. George Arthur Buttrick (New York: Abingdon Press, 1962), 4:295. For the number's relation to the menorah, see Annemarie Schimmel, "Numbers: An Overview," in *The Encyclopedia of Religion*, ed. Mircea Eliade (New York: Macmillan, 1987), 11:16.

life. This motif, where the sacred garden and temple were intricately linked, was long-lived and widespread in the ancient Near East. It is seen, for example, in "Assyrian palace reliefs from Nineveh and Dur-Sharrukin (about 700 B.C.). Here the temple is usually depicted with a sacred grove and a river . . . , thus by all accounts a realistic representation of a temple garden."[19] The biblical Eden was nothing less than a garden temple.

Beyond Genesis

Outside of Genesis, the only other attestations of the phrase *ētz-hayyim* (tree of life) in the Hebrew Bible occur in Proverbs, to which we shall turn momentarily. However, it is important to note that the Septuagint (Greek) version of Isaiah 65:22 does explicitly mention the tree of life (*xulou tēs zoēs*). The Masoretic Text, as reflected in the King James Version, reads (with emphasis added):

> They shall not build, and another inhabit; they shall not plant, and another eat: for as *the days of a tree* are the days of my people, and mine elect shall long enjoy the work of their hands.

Compare the Septuagint rendition (with emphasis added):

> They shall not build, and others inhabit; and they shall not plant, and others eat: for as *the days of the tree of life* shall be the days of my people, they shall enjoy the fruits of their labors.

In the Septuagint the enduring nature of the restoration of the Lord's chosen people in a coming millennial or new age renewal is clearly alluded to. As to why there is a difference between the Septuagint rendition of this passage and the Masoretic Text (from which much of our King James Version was translated), I think there is a probable reason. The Septuagint was translated from a Hebrew text (one extant in the third century BC) that was different from the one that has come down to us as the Masoretic Text. Evidence confirms that the Septuagint and the Masoretic Text were two different text

19. Yarden, *Tree of Light*, 38.

types existing at the same time and that the Septuagint sometimes preserves an earlier, more original reading of what Christians call the Old Testament.

But whether or not the Septuagint exhibits the earlier, and thus preferred, reading in this case is unclear. The Isaiah material from Qumran (Dead Sea Scrolls) supports thc Masoretic Text and does not explicitly mention the tree of life—only a "tree." However, the theological context of Isaiah 65:22 seems to me to argue in favor of the full phrase, *tree of life*, as the earlier (perhaps even original), preferred reading.

The tree of life has an important connection to Wisdom literature, that genre of sayings in Israelite religion that teaches about God and virtue. The image of the tree of life as a personification of wisdom in Proverbs is a critical indicator of the significance of this symbol in Hebrew thought.

The phrase *tree of life* in Proverbs appears as the personification or symbolic representation of the concept of wisdom. There are four passages in which the expression occurs:

- "She [wisdom] is a tree of life to them that lay hold upon her" (3:18).
- "The fruit of the righteous is a tree of life" (11:30).
- "Hope deferred maketh the heart sick: but when the desire cometh, it is a tree of life" (13:12).
- "A wholesome tongue is a tree of life" (15:4).

There is scholarly debate about how these passages would have been understood in ancient Israel. Professor Ralph Marcus argued in his brief study that in the corpus of Wisdom literature, of which Proverbs is a part, the phrase *tree of life* had acquired a secularized, practical meaning, the same as the late Hebrew phrase *sām hayyim*, "health-giving drug" or "remedy."[20] In other words, in Proverbs the expression *tree of life* has a medicinal meaning, with "health" replacing "life" in the conceptual framework of Israel's wisdom tradition. Marcus writes:

20. Ralph Marcus, "The Tree of Life in Proverbs," *Journal of Biblical Literature* 62/2 (June 1943): 119.

> This non-mythological or medical meaning of the expression [*ētz-hayyim*] in the book of Proverbs has not, of course, escaped the notice of commentators. For example, [Professor] Toy writes, '"Tree of Life' is a figurative expression (probably a commonplace of the poetical vocabulary) equivalent to 'source of long life and peace.'" . . .
>
> The chief point I wish to make is that the mythological associations of the Tree of Life are preserved to a late date in eschatological literature, Jewish, Christian and pagan, while the expression [*ētz-hayyim*] survives only as a secularized term or faded metaphor in Jewish Wisdom literature.[21]

Thus, in Marcus's view, the tendency in Jewish Wisdom literature is "to reclaim some of the older mythological terminology from the eschatologists, and to present the Torah-Hokmah concept as this-worldly rather than other-worldly."[22]

Though Professor Marcus's argument has much to commend it, one still cannot help but wonder if many Israelites did not see Proverbs as simply extolling the virtue of cultivating wisdom, the enduring quality of the faithful. David Stern writes that the term *tree of life* was simply used in Proverbs "to describe wisdom, the fruit of the righteous . . . aspects of eternal life," or qualities possessed by those who seek eternal life.[23]

While the Masoretic Text does not attest the phrase *tree of life* outside of Genesis and Proverbs, scholars believe that the book of Ezekiel alludes to the tree of life without naming it. A passage in Ezekiel 31 echoes refrains of the Sumerian motif of the king as the tree of life, being planted by the Water of Life; and, at the same time, it harks back to the Garden of Eden in Genesis. Consider these verses:

> The word of the Lord came unto me, saying, son of man, speak unto Pharaoh king of Egypt, and to his multitude; Whom art

21. Marcus, "Tree of Life in Proverbs," 119–20.
22. Marcus, "Tree of Life in Proverbs," 120.
23. David H. Stern, *Jewish New Testament Commentary* (Clarksville, MD: Jewish New Testament Publications, 1992), 795.

> thou like in thy greatness? Behold, the Assyrian was a cedar in Lebanon with fair branches, and with a shadowing shroud, and of an high stature; and his top was among the thick boughs. The waters made him great, the deep set him up on high with her rivers running round about his plants, and sent out her little rivers unto all the trees of the field. Therefore his height was exalted above all the trees of the field, and his boughs were multiplied, and his branches became long because of the multitude of waters, when he shot forth. All the fowls of heaven made their nests in his boughs, and under his branches did all the beasts of the field bring forth their young, and under his shadow dwelt all great nations. Thus was he fair in his greatness, in the length of his branches: for his root was by great waters. The cedars in the garden of God could not hide him: the fir trees were not like his boughs, and the chestnut trees were not like his branches; nor any tree in the garden of God was like unto him in his beauty. I have made him fair by the multitude of his branches: so that all the trees of Eden, that were in the garden of God, envied him. (Ezekiel 31:1–9)

Later on in Ezekiel 47 the prophet describes a vision in which he sees trees with healing properties growing alongside a river of life-giving water that flows out from the temple (vv. 1–12). Allusions here to the tree of life motif are substantial. Note again the connection between trees of life, the temple, and waters of life that flow down to "heal" or restore life to the Dead Sea (v. 8). As alluded to earlier, this intersection of images—temples, waters of life, and trees of life—is a recurring theme in ancient Near Eastern literature.[24]

The image of the tree of life is strongly implied in the opening verses of the Psalms: "Blessed is the man that walketh not in the counsel of the ungodly, nor standeth in the way of sinners, nor sitteth in the seat of the scornful. But his delight is in the law of the Lord; and in his

24. See, for example, John M. Lundquist, "What Is a Temple? A Preliminary Typology," in *Temples of the Ancient World: Ritual and Symbolism*, ed. Donald W. Parry (Salt Lake City: Deseret Book and FARMS, 1994), 88–89.

law doth he meditate day and night. And he shall be like a *tree* planted by the *rivers of water*, that bringeth forth his fruit in his season; his leaf also shall not wither; and whatsoever he doeth shall prosper" (Psalm 1:1–3, emphasis added).

Here the relationship between obedience to God and immortality is expressed in the analogy of the tree, again planted by the rivers of water, whose leaf does not wither (Psalm 1:3). The obedient, unrebellious, Torah-centered man becomes as a tree of life. The language of this text recalls the Garden of Eden in Genesis 2–3, wherein the same relationship between obedience and enjoyment of the fruit of the tree of life—immortality—is implied.

Some scholars see extensions of, and direct allusions to, the tree of life in other Old Testament episodes. "The tree [of life] symbolizes not only eternal life but also God's presence. . . . Thus, whenever man regained God's presence, a tree of life representation was used to symbolize that reunion. When Moses went to the mountain of God, the Lord spoke to him out of a bush that burned with fire but was not consumed. (See Ex. 3:1–6.) The rod of Aaron similarly represented that God was with Moses and Aaron as it swallowed the rods-turned-serpents of the Egyptian magicians. (See Ex. 7:10–12.)"[25] Thus the burning bush and Aaron's rod are seen as symbols of the tree of life. It will be remembered that God later caused Aaron's rod to bud and yield almonds—a sure sign that the rod was continually filled with life (Numbers 17:2–10). The images of planting and almond trees also appear in Jeremiah's prophetic call (Jeremiah 1:10–12).

Professor Wilfred Griggs believes that messianic prophecies in the Old Testament often speak of the Messiah in terms of a tree of life. For example, Isaiah prophesied that a rod would come out of the stem of Jesse and a "Branch" would grow out of his roots (Isaiah 11:1). Zechariah saw in vision that Joshua the high priest would walk with the Branch, or Messiah (Zechariah 3).[26]

---

25. Griggs, "Tree of Life in Ancient Cultures," 27–28.
26. Griggs, "Tree of Life in Ancient Cultures," 28.

By the end of the biblical or Old Testament period (after 400 BC), Israel, or rather its surviving Jewish remnant, had been through periods of apostasy and exile. But the tree of life remained a powerful and vibrant image and cultural icon.

Postbiblical Literature

In the words of one scholar, the postbiblical literature of the Apocrypha and Pseudepigrapha took the tree of life and transplanted it, so to speak, "from the Garden of Eden to paradise in the afterlife."[27] It should not be surprising that such a powerful image was attached to the concept of the afterlife since discussions about the latter became a passion among postbiblical leaders and teachers, owing, undoubtedly, to the challenges and confrontations Jews increasingly encountered and, thus, the need for encouragement leaders felt they had to give to everyone to remain steadfast and anticipate a better existence beyond mortality. Generally speaking, the authors of the Apocrypha and Pseudepigrapha, as most all Jews of this period, regarded the tree of life in a literal sense. The attribute of being able to convey immortality was still inherent in the tree of life, but it was reserved only for the righteous who would enjoy God's presence in a risen state.

An interesting bridge between the Genesis story and intertestamental descriptions of the paradisiacal conditions of the afterlife, wherein is found the tree of life, comes from the pseudepigraphic *Testament of Levi*:

> Then shall the Lord raise up a new priest. And to him all the words of the Lord shall be revealed; and he shall execute a righteous judgement upon the earth for a multitude of days. . . . And he shall open the gates of paradise, and shall remove the threatening sword against Adam. And he shall give to the saints to eat from the tree of life, and the spirit of holiness shall be on them. (*Testament of Levi* 18:2, 10–11)

27. Geoffrey Wigoder, ed., *The Encyclopedia of Judaism* (New York: Macmillan, 1989), 714.

As noted by one of the true experts on intertestamental literature, R. H. Charles, the tree of life is "one of the striking features of the heavenly Paradise on which the apocalyptists love to dwell."[28] The conditions of the future age of joy and immortality are described in several other pseudepigraphic works. From *4 Ezra* (2 Esdras), where the prophet is assured that his lot is with the blessed and that he should think about their glorious condition rather than the fate of sinners, we read:

> For for you
> is opened Paradise,
> planted the Tree of Life;
> the future Age prepared,
> plenteousness made ready;
> a City builded,
> a Rest appointed;
> Good works established
> wisdom preconstituted;
> The (evil) root is sealed up from you,
> infirmity from your path extinguished;
> And Death is hidden,
> Hades fled away;
> Corruption forgotten,
> sorrows passed away;
> and in the end the treasures of immortality are
> made manifest.[29]

Here one discerns striking connections to Isaiah's discussion of millennial conditions. Explicit mention of the tree of life in the

---

28. R. H. Charles, *Apocrypha and Pseudepigrapha of the Old Testament* (Oxford: Clarendon, 1913), 2:597.

29. *4 Ezra* 8:52–54. See the alternative translation in Bruce M. Metzger and Roland E. Murphy, eds., *The New Oxford Annotated Apocrypha: The Apocryphal/Deuterocanonical Books of the Old Testament* (New York: Oxford University Press, 1991), 323: "Because it is for you that paradise is opened, the tree of life is planted, the age to come is prepared, plenty is provided, a city is built, rest is appointed, goodness is established and wisdom perfected beforehand. The root of evil is sealed up from you, illness is banished from you, and death is hidden; Hades has fled and corruption has been forgotten; sorrows have passed away, and in the end the treasure of immortality is made manifest."

Septuagint version of Isaiah 65:22 fits well with the paradisiacal environment with which the intertestamental authors were so taken.

In the Enoch narratives, the noted seer saw the tree of life in a visionary journey to the ends of the earth. It was planted on the mountain of God's throne, incredibly beautiful and fragrant (*1 Enoch* 24:6–25:6). The archangel Michael explains to Enoch the nature of God's mountain throne, the tree of life, and the fruit thereof, which provides nourishment to the righteous and the holy ones (i.e., the saints). Michael acts as tutor and revealer because he is caretaker of the grove of trees encircling God's throne—an image somewhat reminiscent of the trees in the midst of the garden described in Genesis. Enoch learned that no mortal is allowed to touch the tree of life until after the great judgment, when God will "bring everything to its consummation for ever" (*1 Enoch* 25:4). Continuing with verse 5 of this Enoch passage, we again see the connection between the tree of life and the temple, similar to the connection drawn in Sumerian literature between the tree of life and the temple of the god-king. Says Michael to Enoch in *1 Enoch* 25:5–7:

> It [the tree of life] shall then [after the great judgment] be given to the righteous and holy. Its fruit shall be for food to the elect: it shall be transplanted to the holy place, to the temple of the Lord, the Eternal King. Then shall they rejoice with joy and be glad, and into the holy place shall they enter; and its fragrance [from the tree of life] shall be in their bones, and they shall live a long life on earth, such as thy fathers lived: And in their days shall no sorrow or plague or torment or calamity touch them. Then blessed I [Enoch] the God of Glory, the Eternal King, who hath prepared such things for the righteous, and hath created them and promised to give to them.

Other Enoch narratives describe similar things. In the *Secrets of Enoch* 9:1, the seer beholds the heavenly abode of the righteous, wherein is placed the tree of life.

> This place, O Enoch, is prepared for the righteous, who endure all manner of offence from those that exasperate their souls, who avert their eyes from iniquity, and make righteous judgement, and give bread to the hungering, and cover the naked with clothing, and raise up the fallen, and help injured orphans, and who walk without fault before the face of the Lord, and serve him in the midst of Paradise, and a place unknown in goodness of appearance.
>
> Every tree sweet-flowering, every fruit ripe, all manner of food perpetually bubbling with all pleasant smells, and four rivers flowing by with quiet course, and every growth is good, bearing fruit for food, and the tree of life is at that place, at which God rests when he goes up into Paradise, and that tree is ineffable for the goodness of its sweet scent, and another olive tree alongside was always discharging the oil of its fruit.

In *1 Enoch* 25:5 the fruit of the tree of life is described as being food for the elect. Only the elect will enjoy eternal life. No color of the fruit is mentioned. However, in a text called the *Creation Apocryphon*, "the tree of life is described as a cypress that has fruit that is perfectly white."[30] As Professor Hugh Nibley notes, because this is not a common image, it is a striking one.[31] Indeed! That is why Book of Mormon statements about the tree of life deserve so much more of our attention, especially the perfect whiteness of the tree and its fruit: "the whiteness [of the tree] . . . did exceed the whiteness of the driven snow" (1 Nephi 11:8), and "the fruit thereof was white, to exceed all the whiteness that I had ever seen" (8:11).

Rabbinic literature, specifically the collections of Midrash (exposition of scripture), is very interested in the tree of life and provides graphic commentary on its physical size. The tree was so huge that it

---

30. Hugh Nibley, *Temple and Cosmos: Beyond This Ignorant Present*, ed. Don Norton (Salt Lake City: Deseret Book and FARMS, 1992), 244.

31. Nibley, *Temple and Cosmos*, 244.

"spread over all living things."[32] In another comment, R. Judah ben R. Ilᶜai said it took five hundred years to encircle the tree of life: "The tree of life covered a five hundred years' journey, and all the primeval waters branched out in streams under it. . . . Not only its boughs but even its trunk was a five hundred years' journey."[33] It seems it would require the sustenance provided by the fruit of the tree for a person to live long enough to make such a circumferential journey! Rabbinic descriptions of the size of the tree of life may be a symbolic way to emphasize its importance, its centrality in God's divine scheme.

A midrashic explanation of Exodus 16:14—"Behold I will cause to rain bread from heaven for you"—interprets the tree of life as being the source of divine nourishment: "He [God] will bring them fruit from the Garden of Eden and will feed them from the Tree of Life."[34]

Perhaps the most interesting of the midrashim relating to the tree of life is the explication of Song of Solomon 6:8, "There are threescore queens, and fourscore concubines, and virgins without number": "R. Judah b. R. Ilᶜai applied the verse to the Tree of Life and the Garden of Eden. There are threescore queens: these are the sixty companies of the righteous who sit in the Garden of Eden under the Tree of Life and study the Torah."[35]

Thus, as might be expected, the rabbis connected the tree of life to the study of Torah—the central activity of their world after the destruction of the temple. The next step in the interpretation of the tree of life is taken by a text called the *Targum Neofiti*, wherein "the Law is a Tree of Life to all who study in it, and those who guard its commandments will live and rise up like a Tree of Life in the world to come."[36]

---

32. *Midrash Rabbah* Genesis 15:6, in H. Freedman and Maurice Simon, eds., *Midrash Rabbah*, 3rd ed., trans. S. H. Freedman (New York: Soncino, 1983), 1:122 (subsequent references to the *Midrash Rabbah* are to this and other volumes edited by Freedman and Simon).

33. *Midrash Rabbah* Genesis 15:6, 1:122.

34. *Midrash Rabbah* Exodus 25:8, 3:310.

35. *Midrash Rabbah* Song of Songs 6:2, 9:266.

36. *Targum Neofiti* commentary on Genesis 3:24, in Derek R. G. Beattie and Martin J. McNamara, eds., *The Aramaic Bible* (Sheffield, England: JSOT Press, 1994), 64.

Dura Europos

Archaeological evidence is instructive in helping us to understand how certain Jews viewed the tree of life during the first centuries of the Christian era.

In 1921 an ancient city was discovered in the desert plains of southern Syria, on the west bank of the Euphrates River, halfway between Aleppo and Baghdad. Its discovery was made accidentally by a British officer during operations against the Arabs. Systematic excavation of the site took place from 1928 to 1937 by Yale University.

Now known as Dura Europos, the locale was originally a Roman military outpost—hence the term *Dura*, which preserves a Semitic term for "fortress." Among the finds were pagan temples, a Jewish synagogue, and a Christian church. All four walls of the synagogue, discovered in 1932, were covered with paintings or murals in five horizontal, parallel bands. The three middle bands consist of at least twenty-eight panels portraying fifty-eight biblical scenes. The bands of murals converge on the image of the Torah shrine on the west wall of the synagogue. These paintings, dated to AD 249, have been called "the most exciting and revolutionary discovery of early Jewish art."[37] It is here we turn to Professor Erwin R. Goodenough, whose massive multivolume reference work, *Jewish Symbols in the Greco-Roman Period*, has become a standard in the field:

> Before the discovery of the Dura synagogue in 1932 anyone would have been thought mad who suggested that Jews could have made such a place of worship[,] . . . but we do not return to sanity when we force the synagogue to conform *a priori* to Jewish literary traditions.[38]

Why? Because the most important figures in the Dura synagogue paintings do not conform to "normative" or rabbinic literary patterns—the dominant Judaism of that period. Professor Goodenough

37. *Interpreter's Dictionary of the Bible*, supplementary volume, 68.

38. Erwin R. Goodenough, *Jewish Symbols in the Greco-Roman Period* (New York: Pantheon, 1953–1968), 10:197.

explains: "In an atmosphere where identification [with other cultures] rather than distinctions, [where] mingling rather than separation, ruled the thoughts of men . . . [we see that] out of the Torah shrine . . . grew the *tree of life* and salvation which led to the supernal throne."[39]

High in the branches of the tree of life we see the familiar figure of Orpheus as he sits playing his lyre to a lion and a lamb. Goodenough believes that this Orpheus image probably represents David, through whose "heavenly, saving . . . music . . . Israel could be glorified."[40] In addition, "[the artist is] trying to show . . . the glorification of Israel through the mystic tree-vine, whose power could also be represented as a divine love which the soul-purifying music of an Orpheus figure best symbolized."[41]

Furthermore, above the tree of life in this final mural there is depicted the throne of God itself, in which God is shown enthroned in heaven, surrounded by his heavenly hosts. Professor Goodenough finds the idea both surprising and compelling: "The enthroned king surrounded by the tribes in such a place reminds us much more of the Christ enthroned with the saints in heaven . . . than of any other figure in the history of art. Let me repeat," says Goodenough, "that before the discovery of the synagogue all sane scholars would have agreed that 'of course' no such synagogue paintings as these could have existed at all."[42]

At Dura Europos we seem to have an artist who understood his Torah differently and who valued eclecticism. Jewish, Greek, and Christian cultural constructs combine in a mix designed to emphasize salvation in God's presence as understood in the syncretistic world of interwoven cultural images in the Near East in late antiquity. And front and center in the murals, associated with the throne of God and the divine presence, is the expansive image of the tree of life with its overflowing boughs.

Just as the tree of life scene is the high point in the Dura murals, so it is in Lehi's and Nephi's vision recorded in the Book of Mormon. And

39. Goodenough, *Jewish Symbols*, 10:200, emphasis added.

40. Goodenough, *Jewish Symbols*, 10:201.

41. Goodenough, *Jewish Symbols*, 10:201.

42. Goodenough, *Jewish Symbols*, 10:201.

Nephi's comment reads even more like it could have been a caption for the central image of the Dura murals: when the angel asks Nephi about the tree of his vision, "Knowest thou the meaning of the tree which thy father saw?" the young man answers, "Yea, it is the love of God, which sheddeth itself abroad in the hearts of the children of men; wherefore, it is the most desirable above all things" (1 Nephi 11:21–22); and hence, I would add, because the tree of life is desirable above all other things, it is the centerpiece of the Dura synagogue paintings.

Medieval and Modern Periods

Among the ancient writers, only Philo seems to have interpreted the tree of life completely allegorically.[43] He foreshadowed the medieval Jewish philosophers who interpreted both the tree of life as well as the entire Garden of Eden allegorically. One of these was Maimonides.

As one of the greatest intellects of the age, Maimonides included comments on aspects of the Garden of Eden story in his *Guide to the Perplexed*. He was concerned with the questions about what constituted Adam's sin and why Adam's condition changed. Man's sin was that he pursued his own desires. His punishment was the loss of the power of intellectual apprehension. "In its place, he acquired the power to apprehend generally accepted opinions and became absorbed in 'judging things to be bad or fine' . . . instead of contemplating intelligibles."[44] The tree of life represented man's opportunity to attain the state of complete intellectual comprehension.

During the later Middle Ages, interest in the tree of life underwent a resurgence, becoming a cardinal symbol for Jewish mystics and Kabbalists. Kabbalah is rich in tree of life imagery, though it interprets the tree of life in a mystical-allegorical manner. *Kabbalah* is a Hebrew word meaning "received tradition." It is a form of Jewish mysticism that attempts to reveal hidden, esoteric insights about the text of the

43. Philo Judaeus, *Questions and Answers on Genesis*, trans. Ralph Marcus (Cambridge, MA: Harvard University Press, 1929), 6 (1.10).

44. Kenneth Seeskin, ed., *The Cambridge Companion to Maimonides* (New York: Cambridge University Press, 2005), 265.

Hebrew Bible. According to Kabbalistic tradition itself, Kabbalah dates from the time of Adam.

Adherents maintain that Kabbalah began with secrets that God revealed to Adam. When read with true understanding, the Torah's description of the creation reveals mysteries about the nature of God, Adam and Eve, the Garden of Eden, the tree of life, and other hidden truths. However, modern scholarship dates Kabbalah to the twelfth century. In the *Book of Bahir*, the oldest known Kabbalistic text, written in southern France around AD 1180, God's powers and the revelations about them are described as forming "a succession of layers and are like a tree."[45] In fact, one of the fascinating aspects of the configuration of the tree of life in the Kabbalistic worldview is that it possesses both "roots," extending downward, as well as "branches," extending upward. Most, if not all, other depictions of the tree of life do not emphasize the roots, which, for Kabbalists, connect earth and heaven in an unbroken continuity but can only be understood (though not completely) through receipt of mystical information as one enters into a state of communion with the Divine.[46] In the most important Kabbalistic text of all, the *Book of Zohar*, composed by Moses de León in the thirteenth century, we read: "Now the Tree of Life extends from above downwards, and is the sun which illuminates all."[47]

Thus at the heart of Kabbalistic thought is the tree of life, consisting of, or disclosing, ten *Sefiroth*, the so-called ten enumerations or emanations of God, ten outward manifestations of God's inner being and his world. These Sefiroth, or "spheres of God," may be thought of as divine attributes and powers arranged into three categories or groups called "pillars." (See fig. 5.)

> There are three vertical columns: the Pillar of Judgment, consisting of Binah (Intelligence), Din or Gevurah (Judgment),

---

45. Quoted in Roger Cook, *The Tree of Life: Image for the Cosmos* (New York: Avon Books, 1974), 18.

46. Here I use *communion* in a broad sense, "sharing one's thoughts and emotions with another"—in this case the Other—and not in the ritual sense in which some Christians use the term.

47. Quoted in Cook, *Tree of Life: Image for the Cosmos*, 18.

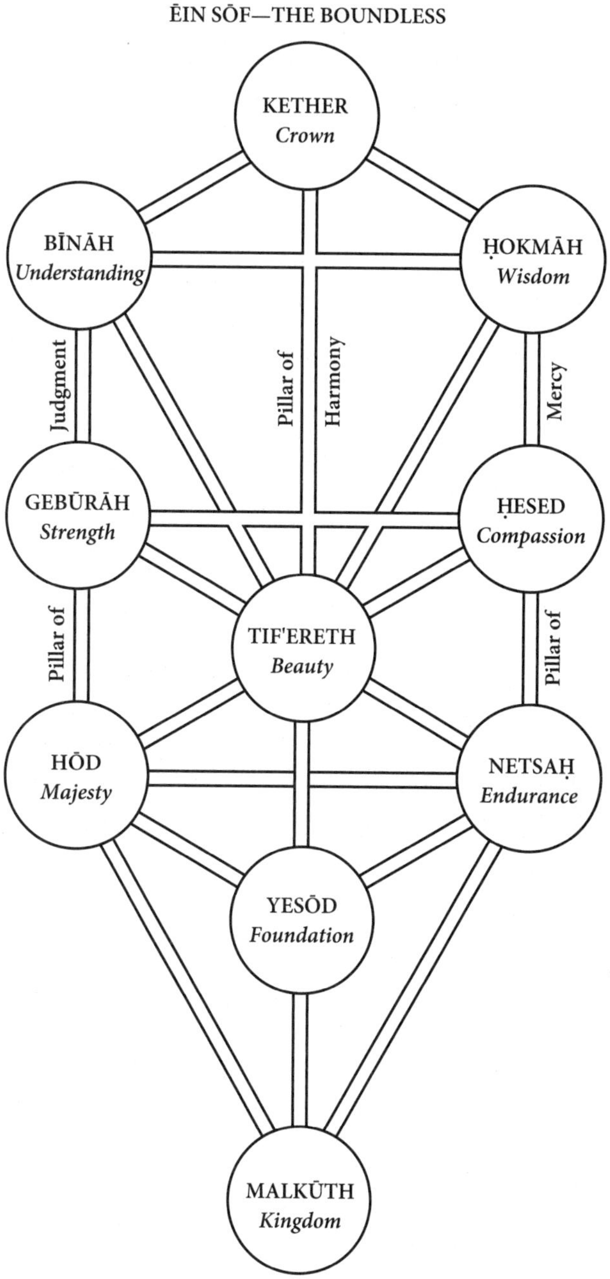

ĒIN SŌF—THE BOUNDLESS

KETHER
Crown

BĪNĀH
Understanding

ḤOKMĀH
Wisdom

Judgment

Pillar of Harmony

Mercy

GEBŪRĀH
Strength

ḤESED
Compassion

Pillar of

TIF'ERETH
Beauty

Pillar of

HŌD
Majesty

NETSAḤ
Endurance

YESŌD
Foundation

MALKŪTH
Kingdom

Fig. 5. Kabbalistic tree of life showing the ten Sefiroth.

> and Hod (Splendour); the Pillar of Mercy, consisting of Hokhmah (Wisdom), Hesed (Love) and Netsah (Firmness); and between them the reconciling column, the Middle Pillar, sometimes called the Balance, consisting of Kether (Crown), Rahamin (Compassion) or Tifereth (Beauty), Yesod (Foundation) and Malkuth (Kingdom). These also read across to form the three interdependent worlds of Intellect (Kether, Binah, Hokhmah), Imagination (Din, Hesed, Tifereth, Hod, Netsah and sometimes Yesod) and Matter (Yesod and Malkuth). There is, further, a sexual symbolism evolved in the web of relationships between these ten Sephiroth, for each represents a masculine and active or a feminine and passive potency of God.[48]

The ten Sefiroth do not come close to describing all that God is, his unfathomable essence, or the infinite nature of his world, what the Kabbalists call the *En Sof*, the Endless or Infinite. Human (and therefore finite) consciousness cannot comprehend that which is infinite and, ultimately, incomprehensible in our sphere of existence. The symbolic nature of the mystical tree of life is intended to convey this recognition of the En Sof.

In addition, the *Zohar* interprets Adam's fall as the result of his failure to understand the nature of the tree of life, specifically the unity that exists among the ten Sefiroth, and therefore his flaw of worshipping something different. He worshipped the *Shekhinah* (literally "dwelling"), which is equated with the Sefirah known as Malkuth and which refers to God's presence in space and time. The Shekhinah is also most closely identified with the material world. "By worshipping the Shekhinah and failing to understand its unity with the other Sefirot, Adam became attached to the temporal, material world as opposed to the values that world instantiates or represents. In this way he worshipped the Tree of Knowledge (of good and evil) and ignored the 'Tree of Life' (the sefirotic values embodied in the Torah)."[49]

48. Quoted in Cook, *Tree of Life: Image for the Cosmos*, 19–20.

49. Sanford L. Drob, *Symbols of the Kabbalah: Philosophical and Psychological Perspectives* (Northvale, NJ: Aronson, 2000), 368.

Another strand of Jewish mysticism, standing alongside that found in the *Zohar*, is represented by a work entitled *Raya Mehemna* and is much more anti-legalistic in its orientation, as noted by the great twentieth-century expert on Jewish mystical thought, Gershom Scholem.

> The latter [*Raya Mehemna*] is full of references to the "two trees": the "tree of knowledge of good and evil" which dominates our world age, and the "tree of life" which is to preside over the coming Messianic aeon. The difference between these two cosmic forces is vividly described, and it is obvious that the writer [of *Raya Mehemna*] is greatly fascinated by the idea of the coming liberation from the yoke of commandments and prohibitions. Nothing of the sort is to be found in the genuine Zohar. Nor is a very pointed social criticism in an apocalyptical vein typical of the Zohar, whereas it is an outstanding feature of the *Raya Mehemna* whose burning hate of the oppressive groups in contemporary Jewish society is unmistakable.[50]

Much more recent attempts to explore and describe Jewish mysticism have theorized that some of the oldest aspects of Kabbalah go back to ancient Assyrian civilization. This has involved comparing the Sefiroth of the Kabbalistic tree of life with the gods of Assyria and the characteristics and descriptions ascribed to them in their ancient cultural setting. The Assyrians assigned specific numbers and values to their gods, somewhat similar to the numbering of the Sefiroth. Corresponding ultimately to the Hebrew En Sof was the god Assur, usually positioned above the Assyrian tree of life. A reconstructed Assyrian antecedent to the Kabbalistic tree of life and its Sefiroth has been the work of Dr. Simo Parpola, who has noted parallels to the Assyrian pantheon.[51]

However, such reconstructions strike one as a poorly aimed attempt to read Kabbalah back into Assyrian civilization of the ancient Near East. The idea that the Kabbalistic tree of life, with its concepts

50. Gershom G. Scholem, *Major Trends in Jewish Mysticism* (New York: Schocken Books, 1961), 180.

51. Simo Parpola, "The Assyrian Tree of Life: Tracing the Origins of Jewish Monotheism and Greek Philosophy," *Journal of Near Eastern Studies* 52/3 (1993): 161–208.

of ten Sefiroth, originated with the Assyrians (ninth to seventh centuries BC), was transferred to Judaism, and then existed undocumented for some eighteen hundred years when it surfaced with the publication of the *Book of Bahir* seems far-fetched indeed. Kabbalah as phenomenon can be traced to a specific period. It started to develop seriously only in the late Middle Ages and is undocumented as a cohesive system prior to the twelfth century.

Conclusion

The tree of life has remained a powerful and profound image and symbol throughout all the periods of Israelite and Jewish history up to modern times. It has always, at some level, conveyed the concepts of immortality and God's divine presence. But the tree of life also became associated with, and a symbol for, other themes or central cultural concepts that faded in and out of dominance during the successive periods of Israelite-Jewish history. Thus, the tree of life served as an object of accommodation to emphasize the prominent religious issues of the day.

During the biblical period, the tree of life not only was the premier symbol of humankind's quest for immortality, the kind of existence experienced by God, but it also represented the sanctuary or temple of God, the repository of his presence. At some point, the tree of life became the symbol and personification of wisdom. It also stood for health and well-being, which derive from wisdom's path; it moved away (in some Jewish circles) from the connotation of immortality and acquired a practical sense of wholeness.

The postbiblical period witnessed the transplanting of the tree of life, so to speak, from Eden to the afterlife so that it became the embodiment of the promises made to the righteous. Intertestamental Jewish thought was preoccupied with the concept of rewards and punishments in the world to come, and that preoccupation forms an important link with New Testament apocalyptic expressions of the tree of life. As reported in postbiblical apocryphal literature, the tree of life and the paradise of God were intertwined in the multiple visions of the next life, which culminate in John's revelation to the Christian community: "To him that overcometh will I give to eat of the tree of life, which is in the midst of the paradise of God" (Revelation 2:7). Such a statement might have been plucked straight out of Enoch's narratives.

Given the postbiblical Jewish fixation on rewards for righteousness, it seems only natural that the rabbis would wed the study of Torah with the image of the tree of life so that, eventually, the tree of life and the Torah were one. As *Targum Neofiti* says, "The Law is a Tree of Life to all who study in it, and those who guard its commandments will live and rise up like a Tree of Life in the world to come."[52]

Medieval and early modern Jewish literature disclose two strains of thought on the tree of life. One is allegorical but rooted in this world, and the other mystical, rooted in the otherworldly. Central to Kabbalah is the tree of life—the representation of the En Sof, the ten emanations of God, the Sefiroth, "the outward manifestation of the inner world of God,"[53] all of which are knowable only through a kind of personal revelation that brings humans into communion with the Infinite. To express this system of thought, the tree of life was the perfect image, "for, just as the seed contains the tree, and the tree the seed, so the hidden world of God contains all Creation, and Creation is, in turn, a revelation of the hidden world of God."[54]

Perhaps the most compelling context in which we find the tree of life image is the murals at Dura Europos. In that syncretistic setting—pagan, Jewish, and Christian—the tree of life serves as a kind of metaphor for what it had become throughout Jewish history: the great symbol of peace and rest and everlasting life in God's presence.

Andrew C. Skinner, former dean of Religious Instruction at Brigham Young University (2000–2005), served as executive director of the Neal A. Maxwell Institute for Religious Scholarship at BYU from 2005 to 2008. A professor of ancient scripture and a member of the international editorial group working on the Dead Sea Scrolls, he is the author of the acclaimed three-volume series

52. *Targum Neofiti* commentary on Genesis 3:24, in Beattie and McNamara, *Aramaic Bible*, 64.

53. Cook, *The Tree of Life: Image for the Cosmos*, 18.

54. Cook, *The Tree of Life: Image for the Cosmos*, 18.

Gethsemane, Golgotha, and The Garden Tomb. *He holds MA degrees from the Iliff School of Theology and Harvard University in Hebrew Bible and theology and a PhD in European and Near Eastern history from the University of Denver. He pursued graduate studies at Hebrew University in Jerusalem. He has served as a member of the LDS Church's Materials Evaluation Committee and as a member of the Sunday School General Board.*

The Fragrant Tree

Margaret Barker

The theology of the temple is recorded in symbols and stories. These are not primitive attempts at Bronze Age or Iron Age theology; they are the way profound issues were expressed in a culture that had storytellers rather than philosophers. The furnishings of the temple, for example, were the setting within which great questions were debated. Irenaeus,[1] who opposed the heresies of his time, wrote a manual of essential Christian teaching, *The Demonstration of the Gospel*; and for him, material based on temple symbolism was the first essential. Origen,[2] the greatest biblical scholar in the early church, emphasised that certain key teachings had been handed down unwritten and were encoded in the temple furnishings. Only Aaron and his sons had seen the furnishings (i.e., had knowledge of this tradition), and Origen emphasised that there were similar unwritten teachings in the church that had been "handed down and entrusted to us by the high priest and his sons."[3] The fragrant tree was one of those temple symbols, gathering around itself a whole complex of sophisticated theology expressed in subtle stories and vivid pictures.

The Two Trees of Enochic Tradition

On his second heavenly journey with the archangels, Enoch saw a fragrant tree set among other trees but surpassing them all. Its fragrance was sweeter than that of the other trees; its leaves, wood, and

1. Irenaeus wrote in the late second century CE.
2. Origen died in 253 CE.
3. Origen, *On Numbers*, homily 5.

blossoms did not wither; and its fruit hung in clusters like the fruit of a palm. The fragrant tree stood by a mountain that was like the seat of a throne, and there were three other mountains on each side of it (*1 Enoch* 24:1–25:7). The lesser mountains were made of coloured precious stones and pearls, but the central mountain was made of antimony and capped with sapphire (18:6–8).[4] Enoch was amazed at the tree and the mountain, and Michael explained to him what he saw: the mountain was the throne of the Great Holy One, and the tree would one day give life to the chosen ones (24:5–25:5). The tree is not named, but we assume it is the tree of life because it is depicted as being the source of life.

This section of *1 Enoch* (Ethiopic version) describes several heavenly journeys, and it is not always clear how they relate to each other. On another journey, Enoch saw huge fragrant trees growing in the Paradise of Righteousness, one of which was the tree of knowledge, the source of great wisdom. This tree was also fragrant, with fruit like clusters of grapes and with leaves like those of a carob tree. The archangel Raphael explained that this was the forbidden tree from which Adam and Eve had eaten before they were driven from the garden (32:1–5). The two trees—the tree of life and the tree of knowledge—did not stand in the same garden, as they do in the Genesis story. The Enoch tradition was careful to distinguish between them.

In both cases, Enoch cried out in delight. When he saw the tree of life, he said: "How beautiful this tree is, and fragrant! And pleasant are its leaves, and its blossoms are a pleasure to behold!" (*1 Enoch* 24:5). When he saw the tree of knowledge, he said: "How beautiful this tree is! What a delight to the eye!" (32:5), echoing the story of Eve, who saw that the tree was good for food and a delight to the eyes (Genesis 3:6), even though it had been forbidden. The trees were very similar.

The visionary journeys went in different directions. When he saw the tree of life, Enoch was looking towards a range of mountains

4. There are problems translating the names of the precious stones. The Ethiopic text says the throne was alabaster, but the word looks like a transliteration of the Hebrew/Aramaic word for "antimony." See Daniel Olson, *Enoch: A New Translation* (North Richland Hills, TX: Bibal Press, 2004), 52.

in the south. There are considerable problems in the text here, but if this central mountain was the throne of God, to which he came when he visited the earth (*1 Enoch* 25:3), it must have been the mountain described also in *1 Enoch* 18:8, the throne of God in the south.[5] The dwelling of the Great One in the south is known elsewhere in *1 Enoch*: he comes forth to dwell on the earth on Mount Sinai (1:4), and the south is so called because the *Great One dwells* there, wordplay on the word for "south" (77:1).[6] The mountain and the throne are usually located by scholars in the north, but recovering the southern location is important. After the Great Judgement, said the archangel Michael, the tree of life would be transplanted northwards, to a holy place beside the House of the Lord (25:5). In other words, the tree of life, or whatever it represented, was seen by Enoch to the south of Jerusalem but was destined to be set in the temple. The tree of the knowledge of good and evil, from which Adam and Eve had eaten, was in the east. Enoch passed over the Erythraean Sea (the Persian Gulf) before he saw it, standing among other huge trees (32:1–5).

What tree might have belonged in the temple, which was associated with the heavenly throne? Its fruit was to feed the chosen ones, but the tree was not, at the time of Enoch's journey, in the temple. Had the fragrant tree perhaps been removed from the temple? In the book of Revelation, the tree of life is seen in the temple, in the holy of holies, beside the throne (Revelation 22:1–2), and its fruit was food for the faithful (v. 7). The tree of life in the temple (perhaps *restored* to the temple?) was an important part of early Christian belief.

The temple represented the Garden of Eden, and the tree of life had certainly been there. Throughout the era of the monarchy, however, there had been a struggle over what was appropriate furnishing

5. See Olson, *Enoch: A New Translation*, 266–68; and Roger T. Beckwith, "The Earliest Enoch Literature and Its Calendar: Marks of Their Origin, Date and Motivation," *Revue de Qumran* 39 (February 1981): 395–96.

6. Olson, *Enoch: A New Translation*, 160, suggests wordplay on *drwmʾ* (south) and *dʾr rbʾ* (the Great One dwells). Robert Henry Charles, *The Book of Enoch* (Oxford: Clarendon Press, 1912), 165, suggested that the wordplay was on *yered ram* (the Great One will descend).

for the temple/Garden of Eden. In the northern kingdom of Israel as well as in Jerusalem, there had been struggles over the asherah, a tree-like symbol that had been constantly set up and then removed and destroyed (1 Kings 15:13; 16:33; 2 Kings 13:6; 17:16; 18:4; 21:7; 23:6, 15). The asherah had been a tree or piece of wood[7] set beside the altar (Deuteronomy 16:21). Asherah was the name of a Canaanite goddess, and this is the form of the name that appears, for example, in 1 and 2 Kings, works that are hostile to the temple and most of the kings and that link Asherah and Baal. In the random survivals among Hebrew inscriptions, however, the name has the form *Ashratah* and is associated with Yahweh.[8] The Lady in Israel may have been identified by her enemies as the Canaanite Asherah rather than by her own name.

The greatest triumph of those opposed to Asherah was the cultural revolution in the time of King Josiah. The asherah was removed from the temple, burned by the brook Kidron, and then beaten to dust and cast on common graves. It was utterly desecrated. Why this fury? The same event was described by Jewish refugees in Egypt as abandoning the Queen of Heaven, who had protected them and their city and given them food (Jeremiah 44:16–19). Enoch described the event as abandoning wisdom (*1 Enoch* 93:8). Since the tree of life was identified in the Bible as wisdom (Proverbs 3:13–18), the accumulated evidence makes it likely that the asherah that was removed from the temple and destroyed had represented the tree of life.

Enoch's heavenly journeys probably identify two communities: those of the tree of knowledge, who lived in the east, and those of the tree of life, who lived in the south. Only the tree of life was destined to be taken to (i.e., returned to) the temple. When the Lord of Glory, the Eternal King, descended to earth, he would sit on his mountain throne by the tree of life; and after the great judgment, the fruit of the tree

7. The Hebrew *'eṣ* means either a tree or a piece of wood, and one has to guess from the context which meaning is appropriate. Revelation 22:2 keeps the ambiguity by using *xulon* (which usually means "wood" but can mean "tree") rather than *dendron*, which means simply "tree."

8. Graham I. Davies, *Ancient Hebrew Inscriptions: Corpus and Concordance* (Cambridge: Cambridge University Press, 1991), 1:8.017, 8.021; 81.

would give life to the chosen ones. They would rejoice in the holy place and live long and happy lives, and their very bones would be permeated with the fragrance of the tree (*1 Enoch* 25:2–6). Those who continued to honor the Queen of Heaven, the tree, and who longed for its return to the temple had fled south. Some had been refugees with Jeremiah in Egypt; others had been temple priests who settled in Arabia. As late as the fourth century CE, people remembered that the priests who had opposed Josiah's purges had fought with Nebuchadnezzar against Jerusalem and then settled in Arabia.[9]

After seeing the tree of life, Enoch traveled to the centre of the earth—that is, to Jerusalem—and saw the holy mountain. From its eastern side, water issued and flowed to the south by way of the Gihon Spring and the brook Kidron (*1 Enoch* 26:1–3). This means that for Enoch the holy mountain was not the area we nowadays call the Temple Mount. It must have been the hill to the southeast of it, the Ophel, from which the Gihon gushes. Before Hezekiah built the tunnel that brought its water into the city (2 Kings 20:20; 2 Chronicles 32:30), the water of the Gihon probably created a real stream in the Kidron Valley. It is interesting that Enoch's journey describes accurately the geography of Jerusalem before the time of Hezekiah,[10] that is, in the early ministry of Isaiah. Enoch knew the temple *on a different site*, and this is where the tree would be transplanted. What he saw was a blessed place in which there were living branches that had survived from a felled tree. The text does not say that it was the tree of life, but the vision of the surviving branches follows immediately upon the vision of the tree that was to be planted (again) in the temple.

The two heavenly journeys and the two trees suggest that the Enoch tradition was preserved by a community that had moved to the south, had not been tempted by the tree of knowledge, and had lived with the hope that they and their tree of life would return to the temple. This community could have been people who emigrated to Egypt, perhaps those who built the temple at Yeb/Elephantine around

9. Jerusalem Talmud *Taʿanit* 4.5.

10. Olson, *Enoch: A New Translation*, 70.

600 BCE. The "branches" remembered a holy site that was not the Temple Mount. The other group was in the east, which suggests the exiles in Babylon. They had with them the tree of knowledge that had led to the loss of Eden, to the loss of their angel state, and to a world of dust and death, thorns and thistles (Genesis 3:17–19).

Memories of the Tree of Wisdom

The community of living branches appears in the Qumran Hymns, and its members apparently saw themselves as the guardians of true teaching who were preserving, or who were, the true temple. In the era of wrath, after Israel had been given into the hand of Nebuchadnezzar, king of Babylon, in 597 BCE, a faithful remnant had survived (*Damascus Document* I). The singer of one hymn rejoices that he has been placed among these branches of the council of holiness (*Thanksgiving Hymns* XV). Another voice—possibly the same person—gives thanks that he has been set by a fountain of streams, by a spring of waters, beside a watered garden (XVI). The Lord had established a plantation of trees beside this water source, and these trees had produced a shoot of the everlasting Plant. Beasts and birds had devastated the shoot, but it had been hidden and protected by "spirits of holiness and the whirling flame of fire" (XVI). The hymn is enigmatic, but the imagery recalls Eden. The precious shoot was guarded in the same way as the tree of life had been guarded in Eden, by cherubim and a flaming sword. In the biblical story, the angels guard the tree of life to prevent Adam and Eve from having access; in the Qumran hymn, the angels protect the tree from those who might harm it. The speaker seems to be the one who irrigates the garden with his teaching: "Thou O God hast put into my mouth as it were rain . . . and a fount of living waters that shall not fail" (XVI).

The voices from Qumran, if they represented one community, frequently used this image of planting. They were, in some sense, Eden, and in their midst a plant sprang up (*Damascus Document* I). The *Rule of the Community* expresses a similar idea: the Council of the Community is the Everlasting Plantation, a House of Holiness for Israel. In other words, this Edenic place was the true temple (*Rule of the*

Community VIII). Eden as the temple is a well-known image.[11] Adam was the original high priest, set in the garden to tend it, and the word for "tend," *ʿabad*, is the same as that for temple service (Genesis 2:15). Adam and Eve driven from Eden was, as we shall see, a description of why the priests were driven from the temple: they had chosen to eat from the wrong tree; they had rejected the tree of life.

The "branches" appear in the later prophecies of Isaiah. An anointed figure—possibly the prophet himself—has been called to proclaim good tidings, to give to those who mourn in Zion "a garland instead of ashes" and "the oil of gladness" (Isaiah 61:3).[12] They were to be called the oaks of righteousness and *the planting* of the Lord. They would build up the ruins and restore the devastation, and they would be recognized as priests of the Lord (v. 6). If the second temple had already been built by that time (66:1), were the ancient ruins the original temple that the anointed one would rebuild? Rebuilding the temple was a task for the Messiah (Zechariah 6:12–13). And would the ousted priests (those banished by Josiah) be returned to their former status? These could have been Enoch's community of branches around the original holy site.

The first Christians hoped to join this blessed company of trees and branches. In one of the *Odes of Solomon*, a collection of early hymns, the singer tells how his eyes were enlightened and his face received the dew, how his breath/soul was refreshed with the fragrance of the Lord (Ode 11:14–15). Then he was taken to paradise, where he saw wonderful, fruitful trees watered by a river of gladness. "Blessed O Lord are they who are planted in your land" (v. 18).[13] The description of paradise is like that in *2 Enoch*, where Enoch, having ascended to the third heaven, saw the trees of paradise in full flower, with ripe and

11. See my book *The Gate of Heaven: The History and Symbolism of the Temple in Jerusalem* (London: SPCK, 1991), 57–103.

12. All scripture quotations are from the Revised Standard Version unless otherwise noted.

13. Translation in James H. Charlesworth, ed., *The Old Testament Pseudepigrapha* (Garden City, NY: Doubleday, 1983), 2:74. There is a similar line in *Psalms of Solomon* 14:3: "The Lord's Paradise, his trees of life, are his devout ones," in Charlesworth, *Old Testament Pseudepigrapha*, 2:663.

pleasant fruits. Four streams—of honey, milk, oil, and wine—flowed from paradise, and at the centre was the tree of life, where the Lord used to rest when he entered paradise. It was the most fragrant of all and the most beautiful, red and gold, looking like fire. It spread far out over paradise, and it had "something of every orchard tree and of every fruit" (*2 Enoch* 8:1–4).[14]

It is important to note that the tree of life did not resemble any one tree. Ben Sira's description of Wisdom, when she compares herself to a tree, is similar: "I grew tall like a cedar . . . like a cypress . . . like a palm tree . . . like rose plants . . . like a beautiful olive tree . . . like a plane tree" (Sirach 24:13–14). One of the Nag Hammadi texts, whose modern title is *On the Origin of the World*, describes the tree of life in the north of paradise, standing beside the tree of knowledge: "The colour of the tree of life is like the sun, and its branches are beautiful. Its leaves are like those of the cypress, its fruit is like clusters of white grapes, its height rises up to heaven" (Coptic Gnostic Library II,5 110). The tree of life also marked the place where the Lord's throne rested in paradise. In the *Apocalypse of Moses*[15] the Lord returned to paradise on the chariot throne, which rested by the tree of life (22:4).

These later texts have an uncertain pedigree, but they do preserve interesting and consistent memories about the tree. It was huge, with wide-spreading branches that bore many sorts of fruit. It was fiery, red and gold, and it stood near the throne of God. In the book of Revelation, the tree of life stood by the throne of God and bore twelve kinds of fruit (22:1–2). If the temple had represented the Garden of Eden, what had represented the tree of life? The most obvious answer would be the menorah. The prescriptions for the tabernacle menorah (recorded in their present form in the Second Temple period and therefore almost certainly influenced by memories of the first temple) say that the lamp was golden, with seven branches on which were cups and flowers like almonds. This was the fiery tree.

---

14. Translation in Charlesworth, *Old Testament Pseudepigrapha*, 2:114.

15. The *Apocalypse of Moses* is a Greek text that corresponds to a large degree to the Latin text *The Life of Adam and Eve*.

There is, however, a problem about its location. The menorah stood in the main part of the tabernacle, on the south side (Exodus 40:24); but in the book of Revelation the tree stood in the holy of holies, by the throne. And there is another problem: descriptions of the first temple do not mention the menorah, but the prophet Zechariah saw a sevenfold lamp that represented the watching presence of the Lord (Zechariah 4:2, 10). Since he prophesied before the second temple had been built, this must have been a memory of the earlier temple. The form of Zechariah's lamp may not have been the familiar menorah; he seems to be describing a single lamp bowl with seven wicks, but this too could have represented the tree.[16] The asherah was described as a pole, so a pillar lamp would have been similar.

Where was the tree of Wisdom? In which community? Ben Sira, writing in Jerusalem about 200 BCE, claimed that Wisdom had taken root in Zion and was still there, growing like a mighty tree and watering her garden with her teaching. She had been identified with the law of Moses, and what had originally been a poem in praise of Wisdom had been transformed into a eulogy of the law (Sirach 24:1–34). Baruch 3–4 is similar. Why was Israel in exile, growing old in a foreign land? The people had forsaken Wisdom (3:12). Wisdom appearing on earth was the giving of the law, because "she is the book of the commandments of God" (4:1). The Enoch tradition disagreed: Wisdom had found no dwelling place on earth and so had returned to her place among the angels (*1 Enoch* 42:2). In her place the thirsty earth had drunk the water of iniquity.[17] Enoch saw the tree—Wisdom—far away in the south, among the trees around the throne of God.

Memories of the first temple persisted for centuries, as did hopes for the true temple to be restored in the time of the Messiah. At that time the menorah, the ark, the spirit, the fire, and the cherubim would be returned (*Rabbah* Numbers XV:10). There *had* been a menorah in

---

16. See Robert North, "Zechariah's Seven-Spout Lampstand," *Biblica* 51 (1970): 183–206. "All experts agree" that the earlier menorah was not like the lamp depicted on the Arch of Titus (p. 206).

17. Olson, *Enoch: A New Translation*, 84, suggests that Wisdom leaving the earth may be the Enochic version of Genesis 6:3, "My Spirit shall not abide with human beings for ever."

the second temple; it was among the Roman loot carried away from the devastated temple in 70 CE and is famously depicted on the Arch of Titus. In what way, then, was this not a genuine menorah? It could have had a different form or meaning, or it could have stood in a different place in the temple. There are other mysteries: in the late Second Temple period, the menorah was widely employed as a Jewish symbol, and yet the Rabbis forbade its use.[18] No passage in the Talmud[19] or in the great commentaries (*Mekilta*, *Rabbah* Exodus) explains its symbolism. Why was the tree/lamp such a sensitive matter?

The asherah also remained a threat. As late as the Mishnah,[20] there were detailed rules defining the asherah—how it can be recognized as a tree grown or pruned for idolatrous worship. It could pollute even the unwary; its wood was forbidden to fuel an oven or make a weaver's shuttle, and nobody could sit in its shade.[21] Objects that Jews described as asherahs were all over Palestine in the sixth century; they may have been Christian crosses since the tree and the cross were symbols that coalesced[22] and Jesus reigning from the tree was a natural development from the idea of the throne of God beneath the tree of life. The Letter of Barnabas[23] alludes to the tree as the throne: "the royal realm of Jesus was founded on a tree"; and Justin Martyr[24] maintained that the Jews had removed certain key texts from the Hebrew scriptures, for example, part of Psalm 96:10, which had originally read, "The Lord reigns *from the tree*" (*Dialogue with Trypho* 73).[25] Since one of the synagogue frescoes at Dura-Europos shows the Messiah enthroned in a tree, this could well have been the original

18. Babylonian Talmud *Menaḥot* 28b, *ʿAboda Zarah* 43a, *Roš Haššanah* 24ab.

19. See Erwin R. Goodenough, *Jewish Symbols in the Greco-Roman Period* (New York: Pantheon Books, 1954), 4:88.

20. Compiled from earlier tradition about 200 CE.

21. Mishnah *ʿAboda Zarah* 2:7–9.

22. Suggested by Robert L. Wilken, *The Land Called Holy* (New Haven and London: Yale University Press, 1992), 211.

23. Late first century CE.

24. Mid-second century CE.

25. The Greek is *xylon*, literally "wood," but *xylon* appears in Revelation 22:2 with the meaning "tree," reflecting the ambiguity of the underlying Hebrew *ʿeṣ*, which can mean either "wood" or "tree."

text. Irenaeus, setting out his system of Old Testament and Christian counterparts (known as "recapitulation"), taught that the cross had been a remedy for the ills brought by the tree of knowledge (*Proof of the Apostolic Preaching* 33–34). The cross as the tree of life was widely used in Christian art, as in the apse mosaic in the Basilica of San Clemente in Rome (see fig. 12).

The Counterclaim of Nonbiblical Books

Embedded within *1 Enoch* is a short, stylised history known as the *Apocalypse of Weeks* (93:1–10; 91:11–17, the Ethiopic text being disordered). Each era of history was a "week." In the first week Enoch was born; in the second, Noah was saved from the flood; in the third, Abraham was born as the chosen plant whose descendants would also be righteous plants. In the fourth week, the law was given; in the fifth, the temple was built; and in the sixth, those in the temple lost their spiritual sight. They rejected Wisdom, and the temple was burned. A man ascended during this week, possibly Isaiah,[26] who saw the throne of God in his temple vision (Isaiah 6). Thus the rejection of Wisdom and the loss of vision represented the struggle to remove the tree. After the temple was burned, the race of the chosen root was scattered. The seventh week saw an apostate generation, who, as we learn elsewhere in *1 Enoch*, built the second temple;[27] but at the end of that week the chosen ones from the eternal plant were called as witnesses to righteousness and given sevenfold wisdom. The Ethiopic version of *1 Enoch* at this point inserts a wisdom poem[28] detailing what knowledge would be restored to the chosen plants. It was the esoteric knowledge revealed to Enoch on his heavenly journeys and widely attested elsewhere: knowledge of the works of heaven, the stars, the spirits, the whole pattern of the world (*1 Enoch* 93:11–14).

---

26. The man is usually identified as Elijah, but there is no compelling reason to make this identification.

27. *1 Enoch* 89:72–74 describes the return from exile and the rebuilding of the temple as a time of polluted and impure worship when the people and their leaders lost their sight.

28. This poem is not in the Qumran fragments at this point, so it must have been from another version of *1 Enoch*.

The *Apocalypse of Weeks* raises several questions, not least of which is, where is Moses? There is no reference to the exodus, and the section about giving the law does not mention any one figure. Most summaries of history in the Hebrew scriptures focus on Moses and the exodus and omit Sinai.[29] They are, in fact, the exact opposite of the *Apocalypse of Weeks*, which emphasises Abraham and his children and the fate of the first temple. This is confirmed by the curious "Animal History" in *1 Enoch*, which tells the story of Israel as an animal fable. From Adam to Isaac, the patriarchs are described as bulls, but Esau is a black boar and Jacob a white ram. Moses is a sheep, and Israel is a flock of sheep, until the corrupt second temple is destroyed and the new temple built. Then a new Adam is born, in the form of a white bull, and all the other animals—sheep as well as the unclean ones—are transformed into bulls. In other words, when Eden is restored, the Moses religion is transformed, along with all others, into the original faith of Adam and Abraham.

Nonbiblical texts emphasise that many of the important laws and customs did not derive from Moses. They should not be seen as "rewriting" the biblical version of the story, but rather as a counterclaim to the origin of the traditions and customs of Israel by those who denied that they came from Moses. The prescriptions in *Jubilees*, for example, a text found at Qumran, are usually read as rewritten Genesis, the normative biblical text. According to *Jubilees*, Noah learned from his ancestors about the firstfruits and the Sabbath year (7:34–39), and he himself recorded angelic teaching about healing with herbs (10:13). Abraham followed the teachings of Enoch and Noah (21:1–26), shunning idols, offering sacrifices in the correct way, and observing food laws and rules for ritual washing. Isaac passed these instructions to his grandson Levi (*Testament of Levi* 9:1–14). Ancient Noachian texts are embedded in *1 Enoch*,[30] and *2 Enoch* has the wife of Noah's brother Nir giving birth miraculously to Melchizedek (70–71). These

29. Gerhard von Rad, *The Problem of the Hexateuch and Other Essays*, ed. E. W. Trueman Dicken (Edinburgh and London: Oliver and Boyd, 1966), 1–78.

30. Identified by Charles, *Book of Enoch*, p. xlvii, as *1 Enoch* 6–11; 54–55:2; 60; 65–69:25; 106–7.

are all echoes of the first temple, the time before the great flood, which now encodes the disaster that swept over Jerusalem in 597 BCE. Adam, Enoch, Noah, and Melchizedek represented older traditions that the Second Temple–era compilers of the Pentateuch attributed to Moses.

According to 2 Esdras, when the canon of Hebrew scriptures was defined, "Ezra" restored the lost scriptures to his people. The story is set in the time of the biblical Ezra, but there are indications (e.g., 2 Esdras 3:1) that the actual date was thirty years after the destruction of the temple in 70 CE. Ezra sat under an oak tree and heard a voice from a nearby bush (14:1–2) telling him that the scriptures, lost in the recent war and destruction, would be restored through him. In a state of rapture, Ezra then dictated ninety-four books. God Most High told him to make twenty-four books public but to keep the other seventy only for the wise: "For in them is the spring of understanding, the fountain of Wisdom and the river of knowledge" (vv. 45–48). These seventy other books sound remarkably like the teaching claimed by the community of the living branches. By definition, they are not in the Hebrew canon, and so we probably have to look outside the Old Testament for the teachings associated with the fragrant tree and its branches.

Eden and the Fallen Priests

The Bible begins with the story of creation and then the Garden of Eden. It is one of the more curious aspects of the Old Testament that this story, which apparently sets the stage for all that follows, is not mentioned elsewhere. There is another Eden story in Ezekiel 28:12–19, where a heavenly figure was expelled from Eden, the holy mountain garden of God, because of pride and corrupted wisdom. The heavenly figure was no longer an angel but profane (v. 16), and the sanctuaries that were profaned as a result were burned. This heavenly being, who was reduced to a mortal state and died as ashes on the earth, is currently described as the king of Tyre, but this could be an example of a reworked and reused prophecy.[31] The original seems to

31. The original heavenly being of the Ezekiel account seems to be feminine, hence my attempt not to use masculine or feminine pronouns.

have been about the ruler of Zion, since *Tyre* and *Zion* can look very similar in Hebrew.[32] What is certain is that the Greek text of Ezekiel 28:13 is longer and lists, in correct order, all the precious stones of the high priest's breastplate, as they appear in the Greek text of Exodus 28:17–20. The translator of Ezekiel knew that the splendid figure thrown from Eden was the high priest. Adam was remembered as the original high priest, and so this was Ezekiel's way of telling the story of how and why the high priest was driven out of Eden—thrown down because of pride and corrupted wisdom.

Isaiah knew the same story. "Your first father sinned, and your *** transgressed against me. Therefore I profaned the princes of the sanctuary, and I delivered Jacob to utter destruction and Israel to reviling" (Isaiah 43:27–28). Thus in the Hebrew, where *** represents a word with several meanings ("interpreter," as in Genesis 42:23; "a mediator," as in Job 33:23, where the word is in parallel with *angel*; or "one who mocks," as in Isaiah 29:20, with the noun form in Habakkuk 2:6), Isaiah's style often includes wordplay, and so all these meanings are probably intended here. Those who should have been the angel mediators for the people (i.e., the priests) had become mocking transgressors, and so the Lord had profaned the princes of the sanctuary,[33] reducing them from their angel state to that of mortals, exactly the fate of the heavenly being in Ezekiel's oracle. As a result, Jacob/Israel was destroyed. The Greek text here is different: "Your first fathers and rulers transgressed against me, and the rulers desecrated my sanctuary. And I delivered Israel to destruction." The meaning is the same. Something had happened to the priests and to the temple, such that the Lord destroyed both.

The Genesis story of Eden has two trees, but neither is described in any detail (we do not know about any fragrance, for example).

---

32. *Tyre* is *ṣwr*, and *Zion* is *ṣywn*, and Hebrew *r* and *n* are similar forms.

33. The "princes of the sanctuary" appear in the Qumran *Songs of the Sabbath Sacrifice*. Consider, for example, "The sovereign princes . . . the seven priest[***] in the wonderful sanctuary" (4Q403 1.II) and "The princes of those marvellously clothed for service, the princes of the Kingdom . . . in all the heights of the sanctuaries of His glorious kingdom" (4Q405 23.II).

Only the tree of the knowledge of good and evil was forbidden, which implies that the Wisdom of the tree of life had been intended as food for Adam and Eve. Eliphaz's mocking words to Job imply this: "Are you the first man to be born? Have you listened in the council of God? Are you the only one with Wisdom?" (Job 15:7–8, my translation). The great restoration described in the book of Revelation also implies this: the faithful Christian will once again eat from the tree of life (2:7); the blessed have access to the tree of life (22:14). The story of the Garden of Eden is often interpreted simply as a story of disobedience, of Adam and Eve breaking the one commandment they had been given. It is far more than that. The story of Adam and Eve is about people who chose the knowledge of good and evil and then discovered that they could no longer have access to the Wisdom of the tree of life. The grand narrative of the Bible is about rejecting the tree of life and then regaining access to its fruit.

The writer of Genesis is more sympathetic to the fallen priests than are Ezekiel and Isaiah. The prophets described their sins as pride, abuse of wisdom, mockery, and defiling the holy place. The writer of Genesis recognized that they had been deceived, and in the telling of the story we see what was at stake. "God knows that when you eat of [the fruit of the tree] your eyes will be opened, and you will be like God, knowing good and evil" (Genesis 3:5). This is exactly the opposite of the Enochic account of the sixth week, when the temple was destroyed. The eyes of the priests were closed, and they abandoned Wisdom (*1 Enoch* 93:8). They chose the wrong tree. They were the first victims of the rebel angels who came to earth to offer knowledge in rebellion against the Great Holy One. Mortals then had knowledge and skills without the constraint of morality, and the result was bloodshed and cries of despair (9:1–2). The fallen angels also taught how to "change the world" (8:1), which traditional Ethiopian commentaries explained as changing a man into an animal.[34] This sounds like a memory of the original tradition in which a "man" indicated an angel and an "animal" indicated a mortal. Great heroes were born as

34. E. Isaac, *1 Enoch*, in Charlesworth, *Old Testament Pseudepigrapha*, 1:16.

animals and became "men." Noah was born a white bull and became a man (89:1). To turn men into animals meant reducing angels to mortals, which is exactly what the fallen angels did. Adam and Eve were tempted by the leader of the fallen angels, and as a result they left the garden and learned they were mortal.

The two trees represented two ways of knowing, perhaps two attitudes to knowledge, and the state that arises from each. The tree of life represented Wisdom, and those who ate from it were angels, "men." The other tree represented knowledge that could be used for good or for evil, and those who ate from it were mortals, "animals." The story of the two trees is the story of a clash of cultures: the life of the angels or the life of mortals. The *Gospel of Philip*, an early Christian text, shows that these ideas were known in the church. Unfortunately, the relevant part is damaged, and so some parts are uncertain. "There are two trees growing in Paradise. The one bears [animals], the other bears men. Adam [ate] from the tree which bore animals. He became an animal" (Coptic Gnostic Library II,3 71).[35]

The Tree in Isaiah's Temple Vision and Mysterious Oracle

The conflict over the tree breaks the surface in some Old Testament texts and can be detected in the earliest parts of the writings of Isaiah, who prophesied in the reigns of four kings: Uzziah (also called Azariah), Jotham, Ahaz, and Hezekiah. Uzziah "did what was right in the eyes of the Lord" (2 Kings 15:3); Jotham too "did what was right in the eyes of the Lord" (v. 34), although the writer noted that both of them allowed the high places to remain, clearly something of which he disapproved. Ahaz "did not do what was right in the eyes of the Lord . . . and even sacrificed his son" (16:2–4), but Hezekiah did what was right in the eyes of the Lord, removing the high places and cutting down the asherah; he followed the religion of Moses (18:3–7). These accounts in 2 Kings, however, were written by someone who inclined to the Mosaic element in Israel's religion.

35. *The Nag Hammadi Library in English*, trans. James M. Robinson (New York: Harper and Row, 1977).

Isaiah saw things differently. Ahaz was not condemned for sacrificing his son but chided only for lack of faith (Isaiah 7:4). Hezekiah was seen as the one who had destroyed the altars of the Lord rather than purified the religion of his kingdom (36:7). He was smitten with plague, a sure sign of divine wrath (38:1), but was miraculously restored to health. His recovery probably inspired the Fourth Servant Song (52:13–53:12).[36] And something had happened during the reign of Uzziah that had been heavy on the conscience of Isaiah. In his great vision of the Lord enthroned in the temple, the prophet cried out, "Woe is me, for I kept silent" (6:5).[37] His lips were then purified by the seraph with a coal, suggesting that it was a sin of his lips that had caused his anguish. What was the silence that Isaiah so regretted?

From his attitude towards Ahaz and Hezekiah, we can guess that Isaiah was not sympathetic towards the changes in Jerusalem, the purges that the writer of Kings regarded as "doing what was right in the eyes of the Lord." His guilty conscience may indicate that he had not spoken out about similar events in the reign of Uzziah, a king who "did what was right in the eyes of the Lord." Uzziah had been in conflict with the temple priesthood (2 Chronicles 26:16–21), and there is good reason to believe that Isaiah himself was a temple priest.[38]

The punishment prophesied for Jerusalem and Judah after Isaiah's temple vision suggests what Uzziah had done. The people would be condemned to hear but not understand, and to see but not perceive, so that they would not turn and be healed (Isaiah 6:10). Had Uzziah rejected the tree and its wisdom, this would have been the result, not so much a punishment from the Lord as allowing the people to experience the consequence of their choice. Understanding, *biynah*, and perception/knowledge, *daʿat*, were the fundamentals of wisdom teaching,

36. See my article "Hezekiah's Boil," *Journal for the Study of the Old Testament* 95 (September 2001): 31–42.

37. Usually translated "I am lost," but the Hebrew verbs *dmh*, "be destroyed," and *dmm*, "be silent," are identical in some forms. Symmachus the Ebionite, that is, a Jewish Christian, read it as *esiopēsa*, "kept silent," as did the Vulgate, *tacui*.

38. His call vision, for example, is set in the temple (Isaiah 6). Even though he may not have been physically in the temple, he was familiar with the interior where only the priests could go.

as can be seen in Proverbs 1:2. "That men may know [*ladaᶜat*] wisdom and instruction, understand [*lᵉhabiyn*] words of insight." According to the *Apocalypse of Weeks*, the ascension of a man in the "sixth week" was linked to the priests (those who "live in the temple") abandoning wisdom and losing their spiritual sight (*1 Enoch* 93:8). This man is usually said to be Elijah, but Isaiah is more likely, as his call vision—his ascent to stand before the throne—is linked to the loss of wisdom. "All who lived in it lost their sight" is very similar to "Hear, hear and do not *understand*; see, see and do not *perceive*" (Isaiah 6:9).

At the close of the sixth week, the temple was burned and the "entire race of the chosen root" was scattered.[39] The next part of Isaiah's prophecy was similar: "How long, O Lord?" (Isaiah 6:11). How long would this spiritual blindness continue? "Until cities lie waste without inhabitant, and houses without men, and the land is utterly desolate, and the Lord removes men far away" (vv. 11–12). "Until the forsaken places are many in the midst of the land" is the usual translation of the next line, and this makes good sense. But the same Hebrew words can also be read: "Until the Deserted One is great in the midst of the land." The Deserted One would have been Wisdom, the female figure in the Jerusalem temple cult. She was described and represented in many ways: as the city, as the bride, as the heavenly mother of the Davidic king, and as the tree. Isaiah's use of the same vocabulary in later oracles suggests that Isaiah 6:12 was indeed about the Lady. *Deserted*, *ᶜᵃzubah*, is used elsewhere to describe the city as the forsaken wife of the Lord (Isaiah 54:6), the forsaken city, depicted as an abandoned woman (60:15), the name she is to use no more once she has been restored (62:4). Her land will no longer be called desolate, *šᵉmamah*, as it was in Isaiah 6:11b. In the future she was to be called *hephṣiybah*, "my delight is in her," the name later used for the mother of the Messiah.[40]

39. Olson, *Enoch: A New Translation*, 221.

40. In the *Book of Zerubbabel*, a Jewish apocalypse from the sixth or seventh century CE, Hephzibah is obviously the Jewish counterpart to the Byzantine Mary, the Mother of God. This was suggested by Martha Himmelfarb in *Rabbinic Fantasies:*

The variety of translations offered for Isaiah 6:13 gives an idea of the problems it presents. It is about a tree that has been felled, "a tenth," and the holy seed surviving in the stump of the tree. The Deserted One is linked to a tree. The Authorised Version offers this reading: "But yet in it shall be a tenth, and it shall return, and shall be eaten: as a teil tree, and as an oak, whose substance is in them, when they cast their leaves: so the holy seed shall be the substance thereof." The Jerusalem Bible reads, "Though a tenth of the people remain, it will be stripped like a terebinth of which, once felled, only the stock remains. The stock is a holy seed." The New English Bible reads: "Even if a tenth part of its people remain there, they too will be exterminated [like an oak or a terebinth, a sacred pole thrown out from its place in a hill-shrine]." The word *tenth*, *ʿaśryh*, is a suggestive set of letters, being very similar to the word *asherah*, the treelike object commonly associated with the Canaanite worship. Reference to a terebinth and an oak confirms that the verse is about a tree, and the New English Bible term *sacred pole* shows that the translators also had this association in mind. This was the tree that had been abandoned in Isaiah's time, the tree that represented Wisdom.

If Isaiah 6:13 refers to the fragrant tree, the various translations for that verse echo what we find in *1 Enoch*. If the "tenth" was originally the name *asherah*, then the Authorised Version would read, "In it shall be the sacred tree, and it shall return and be eaten"—the words of Michael to Enoch on his heavenly journey. The Qumran Isaiah has a different reading in 13b, *mšlkt*, "throw, fling, cast," instead of Masoretic Text *bšlkt*, "in the felling." "Shedding" is the reading assumed by the Authorised Version, and since the ancient versions reflect this idea of shedding/spreading, the Qumran text may be the original.[41] In addition, *ʾašer*, "which," could also once have been *asherah*. That line would then read, "Like a terebinth or an oak tree, *asherah* sheds her leaves/spreads her branches." The Greek omits any mention of the

Imaginative Narratives from Classical Hebrew Literature, ed. David Stern and Mark Jay Mirsky (New Haven and London: Yale University Press, 1990), 69.

41. Targum, "when their leaves fall"; Symmachus, "when the leaves have been shed"; Vulgate, "which spread out their branches."

holy seed, but the other ancient versions knew this line. The Targum interpreted the seed as the future of Israel: "So the exiles of Israel shall be gathered together and return to their land, for a holy seed is their plant." Symmachus the Ebionite[42] and the Vulgate both understood that the holy seed was within her, that is, the tree.

Isaiah's temple vision and mysterious oracle refer to the tree and those who had abandoned her. The tree was the symbol of Wisdom, and Isaiah had kept silent when she was abandoned. There had been disputes over the tree symbol for generations before the time of Isaiah: King Asa had removed a tree symbol from the temple (1 Kings 15:9–15) some 150 years before the time of Isaiah's call in 742 BCE, "the year that King Uzziah died" (Isaiah 6:1). The Queen mother had had a special devotion to the sacred tree and had set up an asherah. We are not told it was in the temple, but her son cut it down and burned it. It must have been restored, because King Hezekiah also removed the asherah in the time of Isaiah (2 Kings 18:4).

Further Tree and Branch/Shoot Imagery

The clearest description of the tree of life is found in the book of Proverbs, where a short poem describes Wisdom as the tree of life (3:13–18). The poem begins and ends with play on the word *asherah*, which would not have been appropriate had this not been legitimately linked to the tree of life. *Asherah* is very like the Hebrew word *ʾašar*, which means "happy/blessed/walking the straight path."[43] Thus the poem describes the happy person who finds wisdom: "How happy/blessed/on the straight path is the human who finds wisdom, the human who gets understanding." The word for "human," here and in Genesis, is *Adam*: "How blessed is Adam who finds wisdom." Wisdom is more precious than jewels; she gives long life, wealth, and honour, and her ways are the paths of pleasantness and peace.[44] "She is a tree

42. Late second century CE.

43. Isaiah 9:16 is an example of *ʾašar* meaning "set on the straight path": "the *leaders* . . . they that *are led*."

44. The Greek adds that righteousness comes from her mouth, that she carries the law and mercy on her tongue.

of life to those who take hold of her; he who holds her is made happy/blessed/set on the straight path" (v. 18, my translation).

Isaiah described the Messiah as a shoot, *hoter*,[45] from the stump of Jesse, and as a branch, *nezer*, from his roots (Isaiah 11:1). The stump here is the royal house, but the tree image persists. The Messiah and the Davidic king were both described in branch/shoot imagery.[46] They were (and they held as a sign of their office) a branch from the tree. Ezekiel described the great mother vine, planted by water and full of branches. Her strongest stem was the ruler's sceptre. But she had been uprooted, stripped of her fruit, and left with no strong branch to be a ruler (Ezekiel 19:10–14). Isaiah foresaw a day when the branch, *şemah*, of Yahweh would be beautiful and glorious in Zion (Isaiah 4:2). Jeremiah prophesied of a righteous branch, *şemah* (Jeremiah 23:5; 33:15). Zechariah looked for the branch, *şemah*, the Servant of the Lord who would build the temple (Zechariah 3:8; 6:12).[47]

Various words are used to describe the Branch, just as many trees combine to form the tree of life, suggesting an origin in a pre-written stage of the tradition. The Branch could also be *neşer*, as in Isaiah 11:1, and this may account for the otherwise inexplicable statement in Matthew's account of the Christmas story, in which Jesus is said to have fulfilled the prophecy "He shall be called a Nazarene" (Matthew 2:23). We know of no such prophecy, but there is the prophecy that the Messiah would be called the *neşer*, sufficiently similar in sound to have been a wordplay on "Jesus from Nazareth." The Branch could also be described as the "stock," *kanah*, planted by the Lord's right hand (Psalm 80:15), a word not found elsewhere in the Hebrew Bible. It sounds very like *qaneh*, the word used to describe the branches of the menorah (e.g., Exodus 25:32) and also the Suffering Servant of the

45. The word *hoter* in Phoenician means "sceptre." See Geo Widengren, *The King and the Tree of Life in Ancient Near Eastern Religion* (Uppsala, Sweden: Lundequistska bokhandeln, 1951), 50.

46. The imagery later applied to the Messiah derived from the original royal cult. Memories of the anointed king became prophecies of the future Messiah.

47. Similar imagery appears in the *Damascus Document* I.7 and in the *Testament of Judah* 24:4.

Lord. *Qaneh* literally means "reed" or "hollow stem" and so is appropriate for the branches of the lamp; it is usually translated "reed" in Isaiah 42:3, where the Servant is a bruised reed who will not be broken. Given the context—"a dimly burning wick"—the image in this poem is of the Servant as a broken branch of the great lamp. The lines can then be translated as "A bruised lamp branch, he will not be broken off; a spluttering wick, he will not be put out."[48] Here the Messiah figure is a branch of the lamp that represented the tree. Since the menorah was an almond tree, Aaron's high priestly rod that blossomed and bore almonds must have been another branch of the tree (Numbers 17:8). And Jeremiah saw an almond branch and knew that the Lord was watching (Jeremiah 1:11–12, NIV).[49]

Anointing Oil from the Tree of Life

The tree was fragrant, and the early Christians said that this fragrance had been replicated in the anointing oil. In the *Clementine Recognitions*, attributed to Clement, the bishop of Rome at the end of the first century, Peter teaches Clement about the oil:

> Among the Jews, a King is called Christ. And the reason for the name is this: although He was the Son of God and the beginning of all things, He became man. God anointed him with oil taken from the wood of the tree of life, and from that anointing he is called the Christ. He Himself also, as appointed by His Father, anoints with similar oil every one of the pious when they come to His kingdom . . . so that their light may shine, and being filled with the Holy Spirit, they may be endowed with immortality.
>
> In the present life, Aaron, the first high priest, was anointed with a blended oil which was made as a copy of the spiritual oil of which we have spoken. . . . If this temporal

48. For detail see my book *The Older Testament: The Survival of Themes from the Ancient Royal Cult in Sectarian Judaism and Early Christianity* (London: SPCK, 1987; Sheffield, England: Phoenix, 2005), 229.

49. There is more to this image than just the prophetic wordplay on *šaqed*, "almond," and *šoqed*, "watching."

> grace, blended by men, was so powerful, consider how potent was the oil extracted by God from a branch of the tree of life.[50]

We do not know the age of this belief, but it seems to be as old as the tradition about the tree. Anointing conferred the gifts of Wisdom, and the anointed one was Wisdom's "child."[51] The Branch from the roots of Jesse (Isaiah 11:1; compare Revelation 5:5; 22:16) was given the manifold Spirit of the Lord: wisdom, understanding, counsel, might, knowledge, and the fear of the Lord. This was the gift of Wisdom, given to the Branch from the tree. His delight/pleasure/breath[52] would be the fear of the Lord (Isaiah 11:3). The Hebrew word is *reyah*, "perfume." The anointed one gave forth the fragrance of the tree from which he had been anointed. Paul wrote of the fragrance of the knowledge of Christ that was spread by Christians who were themselves his fragrance. An enigmatic line follows that seems to refer to the two trees. Contrasting those who are being saved and those who are perishing, Paul says that the fragrance for those being saved is "a fragrance from life to life," a reference to the tree of life and its gift (2 Corinthians 2:14–16).

There was a Jewish tradition that the oil had been kept in the holy of holies[53] but had been hidden away in the time of Josiah.[54] This would be consistent with the tree having disappeared from the temple in the time of Josiah, if the tree had been the source of the oil. The only biblical account of making a high priest in the postexilic period, the vesting of Joshua (Zechariah 3:1–10), does not mention that he was anointed. The anointing oil was perfumed with spices, predominantly myrrh (Exodus 30:22–33), and it was absolutely forbidden to use it outside the sanctuary. It was compared to dew (Psalm 133:2–3), and

50. *Clementine Recognitions* 1.45, 46, as found in F. Stanley Jones, *An Ancient Jewish Christian Source on the History of Christianity: Pseudo-Clementine Recognitions*, 1.27–71 (Atlanta, GA: Scholars Press, 1995), 75–78.

51. Compare Luke 7:35, the children of Wisdom.

52. Revised Standard Version, Good News Bible, and Jerusalem Bible, respectively. The New English Bible omits the word and explains it as an insertion.

53. Tosefta *Kippurim* 2:15.

54. Babylonian Talmud *Horayot* 12a.

this comparison opens up the complex of theology associated with the oil.

We have seen that the perfume was intended to imitate the perfume of the tree and that the oil was "extracted" from the tree. It transformed the recipient into an angel, a son of God. This explains the presence of *dew* in the otherwise opaque text of Psalm 110:3. The human king became the divine son "in the glory of the holy ones," that is, in the holy of holies, among the angels; and the Greek text enables us to see what the impossible Hebrew once read: "I have begotten you"—and dew was part of the process. The human being became a Melchizedek priest. A text in *2 Enoch* gives more detail. Enoch—a high priest figure—ascended and stood before the throne; that is, he was in the holy of holies. The archangel Michael was told to take Enoch from his earthly clothing, from his human body, and dress him in garments of the Lord's glory.[55] Michael anointed him: "And the appearance of that oil is greater than the greatest light . . . like sweet dew, and its fragrance like myrrh; and its shining like the sun. And I gazed at all of myself, and I had become like one of the glorious ones, and there was no observable difference" (22:8–10).[56] Enoch the high priest had been anointed and become an angel. He had received the gift of Wisdom, who was herself the oil, according to Ben Sira. He described her as "like cassia and camel's thorn . . . like choice myrrh I spread a pleasant odour" (Sirach 24:15). John wrote: "You have been anointed by the Holy One and you know everything" (1 John 2:20). Memories of the gift of Wisdom from the oil of the fragrant tree appear in a variety of early Christian texts.[57]

55. This was the purpose of the high priest's vestments. They were for beauty and glory (Exodus 28:2).

56. Translation in Charlesworth, *Old Testament Pseudepigrapha*, 1:139. In Proverbs 1:23, Wisdom says, "I will pour out my Spirit on you," translating literally.

57. See my book *The Great High Priest: The Temple Roots of Christian Liturgy* (London: T&T Clark, 2003), 129–36.

> My eyes were enlightened and my face received the dew,
> And my breath [or soul] was refreshed by the pleasant fragrance of the Lord.[58]

> He anointed me with his perfection,
> And I became one of those who are near him.[59]

> [The oil] spreads its sweet fragrance into their mental reception. . . . The transcendent fragrance of the divine Jesus distributes its conceptual gifts over our own intellectual powers.[60]

The fruit of the fragrant tree was the intended food for Adam and Eve, made in the image of God. Decoding all this theological symbolism is a lengthy and complicated process, but what we uncover are extraordinary insights into the role of knowledge/Wisdom in the temple tradition that passed into Christianity.

> Where is the Wisdom we have lost in knowledge?
> Where is the knowledge that we have lost in information?[61]

Margaret Barker read theology at Cambridge, England, specializing in Hebrew. Over many years of independent research, she has developed a new way of doing biblical theology, now known as "Temple Theology." She is a former president of the Society for Old Testament Study and has been for many years a member of the Ecumenical Patriarch's symposium "Religion, Science and the Environment." She was awarded the Lambeth Doctorate in Divinity by the Archbishop of Canterbury for her research in Temple Theology and is currently writing her fifteenth book. Material relevant to her paper in this volume can be found in The Revelation of Jesus Christ *(2000),* The Great High Priest *(2003), and* Temple Theology *(2004).*

58. *Odes of Solomon* 11:14–15; in Charlesworth, *Old Testament Pseudepigrapha*, 2:745.

59. *Odes of Solomon* 36:6; in Charlesworth, *Old Testament Pseudepigrapha*, 2:766.

60. Dionysius, *Ecclesiastical Hierarchy* 476b, 477c; in Colm Luibheid, *Pseudo-Dionysius: The Complete Works* (New York: Paulist Press, 1987).

61. T. S. Eliot, chorus 1 from *The Rock*, in T. S. Eliot, *Collected Poems, 1909–1935* (New York: Harcourt, Brace, 1936), 179.

The Tree of Life in the New Testament and Christian Tradition

John W. Welch

For millennia, the tree of life has been one of the most used symbols by religious writers, artists, and architects worldwide. With its soil, roots, trunk, branches, leaves, fruit, and seeds, the tree of life motif is rich in allegorical potential, making it easily adaptable for religious meanings in virtually all religious traditions, and Christianity is certainly no exception. The tree of life is prominent in the texts and art of ancient, medieval, and modern Christianity, where it is used to communicate metaphorically the life, messages, and atonement of Jesus Christ. Although the book of Revelation contains the only explicit New Testament references to the tree of life, other New Testament passages richly echo tree of life motifs. As early as the second century, Christian authors became more explicit in their use of the tree of life as a Christian metaphor—a use that has continued into modern times.

Three areas of study reveal the use of the tree of life as a metaphor in early Christian textual and artistic traditions: the New Testament, patristic writings, and early and medieval Christian works of art. In each of these fields, the vitality and importance of the tree of life in Christianity becomes increasingly evident, as this motif has been used to represent six important themes: (1) salvation and eternal life, (2) Christ himself, (3) personified wisdom, (4) the cross of Calvary, (5) Christian peoples, and (6) the cosmic world tree. These themes are rarely used in discrete, single-meaning ways but instead overlap and interrelate, especially in medieval art, which typically imbued its subjects with multiple levels of meaning.

Several excellent studies discuss the tree of life in the ancient Near East and examine its connection to Judaism and ancient Christianity.[1] Regarding the meaning of the tree of life in Christianity, Stephen Jerome Reno's book, *The Sacred Tree as an Early Christian Literary Symbol: A Phenomenological Approach*, is the most comprehensive and in many ways the best treatment of this subject, even though it was not produced by a main academic press.[2] Reno studied the corpus of patristic texts and distilled major, recurring themes of the sacred tree in early Christian writings along the lines of several of the categories listed above. This chapter expands upon Reno's framework particularly by tracing back into the New Testament the genealogy of tree of life motifs used by the church fathers and by sampling the way medieval artists have represented these concepts.

Symbol of Salvation and Eternal Life

The tree of life in the Garden of Eden possessed the regenerative power to allow Adam and Eve to live forever (Genesis 3:22).[3] Drawing on this imagery, Christians readily saw in the resurrection of Jesus Christ the culmination of this same saving and immortalizing power.

1. E. O. James, *The Tree of Life: An Archaeological Study* (Leiden: Brill, 1966); Benedikt Otzen, "The Paradise Trees in Jewish Apocalyptic," in *Apocryphon Severini: Studies in Ancient Manichaeism and Gnosticism Presented to Soren Giversen*, ed. Per Bilde et al. (Aarhus, Denmark: Aarhus University Press, 1993), 140–54; Erwin R. Goodenough, *Jewish Symbols in the Greco-Roman Period*, vols. 7–8, *Pagan Symbols in Judaism* (New York: Pantheon, 1953); Robert Starke, "The Tree of Life: Protological to Eschatological," *Kerux* 11/2 (September 1996): 15–31; Daniel K. K. Wong, "The Tree of Life in Revelation 2:7," *Bibliotheca Sacra* 155 (April–June 1998): 211–26; Ingvild Sælid Gilhus, "The Tree of Life and the Tree of Death: A Study of Gnostic Symbols," *Religion* 17 (1987): 337–53; Roger Cook, *The Tree of Life: Image for the Cosmos* (London: Avon, 1974); Robert Masson, ed., *The Pedagogy of God's Image: Essays on Symbol and the Religious Imagination* (Chico, CA: Scholars, 1981); Roland E. Murphy, *The Tree of Life: An Exploration of Biblical Wisdom Literature*, 2nd ed. (Grand Rapids, MI: Eerdmans, 1990); Simo Parpola, "The Assyrian Tree of Life: Tracing the Origins of Jewish Monotheism and Greek Philosophy," *Journal of Near Eastern Studies* 52 (July 1993): 161–208.

2. Stephen Jerome Reno, *The Sacred Tree as an Early Christian Literary Symbol: A Phenomenological Study* (Saarbrücken, Germany: Homo et Religio, 1978). This work appears in a little-known series on anthropology and religious research.

3. Scriptural citations are to the King James Version of the Bible unless otherwise specified.

Fig. 6. *Mystery of the Fall and Redemption of Man*, by Giovanni da Modena, 15th century, Basilica of San Petronio, Bologna, Italy. In the foreground of the verdant tree cross are Mary and Adam and Eve.

Thus, the symbolism of the tree fit snugly together with the gospel message of the earliest Christian writers, not as a later addition to Christian iconography but from the times of the New Testament.

The best-known Christian use of the tree of life is in the book of Revelation, where, as noted earlier, the only two explicit New Testament references to this tree are found. In Revelation 2, John crowns his message to the church at Ephesus with a promise similar to formulas found in royal victory decrees: "To everyone who conquers, I will give permission to eat from the tree (*xylou*) of life that is in the paradise of God" (v. 7, my translation)—a tree that he actually sees

Fig. 7. Apocalypse tapestry, Château d´Angers, 14th century, Angers, France. John the Revelator beholds Eden and the heavenly Jerusalem in vision. See plate 1.

later in vision.[4] Near the end of the book of Revelation, John saw the return and reestablishment of Eden and the heavenly Jerusalem, next to which ran a "river of living water, bright as crystal, flowing out of the throne of God and of the Lamb through the middle of the street of the city. On either side of the river is the tree of life having twelve kinds of fruit, yielding its fruit each month; and the leaves of the tree are for the healing of the nations" (22:1–2, my translation).[5] This passage contains striking parallels to the vision in Ezekiel 47, in which

4. Although the reference to Genesis 2:9 and 3:22 is clear, some scholars see another possible contemporary connection to the temple of Artemis at Ephesus, which was built on a primitive tree shrine. See Raymond E. Brown, *An Introduction to the New Testament* (New York: Doubleday, 1997), 783; Leonard L. Thompson, *The Book of Revelation: Apocalypse and Empire* (New York: Oxford, 1990), 202; and Wong, "Tree of Life in Revelation 2:7," 215.

5. Saint Bonaventure wrote that each leaf corresponds to "one of the mysteries of Jesus' origin, passion, and glorification" and that the river of water originated in Christ's pierced side, making the water efficacious through the incorporation of Christ's blood. John Borelli, "The Tree of Life in Hindu and Christian Theology," in Masson, *Pedagogy of God's Image*, 185–87.

Ezekiel also saw a river, a tree on both banks, monthly fruit, and leaves for healing (v. 12), in connection with his vision of restoration of the house of the Lord, the healing of the Dead Sea (47:8), and the ultimate presence of the Lord (48:35).[6] In his concluding benediction at the end of the book of Revelation, John writes, "Blessed are those who wash their robes, so that it will be authorized for them to come to the tree of life and to enter the city through the gates" (22:14, my translation). Then he warns that alteration of his text will lead God to "take away" that person's "share from the tree of life" (v. 19, my translation).

To John the Revelator, then, the tree of life was of central importance to his vision and the vision's Christology, soteriology, and martyrology. The fruit of the tree was available to all Christian disciples who conquered evil, which at the time meant particularly such things as enduring persecution (Revelation 2:10; 6:9),[7] avoiding sexual sin (2:14), refusing to worship Roman deities (v. 14), and shunning heretics among the Christian ranks such as the Nicolaitans, Balaam, and the prophetess Jezebel (vv. 6, 14, 20).

The Greek wording for the phrase "the tree of life" in these New Testament passages, *ho xylon tēs zōēs*, merits attention, for it shows that the author clearly had Genesis 3:25 in mind here.[8] The Greek translation of Genesis in the Septuagint speaks of "a fiery sword to guard the way (*tēn hodon*) of the tree of life (*tou xylou tēs zōēs*)." The word *xylon* is especially evocative and indicative, being a fairly rare word in the New Testament. It is used about eighteen times and connotes "wood" or "timber," more distinctive than the more generic word for "tree"

6. Wong, "Tree of Life in Revelation 2:7," 212.

7. Although John warns his readers of a specific persecution—"Do not fear what you are about to suffer" (Revelation 2:10, my translation)—no extant data from Asia Minor reveals what his concern was. As Leonard Thompson writes, "It is conceivable that the Book of Revelation was written in response to an otherwise unknown crisis in Asian Christianity, in which Christians were being—or about to be—persecuted in large numbers, but such a crisis does not fit with our other sources for this period." Leonard L. Thompson, *The Book of Revelation: Apocalypse and Empire* (New York: Oxford, 1990), 172. Although some of the references to the martyrs could be to past events, Adela Collins has called the situation "a perceived crisis." See Adela Yarbro Collins, *Crisis and Catharsis: The Power of the Apocalypse* (Philadelphia: Westminster, 1984), 84–110.

8. Wong, "Tree of Life in Revelation 2:7," 222–23.

(*dendron*). Indeed, whenever *xylon* appeared in the Septuagint, it was an open invitation for early Christian writers to think of both the tree of life and the cross of Jesus.

For example, when the children of Israel came upon the bitter waters of Marah, "the Lord shewed [Moses] a tree (*xylon*), which when he had cast into the waters, the waters were made sweet," whereupon the Lord promised to heal the people from the diseases that had been brought upon the Egyptians (Exodus 15:23–26). The intertestamental Jewish/Christian text known as the *Biblical Antiquities* (most likely written as early as the time of Jesus) goes on to state that the tree that Moses used was "the tree of life, from which he cut off and took and threw into Marah, and the water became sweet" (Pseudo-Philo 11:15). This is consonant with Peter's and Paul's uses of the word *xylon* in making explicit reference to the cross of Christ (Acts 5:30; 10:39; 13:29; Galatians 3:13; 1 Peter 2:24).

For centuries, Christian liturgy and art have linked the fruit of the tree of life with the mysteries and ritual ordinances associated with salvation and eternal life. The eucharistic sacrament of partaking of the blood and body of Christ is itself a metaphor—a literal one in some traditions—of partaking of the fruit of Jesus's passion. Strong precedents linking salvation with the eating of the "daily" or living bread (*epousion arton*) and seeing this bread as Jesus himself reach again into the New Testament (Matthew 26:26; John 6:32–35). This was more than enough invitation for some early Christians to see in the tree of life a powerful symbol of salvation and eternal life. In his commentary on the Syriac Jacobite Liturgy, Mesopotamian bishop Moses Bar-Kepha (ca. 813–903) related various interpretations of the liturgical altar, including the following: "Saint Dionysius says that the altar signifies Emmanuel himself, who is the tree of life." In commenting on the same liturgy, George of the Arabs about that same time wrote, "The bread and wine which are upon it [signify] the body of God the Word, wherein was blood also, and they are the fruits of the tree of life."[9] And speaking of the "daily bread"

9. R. H. Connolly and H. W. Codrington, trans. and eds., *Two Commentaries on the Jacobite Liturgy* (Farnborough, England: Gregg International, 1913), 34, 17.

Fig. 8. A pair of rondelles on an illuminated page from the 13th-century Bible Moralisée links the crucifixion of the Savior on a cross of green wood with Adam looking thoughtfully at the fruit of the tree of life in the Garden of Eden.

(*epousion arton*) in the Lord's Prayer, Origen taught, "This daily bread appears to me to have been called by another name in Scripture, namely, 'tree of life', upon which 'whoever puts forth his hand and takes of it shall live forever.'"[10]

Jesus as the Tree of Life

More than thinking of the tree of life as eternal life itself, early Christians identified Jesus as that tree. This identification begins with a poignant saying of Jesus on his fateful way to Golgotha. Along the way to the Place of the Skull, Jesus was followed by a large group of mourners, largely women according to Luke. During the painstaking procession, Jesus told those mourners: "If they inflict these things upon a green, moist, living tree (*hygrōi xylōi*), what will be the case with a dry one (*xērōi*)?" (Luke 23:31, my translation). It would appear that Jesus's statement here echoes the vision of the last days in Ezekiel 17:24 LXX because of the unusually similar combination of words in these two texts. This verse in Ezekiel reads prophetically: "I have dried up the green tree (*xylon chlōron*), and have made the dry tree (*xylon xēron*) to flourish,"

Fig. 9. A blossoming tree of life rooted in Christ intertwines with Mary and the Saints. Holkham Bible, 14th century.

10. Origen, *De Oratione* 27.10, in *Die griechische christliche Schriftsteller der ersten*, 3:359; also J. P. Migne, *Patrologia Graeca*, 11:513, cited in Reno, *Sacred Tree*, 108.

referring to Babylon as the formerly verdant valley tree and to Israel as the formerly dry mountain tree. With his statement, Jesus refers to himself as a living *xylon*. In doing so, he seems to be saying, "My accusers acted so quickly, they moved before I, the living wood, was even dry." His quip holds out a prophetic warning to all Jerusalem: "If these chief priests are so eager to burn green wood, what are they likely to do to the 'dry wood' [meaning all the people planted in the mountain of the Lord]? At least God will wait in righteousness and mercy until after the harvest and after the wood has had time to dry; but when he comes, the tinder will be dry and it will burn as stubble."

On another occasion, Jesus referred to himself in terms of two other salient features clearly associated with the tree of life in the book of Genesis—"the way" and "the life." During the last supper, Thomas asked Jesus how the apostles could find the way to Jesus's Father's house, to which Jesus responded, "I am the way (*hē hodos*), the truth, and the life (*hē zōē*)" (John 14:6). These terms have their corollaries in the garden narratives of Genesis 2–3 (see especially 3:22–23). One can see protological allusions to the Garden of Eden as well as the eschatological goal of eating the fruit of the tree of life in Jesus's tripartite self-identification: "I am the way, the truth, and the life." Inasmuch as the tree was a physical manifestation of the powers of life, so the tree of life symbolized the incarnation of the Son of God in the flesh.

Continuing this understanding of the tree of life motif in the New Testament, New Testament apocryphal and other early Christian writings also interpreted the person of Christ as the allegorical and typological motif of the tree of life. Justin Martyr, Ignatius of Antioch, Origen, Ambrose, and Augustine all saw Christ in this way.[11] The *Acts of Peter* has Peter crying out during his own execution, "Now whereas thou hast made known and revealed these things unto me, O word of life, called now by me wood (*or*, word called now by me the tree of life)."[12] And in the fourth-century writings of Ephrem the Syrian, we read, "Our Savior typified his body in the tree, the one from which Adam did not taste

11. Otzen, "The Paradise Trees in Jewish Apocalyptic," 140.

12. *Acts of Peter* 39, cited in Montague R. James, *The Apocryphal New Testament* (Oxford: Clarendon, 1969), 335.

Fig. 10. *Dream of the Virgin*, by Simone dei Crocefissi, 14th century. Christ hangs on a golden tree of life connected to Mary's womb while Adam and Eve are freed from limbo.

because he sinned." Another Ephrem text reads, "The tree of life which was hidden in paradise grew up in Marjam [Mary] and sprang forth from her, and in its shade creation hath repose, and it spreadeth its fruits over those far and near. Extremely mournful was the tree of life when he saw concerning Adam that he was hidden from him. In the virgin earth he plunged and was hidden, and he arose and shone forth from Golgotha."[13]

This last description of Christ, which sees him as growing as a literal tree of life inside the womb of the Virgin Mary, was also used by Christian artists of the fourteenth century, most famously by the Italian painter Simone dei Crocefissi. He painted at least two works depicting the Dream of the Virgin (a popular medieval legend about the Virgin's prophetic dream of Christ's passion and death), wherein a tree of life cross grows out of the Virgin's midsection. In the version owned by the National Gallery in London (see fig. 10), the cross has been morphed into a resplendent golden tree with broad leaves. A hand reaches from below the tree into limbo to rescue Adam and Eve—symbols of all humanity—from the bondage of death. Christ is, therefore, crucified on a golden tree of life, instantaneously reversing the fall of Adam and Eve through his passion and resurrection.

13. Goodenough, *Jewish Symbols in the Greco-Roman Period*, 120. Bracketed interpolation per Goodenough. For more on the tree in the writings of Ephrem, see Tryggve Kronholm, "The Trees of Paradise in the Hymns of Ephraem Syrus," in *Annual of the Swedish Theological Institute* (Leiden: Brill, 1978): 11:48–56.

In the *Dream of the Virgin* owned by the Pinacoteca Nazionale in Italy (see fig. 11), a nested pelican sits atop the tree of life along with other birds as well as angels. The birds in this and other images of the cross as the tree of life are reminiscent of passages in Ezekiel 17:22–23, Daniel 4:10–12, and Matthew 13:31–32. For example, in the parable of the mustard seed, Matthew writes, "When it has grown it is the greatest of shrubs and becomes a tree, so that the birds of the sky come and take shelter in its branches" (13:32, my translation). The pelican is especially important; it was commonly used as a symbol of Christ because legend taught that pelicans pierced their breasts to feed their young with their own blood. Also, some translations of Psalm 102:6 read, "I am like a pelican in the wilderness."[14]

Fig. 11. *Dream of the Virgin*, by Simone dei Crocefissi, 14th century. Pinacoteca Nazionale, Ferrara, Italy.

The Tree of Life as Wisdom and the *Logos*

Christians in the first few centuries after Christ interpreted the life and ministry of Jesus through Jewish Wisdom literature as well as through the Torah and the Prophets,[15] and the connection between Wisdom and the tree of life opened up another avenue for Christian symbolism, beginning once again on the pages of the New Testament. The preface to the Gospel of John—likely an early christological

14. George Ferguson, *Signs and Symbols in Christian Art* (New York: Oxford, 1959), 9.

15. For a survey of Wisdom literature in Israel, see Roland E. Murphy, *The Tree of Life: An Exploration of Biblical Wisdom Literature*, 2nd ed. (Grand Rapids, MI: Eerdmans, 1996).

hymn—contains one of the most famous of these connections: "In the beginning was the *logos*, and the *logos* was with God, and the *logos* was God" (John 1:1). Thus, Christ is the preexistent source of true wisdom.[16] As Ben Witherington III writes, "It is the use of the Genesis material in the hymnic material about Wisdom both in the Old Testament and in later Jewish sapiential writings that provides the font of ideas and forms used in creating this hymn."[17] Because of connections like these, some scholars also see wisdom personified as "the way" in Jesus's declaration that he is "the way, the truth, and the life" (John 14:6).[18]

This association of the tree of life with the Word, wisdom, or knowledge became more explicit as Christian literary traditions developed throughout the Mediterranean region. Asterius, for example, wrote (probably in Palestine between AD 385 and 410)[19] in the *Commentary on the Psalms*, "The Word is the tree planted by the water's edge which the Father has begotten without intermediary, laden with fruit, flourishing, tall, fair-branched. . . . It was of this tree that Adam refused the fruit and fell victim to its opposite. Christ is the tree of life, the devil the tree of death."[20] Along the same lines, Hippolytus of Rome (ca. AD 170–236) wrote, "In this Paradise were found the tree of knowledge and the tree of life. In the same way today, there are two trees planted in the Church, the Law [the tree of knowledge] and the Word [the tree of life]."[21]

---

16. For a discussion of Wisdom Christology in John 1, see Ben Witherington III, *Jesus the Sage: The Pilgrimage of Wisdom* (Minneapolis: Fortress, 1994), 282–94; and Sharon H. Ringe, *Wisdom's Friends: Community and Christology in the Fourth Gospel* (Louisville, KY: Westminster John Knox, 1999), 46–53. Also see Wisdom excerpts in Sirach 24:21 and Wisdom of Solomon 9.

17. Witherington, *Jesus the Sage*, 284.

18. See, for example, John Ashton, "Riddles and Mysteries: The Way, the Truth, and the Life," in *Jesus in Johannine Tradition*, ed. Robert T. Fortna and Tom Thatcher (Louisville, KY: Westminster John Knox, 2001).

19. See Wolfram Kinzig, *In Search of Asterius: Studies on the Authorship of the Homilies on the Psalms* (Göttingen, Germany: Vandenhoeck & Ruprecht, 1990).

20. Cited in Reno, *Sacred Tree*, 105.

21. Hippolytus, *Commentary on the Book of Daniel* 17, in *Griechische christliche Schriftsteller*, 1:29, cited in Reno, *Sacred Tree*, 108.

Christ as a personification of wisdom may also be found, although indirectly, in other New Testament passages, including Matthew 11:19 and Luke 11:49. This seems only natural since the Old Testament and popular Jewish writings in the first century often personified the idea of wisdom. The description of personified wisdom in Proverbs and in the "The Praise of Wisdom" in chapter 24 of Sirach are some of the best examples of personified wisdom in Second Temple Judaism.[22]

Most directly related to a discussion of the tree of life is Proverbs 3:18: "[Wisdom] is a tree of life to them that lay hold upon her." The book of Proverbs continues: "The Lord by wisdom hath founded the earth" (v. 19). Wisdom was created "in the beginning of his way" (8:22). Wisdom says, "Blessed are they that keep my ways . . . , watching daily at my gates, waiting at the posts of my doors. For whoso findeth me findeth life" (vv. 32–35). And Proverbs 11:30 reads, "The fruit of the righteous is a tree of life."

The Wisdom writings of Ben Sira are likewise rich in tree of life imagery. He wrote that Wisdom "dwelt in high places, and [her] throne is in a cloudy pillar" (Sirach 24:4). The chapter goes on to say that Wisdom is found praising herself as a tree that took up residence in "the beloved city" of Jerusalem:

> And I took root in an honourable people, even in the portion of the Lord's inheritance. I was exalted like a cedar in Libanus, and as a cypress tree upon the mountains of Hermon. I was exalted like a palm tree in En-gaddi, and as a rose plant in Jericho, as a fair olive tree in a pleasant field, and grew up as a lane tree by the water. I gave a sweet smell like cinnamon and aspalathus, and I yielded a pleasant odour like the best myrrh, as galbanum, and onyx, and sweet storax, and as the fume of frankincense in the tabernacle. As the turpentine tree I stretched out my branches, and my branches are the branches of honour and grace. As the vine brought I forth pleasant savour, and my flowers are the fruit of honour and

22. Other references to personified wisdom in Hebrew literature include Proverbs 1:20–33; 8–9; Wisdom of Solomon 7:22–26; and Baruch 3:9–4:4.

> riches. I am the mother of fair love, and fear, and knowledge, and holy hope: I therefore, being eternal, am given to all my children which are named of him. Come unto me, all ye that be desirous of me, and fill yourselves with my fruits. For my memorial is sweeter than honey, and mine inheritance than the honeycomb. They that eat me shall yet be hungry, and they that drink me shall yet be thirsty. He that obeyeth me shall never be confounded, and they that work by me shall not do amiss. (Sirach 24:12–22)

Early Christian authors inherited and incorporated a rich fabric of multilayered interpretative traditions and metaphors. Christ was the Son of God, he was the Messiah, and he was the Great High Priest. He was the embodiment of wisdom and also the tree of life. For example, as early as the second century, Clement of Alexandria wrote in his *Stromata*: "Now Moses, describing allegorically the divine prudence, called it a tree of life planted in Paradise, which Paradise may be the world in which all things proceeding from creation grow. In it also the Word [Christ] blossomed and bore fruit, being 'made flesh', and gave it to those 'who had tasted of His graciousness'; since it was not without the wood of the tree that He came to our knowledge."[23]

In the *Symposium of the Ten Virgins*, by Methodius, a ninth-century Byzantine archbishop of Moravia, the tree of life is the first-born of all wisdom. As Christ is the Firstborn, he is also the tree of life. "'She [Wisdom] is a tree of life to them that lay hold on her', says the prophet [in Proverbs], 'and she is a secure help to them that rest on her as on the Lord'. The 'tree which is planted near the running waters which brings forth its fruit in due season', is none other than instructions and charity and understanding, such as is given in 'due season' to those who come to the waters of Redemption. He who does not believe in Christ and does not perceive that he is the first principle,

23. Clement of Alexandria, *Stromata* 5.11; Otto Stählin, *Griechische christliche Schriftsteller* 2:374–75, cited in Reno, *Sacred Tree*, 106–7.

the tree of life, and is unable to show to God his tabernacle adorned with the loveliest of fruit, how will he be able to rejoice?"[24]

The Cross of Calvary as the Tree of Life

As is commonly affirmed in Christian theology, acceptance of Christ's crucifixion makes it possible to partake of the tree of life. Retrieving Deuteronomy 21:23—"you shall hang him (*kremasēte auton*) upon *a* tree (*epi xylou*), but do not leave his body upon *the* tree (*epi tou xylou*) over night" (LXX, my translation)—Stephen, Peter, Paul, and Luke saw "the tree" (*xylon*) as the cross. The following New Testament passages connect Deuteronomy 21:23 with the cross of Calvary.

- Cursed is everyone who is hung upon a *xylon* (Galatians 3:13)
- Bear our sins in his own body on the *xylon* (1 Peter 2:24)
- Whom ye slew and crucified upon a *xylon* (Acts 5:30; 10:39)
- Took him down from the *xylon* (Acts 13:29)

The further connection between the wooden (*xylon*) cross and the tree (*xylon*) of life was perhaps linguistically irresistible but also theologically compelling. The cross itself was soon interpreted and represented as the tree of life in Christian texts and art. Because the cross was made from a tree, this relationship was easy to correlate and depict. The cross, made of wood, lifted Jesus up so that "whosoever believeth in him should not perish [through the effects of the tree of death or of knowledge of good and evil], but have eternal life [through the tree of eternal life]" (John 3:15). Justin Martyr, Origen, Ambrose, Leo the Great, John of Damascus, and many others elevated the cross from pieces of hewn wood to an effulgent tree of life. A few examples will suffice.

The repeated use of the word *xylon* and the popularity of this way of describing the cross upon which Jesus hung gave readers a specific open invitation to connect the cross not just with execution and death but with the *xylon tēs zōēs*, the tree of life. In the *Dialogue with Trypho*

24. Methodius, *Symposium of the Ten Virgins* 9.3, in *Griechische christliche Schriftsteller*, 27:117, lines 20–24; see Migne, *Patrologia Graeca*, 18:181–86; and also Herbert Musurillo, *Ancient Christian Writers* (Westminster, MD, 1958), 136, cited in Reno, *Sacred Tree*, 103.

the Jew, Justin Martyr writes, "Now gentlemen, I want you to understand how he whom the Scriptures announce as about to return in glory after the crucifixion was symbolized . . . by the tree of life."[25] The symbol is added to in the New Testament apocryphal work *Acts of Andrew,* in which this tree connects the earth below with heaven above. The following is an excerpt from Andrew's martyrdom speech:

> O cross, . . . thou art planted in the world to establish the things that are unstable: and the one part of thee stretcheth up toward heaven that thou mayest signify the heavenly word . . . : and another part of thee is spread out to the right hand and the left that it may put to flight the envious and adverse power of the evil one, and gather into one the things that are scattered abroad . . . : and another part of thee is planted in the earth, and securely set in the depth, that thou mayest join the things that are in the earth and that are under the earth unto the heavenly things. . . . O cross, planted upon the earth and having thy fruit in the heavens![26]

Through the visual representation of the cross as the tree of life, artists also created works with multiple levels of metaphorical meaning. The apse mosaic of San Clemente in Rome is one of these works (see fig. 12). The dark-colored wood cross is set in the midst of the Garden of Paradise. It grows out of a large acanthus plant, from which flow the four rivers of paradise. Stags, sheep, birds, and other animals come to drink from the life-giving waters that originate in the four rivers under this "cross-tree." Birds are nested all over the crossbar of the cross, which now has grown into branches, making this entire image reminiscent of Ezekiel 17:23: "In the mountain of the height of Israel will I plant it: and it shall bring forth boughs, and bear fruit . . . : and under it shall dwell all fowl of every wing; in the shadow of the branches thereof shall they dwell." In this magnificent portrayal, the

25. Justin Martyr, *Dialogue with Trypho the Jew* 86.1, in Edgar J. Goodspeed, *Die ältesten Apologeten* (Göttingen, Germany, 1914), 199–200, cited in Reno, *Sacred Tree,* 106.

26. *Acts of Andrew,* in M. R. James, *Apocryphal New Testament,* 359–60.

Fig. 12. Calvary's cross planted in the Garden of Paradise, apse mosaic, Basilica of San Clemente, Rome, Italy, 12th century.

Fig. 13. *Tree of Life*, by Pacino da Bonaguido, 14th century, depicting with the tree of life several events from the life of Christ.

Calvary of death has become the Eden of life, and the tree of Christ's cross has become an *axis mundi* planted in the navel of the earth.[27]

Another impressive artwork is a fourteenth-century painting by Pacino da Bonaguido entitled *Tree of Life* (see fig. 13). In this image, Christ hangs on an elaborate tree with six leafy branches radiating from each side in parallel fashion. Medallions with miniature scenes (Pacino being one of the founders of Miniaturism) depict events from the life of Christ. The four evangelists are at the bottom of the work recording what they see on the tree. And the narrative of Adam and Eve is depicted underneath the tree, again placing the tree in Eden. The hosts of heaven preside over the scene atop the painting with the Virgin and the Son enthroned.[28] Images as multilayered and meaning-laden as this one possess not just narrative illustration but what Jaime Lara, professor of Christian art and architecture, has spoken of as "visual Christology." The work is theological, protological, eschatological, and anagogical at the same time. The tree of death has become a tree of life, and because the events of Christ's life are connected to the branches of the tree of life, his life's narrative as recorded by the evangelists at the bottom of the page has become a wellspring of life, not just his person. Christ's ministry is the fruit of the tree of life. His death reversed the fall of Adam, thus once again making immortality possible. And as the cross of Calvary is placed atop the Cave of Adam and the Garden Tomb, it supplants the old with the new and that in a golden heaven. Out of two tragedies comes new life—the fall and the crucifixion have, in Pacino's work, become the soil from which the multivalent tree of life springs.

Christian Disciples as Trees of Life

Not only Christ but every true Christian can lay claim to being a tree of life. The tradition of seeing the righteous as trees of life has its roots deep in Israelite soil. Psalm 1:3 promises the blessed obedient, "He shall be like a tree planted by the rivers of water, that bringeth

---

27. For an exhaustive study of San Clemente, see Joan Barclay Lloyd, *The Medieval Church and Canonry of S. Clemente in Rome* (Rome: San Clemente, 1989).

28. John Howett, "Two Panels by the Master of the St. George Codex in the Cloisters," *Metropolitan Museum Journal* 11 (1976): 94–96.

forth his fruit in his season; his leaf also shall not wither." Psalm 92:12–14 reads, "The righteous shall flourish like the palm tree: he shall grow like a cedar in Lebanon. Those that be planted in the house of the Lord shall flourish in the courts of our God. They shall still bring forth fruit in old age; they shall be fat and flourishing." Isaiah 61:3 promises, "They might be called trees of righteousness, the planting of the Lord, that he might be glorified." And Jeremiah 11:16 reads, "The Lord called thy name, A green olive tree, fair, and of goodly fruit: with the noise of a great tumult he hath kindled fire upon it, and the branches of it are broken."[29]

Following this and other imagery, early Christians saw the faithful and the blessed not only as partakers of the fruit of the tree of life but also as trees of life themselves, who in turn become continual bearers of the fruits of Christ. In this vein, Matthew 7:17 speaks of individuals as trees. Near the end of the Sermon on the Mount, after mentioning two now-familiar companions of the tree of life, namely the *apagousa hodos* (the narrow way) that leads unto life (*eis tēn zōēn*), Jesus turns directly to tree imagery: "Do men gather grapes of thorns, or figs of thistles? Even so every good tree bringeth forth good fruit; but a corrupt tree bringeth forth evil fruit" (Matthew 7:16–17). Man having partaken of the tree of knowledge, his life becomes a quest to find the way back and righteously partake of the fruit of the tree of life and live forever. Echoes of the tree of life and of temple and eschatological imagery are discernible in those words of Jesus:

> These good trees are trees of life. One only lives forever by partaking of the fruit of the Tree of Life (see Genesis 3:22). Accordingly, the tree is an important feature in the landscape of all temple literature. It is, therefore, natural and logical that Jesus' thoughts should turn to the imagery of the Tree of Life immediately after he has described the path "which leadeth unto life" (3 Nephi 14:14). . . .

29. See also *Psalms of Solomon* 14:3–4.

> . . . Jesus equates individual people with the Tree, for by partaking of the fruit of the Tree of Life, or by planting the seed of life in oneself, each disciple grows up into a tree of life, as the Prophet Alma describes (see Alma 32:41–42). Each good tree of life has a place in God's paradise, growing up unto eternal life and yielding much fruit—powerful imagery also present in the Old Testament Psalms (see Psalm 1:1–3) and in the earliest Christian hymns. "Blessed, O Lord, are they who are planted in Thy land, and who have a place in Thy Paradise; and who grow in the growth of Thy trees" (*Odes of Solomon* 11:18–24). In other allegories, there is only one tree, Jesus being the root and righteous people becoming the branches (see John 15:1–5; Jacob 5).[30]

Although not as explicit as they will become in later Christian writings, the metaphors of seeds, herbs, and trees are used throughout the Gospels and in the writings of Paul. For example, consider the parable of the mustard seed. Should it not be seen as a tree of life parable? The small seed, "when it is grown, . . . is the greatest among herbs, and becometh a tree, so that the birds of the air come and lodge in the branches thereof" (Matthew 13:32). This is certainly reminiscent of the cosmic tree that is home to birds of the heaven in Ezekiel 17:23.

In 1 Corinthians, Paul writes about bodies, like seeds, being planted in corruption but rising in incorruption and how one cannot tell by looking at a seed what the resultant plant will look like: "What is sown is perishable (*phthorai*), what is raised is imperishable" (15:42, my translation; see vv. 38–44). One might ask, is Paul drawing on the image of the seeds from the tree of life planted in God's Garden of Paradise that will grow up in us, or as us, as heirs of eternal life and glory? Either way, the metaphor of people being sown and growing is reminiscent of other treelike parables and tree of life motifs in general.

---

30. John W. Welch, *The Sermon at the Temple and the Sermon on the Mount: A Latter-day Saint Approach* (Salt Lake City: Deseret Book and FARMS, 1990), 75–76; revised and enlarged edition, *Illuminating the Sermon at the Temple and Sermon on the Mount* (Provo, UT: FARMS, 1999), 94.

In the allegory of the olive tree in Romans 11, Paul discusses the grafting of Gentiles into Israel and draws on a tradition that saw the tree of life as an olive tree—a tree that produces the oils of mercy and anointing and of the Holy Spirit. As part of that olive tree, people become connected to the only root that can make them capable of bearing good rather than bitter fruit.

In explaining baptism as a similitude of death, Paul tells the Christians in Rome that through baptism they are "buried with [Christ] by baptism" (Romans 6:4). He goes on to say, "For if we have been planted together in the likeness [*homoiōmati*] of his death, we shall be also in the likeness of his resurrection" (v. 5). And through the rejection of sin, which leads to death, the Christian reconciled to God will be made "alive unto God through Jesus Christ our Lord" (v. 11).

In the earliest known collection of Christian hymns, the *Odes of Solomon*, Syriac Christians sang: "Blessed, O Lord, are they who are planted in Thy land, and who have a place in Thy Paradise; and who grow in the growth of Thy trees."[31] In the *Epistle to Diognetus*, we read, "Those who love [God] rightly . . . become a paradise of delight, a flourishing tree, rich in every fruit, growing up in them, and adorned with various fruits."[32] And in his *Commentary on the Psalms*, Eusebius of Caesarea wrote that the righteous "may be likened to a tree whose roots are situated near the waters from which streams he is completely watered by spiritual things."[33] Cyprian of Carthage was more specific about the waters: these people would be nourished "with four rivers, . . . with the four gospels."[34]

Optatus of Milevis, a fourth-century bishop in North Africa, also expounded on people as trees of life in *De Schismate Donatistorum*. He writes, "The Church is a paradise, in which garden God sets out small

31. *Odes of Solomon* 11:18–24.

32. *Epistula ad Diognetum* 12.1–3, in J. P. Migne, *Patrologia Latina*, 2:1185–86; see also *Ad Diognetum*, ed. H.-I. Marrou, vol. 33, *Sources chretiennes* (Paris, 1951), cited in Reno, *Sacred Tree*, 95.

33. Eusebius of Caesarea, *Commentary on the Psalms* 1.3, in Migne, *Patrologia Graeca*, 27:77, cited in Reno, *Sacred Tree*, 102.

34. Cyprian of Carthage, *Epistuale* 73.10, in *Corpus Scriptorum Ecclesiasticorum Latinorum*, ed. W. Hartel (1871), 3:2, cited in Reno, *Sacred Tree*, 96.

trees. . . . Certainly the plantings of God are different seeds by virtue of different precepts. The just, the continent, the merciful and the virginal, are spiritual seeds: from such as these God plants small trees in paradise. Grant to God that his garden is long, broad and extensive."[35] Hippolytus of Rome described a "new garden of delights, planted towards the East"—a new Eden—in which "may be seen every sort of tree, the line of patriarchs . . . and prophets . . . the choir of apostles . . . the procession of virgins . . . the order of bishops, priests, and levites." And similar to Cyprian's statement that the Gospels water the trees, Christ himself is the river that waters "God's spiritual garden" in Hippolytus's new Eden.[36]

Fig. 14. Scene from Book of Hours, by the anonymous Rohan Master, 15th century. See plate 3.

The medieval Parisian Book of Hours illustrated by the Rohan Master depicts this idea (see fig. 14, also pl. 3). God is a bearded man with the moon behind his head doubling as a halo. Barefooted in a garden, he is planting a tree a couple feet taller than he. Instead of branches growing from the six stumps on the side, six people are growing out of the trunk of the tree. Only their heads are showing, revealing the people's infancy in the garden of life.[37]

---

35. Optatus of Milevis, *De Schismate Donatistorum*, in Migne, *Patrologia Latina*, 11:964–66, cited in Reno, *Sacred Tree*, 94.

36. Hippolytus, *Commentary on Daniel* 1.17–20, in *Griechische christliche Schriftsteller*, 28, lines 16–18, cited in Reno, *Sacred Tree*, 98.

37. *The Rohan Master: A Book of Hours* (New York: George Braziller, 1973), plate 10.

The Tree of Life as the Cosmic Tree of the World

Finally, the tree of life stands at the center of the universe, and so it was understood that Jesus came and stood at the meridian of all things. The Garden of Eden narrative in Genesis paves the way for this understanding when it says that God made the tree of life grow "in the midst of the garden" (Genesis 2:9). The word *midst* should be understood as meaning "middle" or "center." Although the narrative is clear that the garden was planted in the east of Eden, Christians saw the Garden of Eden as the center of the world; and because some interpreted Golgotha as the center (Cyril of Jerusalem writes, "Golgotha is the very center of the earth"), the two locations were syncretized.[38] Early and medieval Christians, therefore, came to see Jesus, the cross, and Jerusalem as the axis of the universe (*axis mundi*).

The cosmic world tree was seen by ancient artists as the embodiment of the source and regulator of life; as the giver of living water and immortality; and as the personification of the Creator and the dying and rising deity, victor over death and eschatological hope, who came at the midpoint (the meridian) of all time and eternity. New Testament references readily come to mind, proclaiming Jesus of Nazareth as the divine, firstborn Son of God in each of these cosmic, representational tree of life senses.

Early Christian authors also cast the tree of Christ's cross, the events of the passion, and the connection with the Garden of Eden as central to the cosmos. The Syriac *Book of the Cave of Treasures*, for example, says, "That Tree of Life which was in the midst of Paradise prefigured the Redeeming Cross which is the middle of the earth . . . (After Adam's death, his son Shem took his body) and . . . when they arrived at Golgotha, which is the center of the earth, . . . and when Shem had deposited the body of our father Adam upon that place, the four quarters of the earth separated themselves from each other, and

38. Cyril of Jerusalem, *Catechesis* 13.28, in Migne, *Patrologia Graeca*, 33:806, cited in Reno, *Sacred Tree*, 181.

Fig. 15. World cross with tree of life below, apse mosaic, Basilica of San Giovanni Laterano, Rome, Italy, 4th–6th century (later restored). See plate 2.

the earth opened in the shape of a cross, and . . . the four quarters drew quickly together, . . . and that place was called the Place of the Skull."[39]

The apse mosaic in San Giovanni Laterano in Rome depicts the cross as tree of life and cosmic tree in the center of the world (see fig. 15, also pl. 2). The cross is golden, jeweled, and set against a field of intertwining vines. It is set in the Garden of Eden, from which

39. E. A. Wallis Budge, trans., *The Book of the Cave of Treasures* (London, 1927), 62–63 and 126–27, as cited in Reno, *Sacred Tree*, 145.

flow the named four rivers of Paradise (Genesis 2:10). In the garden, a cherub is seen guarding the walled Garden of Eden with Adam and Eve inside. With heaven above and the spirit of God descending, the cross links the world to the waters below. The elements of imagery are further brought together as the mosaic labels the river that runs in front of the cross as the River Jordan. Mary and John the Baptist face the cosmic cross. This world cross is more than the tree of life, for the tree of life is here below, with the archangel guarding the entrance and the way to the tree of life behind the walls of the garden. The cross has become a cosmic tree.

As E. O. James has written, "In the third century A.D. the Tree of Life was described poetically as growing to an immense height, its branches stretching out to encircle the whole world from its centre on Calvary, with a bubbling spring at its foot. Thither all nations would resort to drink its sacred water and ascend to heaven by way of the branches of the tree."[40] The *Shepherd of Hermas* bears out this point. In its eighth similitude, this text describes a large willow tree, "and under the shade of the willow all those called in the name of the Lord had come." The author goes on to interpret the metaphor, saying that the willow is seen as a cosmic tree that spreads over the whole world, "symbolizing," according to E. O. James, "the Son of God."[41]

In a third-century Easter sermon, Hippolytus described the cosmic tree: "This tree, wide as the heavens itself, has grown up into heaven from the earth. It is an immortal growth and towers twixt heaven and earth. It is the fulcrum of all things and the place where they are at rest. It is the foundation of the round world, the centre of the cosmos. In it all the diversities in our human nature are formed into a unity. It is held together by invisible nails of the Spirit so that it may not break loose from the divine. It touches the highest summits

40. E. O. James, *Tree of Life*, 161–62.

41. Carolyn Osiek, *Shepherd of Hermas* (Minneapolis: Fortress, 1999), 194–200, stating, "That the tree is God's law (v. 2), or rather, that the law is compared to a tree of life, is a common Jewish image," 203. Similitude 8 is cited and discussed in E. O. James, *Tree of Life*, 162.

of heaven and makes the earth firm beneath its foot, and it grasps the middle regions between them with immeasurable arms."[42]

Conclusion

The image of the tree of life is a powerful, beautiful, multifaceted, and pervasive Christian symbol. This imagery is not merely decorative or tangential to later Christian traditions; it is part of the fabric of the Christian message from the time of the New Testament apostles. The tree of life assumed many forms, representing various stages of life in the unfolding of God's plan of salvation. This study has explored six ways in which the motif of the tree of life has been used in Christianity: to represent salvation and eternal life, Christ himself, personified wisdom, the cross of Calvary, Christian peoples, and the cosmic tree of the world. In these ways, the tree has represented both God and man, life and death, heaven and earth, the single individual and the totality of the cosmos. This complexity is appropriate, for it instantiates the manifold abundance of the fulness of the Christian message of bringing to pass the immortality and eternal life of mankind and the renewal of this earth to its paradisiacal glory.

John W. Welch is the Robert K. Thomas Professor of Law at the J. Reuben Clark Law School, where he teaches various courses, including Perspectives on Jewish, Greek, and Roman Law in the New Testament. Since 1991 he has also served as the editor in chief of BYU Studies. He studied history and classical languages at Brigham Young University (BA, MA 1970); Greek philosophy at St. Edmund Hall, Oxford (1970–72); and law at Duke University (JD 1975). As founder of the Foundation for Ancient Research and Mormon Studies, one of the editors for Macmillan's Encyclopedia of Mormonism, *and codirector of the Masada and Dead Sea Scrolls exhibition at BYU, he has published widely on biblical, early Christian, and Latter-day Saint topics.*

42. Hippolytus, *De Pascha Homilia*, in E. O. James, *Tree of Life*, 162.

The Tree of Life in John's Gospel

C. Wilfred Griggs

The Gospel of John leads readers to the themes associated with the tree of life in profound and insightful ways. In its pages lie an abundance of images that hark back to the earliest scriptural story, the one found in the opening chapters of Genesis. These images draw their relevance from a living plant (the vine), from the product of living plants (bread from grain), or from that which sustains the lives of plants (water). With images such as these, the Fourth Gospel pulls readers both ancient and modern into the circle of eternal life—the real fruit of the tree of life—through Jesus of Nazareth.

The great amount of tree of life material in the Gospel of John may seem at first somewhat paradoxical, inasmuch as the tree of life is never explicitly mentioned in the Fourth Gospel. Nevertheless, by considering John's development of a few selected themes, it will become clear that the themes of Genesis 1–3 run throughout the Gospel of John, for a person's return to God's presence is possible only by partaking of the fruit of the tree in the garden from which Adam and Eve were driven as a result of their disobedience.

The Prologue and Opening of the Gospel of John

Any ancient person who knew the beginning of the Greek version of Genesis might well have thought for a moment that he was listening to Genesis as he encountered the opening words of John's Gospel. The opening two words (*en archēi*) are the same in both texts, and it is obvious from the following verses that John intended to connect his work to the Genesis story and other Old Testament themes.[1] Just as Genesis celebrates the appearance of light and life in the world, John, after giving the briefest possible summary regarding the creation (1:3),[2] declares that whatever was begotten in or through the Word is life and that this life gives light to mankind (v. 4). Verse 9 is purposefully ambiguous, which is a common characteristic of John's writings. The verse can be understood in two ways: First, he was the true light that illuminates every man who comes into the world, and second, he was the true light that, because he came into the world, illuminates every man. In either translation, the Word brings light and life into the world.

Because it was understood that one cannot partake of the tree of life's fruit in a sinful condition (Genesis 3:22), it is natural that John would emphasize at several points throughout his Gospel the means by which sins can be removed. The testimony of John the Baptist (1:19–36) immediately follows the introduction to the Gospel (vv. 1–18), and twice in his testimony he refers to Jesus as the Lamb of God "who takes away the sin of the world" (vv. 29, 36). John often uses the timeless method of repetition when he wishes to emphasize an idea. In this instance the reader should remember that Adam and Eve, in their sinful condition, were forbidden to eat the tree of life's fruit, so it was necessary for Jesus to take away sin before giving life to God's children. Apart from the symbolic references to the Passover offering in John's testimony, one should also consider the image of innocence and meekness portrayed by the Lamb who will "take away the sin of the world."

Wedding at Cana

Two virtually ubiquitous symbols relating to life—marriage and wine—are brought together in the first of Jesus's seven signs, or miracles, recorded in the Gospel of John: the wedding at Cana. Marriage,

1. See generally G. K. Beale and D. A. Carson, eds., *Commentary on the New Testament Use of the Old Testament* (Grand Rapids, MI: Baker, 2007), 421–23.

2. Abbreviated scriptural references are to the Gospel of John unless otherwise indicated.

instituted by God in Eden with Adam and Eve, brought the man and woman together to become one flesh and thus propagate human life on the earth. Every ancient society recognized and celebrated marriage for its promise that life would continue in the world. Wine, both because of its red color and its presumed ability to revive the body and quicken the mind, was therefore analogous to blood, the fluid of life in mortal bodies. The fermentation of grape juice made it appear as if the resulting wine had a divine life of its own, and many ancients (e.g., Hesiod, an early Greek poet) believed that drinking wine imbued them with the ability to speak heavenly words of wisdom. The wine literally inspired them by warming the body and loosing the tongue.

Jesus and his disciples were invited to the wedding at Cana, and Jesus's mother was also present. At such a large and momentous festival rejoicing in the promise of continuing life, it was with obvious concern that Mary went to Jesus to say, "They have run out of wine" (2:3). (Note by her words and Jesus's reply that, contrary to what many believe, this was not Jesus's wedding, and Mary was not responsible for the hospitality shown to the guests.) His answer, not well translated in the King James Version, was "Woman, of what concern is that to us?" (or, "Woman, is that any of our business?"). The second part of his response at first seems, in view of what follows, to be irrelevant—"My hour has not yet come" (2:4). If it referred simply to the beginning of his public ministry and the performance of miracles as bona fides of his identity and compassion toward people, the immediately ensuing miracle would make no sense. There is, however, much more to consider. Throughout John's Gospel one can discover many embedded layers of meaning, much as one constantly finds a new onion by peeling away the outer layers, but with one striking difference: When one peels away layers of an onion, each "new onion" is smaller than its predecessor. When one uncovers a new layer of meaning in John, it is often grander in scope and more profound in significance than the one preceding it. There are many such levels of meaning in the account of the Cana miracle. We will examine one that has direct relationship to the topic we are considering.

There are two additional references in John to the fact that the hour of Jesus had not come (7:30; 8:20), and at the beginning of the long section dealing with the last supper (chaps. 13–17), John writes, "When Jesus knew that his hour had come, that he would pass over from this world to his Father . . ." (13:1). The connection between Jesus's earlier statement at Cana (and the accompanying miracle) and his knowledge that his hour had come on that fateful Passover eve now becomes clear. Changing water to wine without the normal ingredients of grape juice and fermentation agents and the passage of time was no trivial accomplishment, and through this miracle Jesus displayed his divine power and authority, as well as his compassion toward those whose acute embarrassment caused by running out of wine would have had significant social consequences. John records that Jesus produced six stone waterpots of wine, each having the capacity of some 20 to 30 gallons (Jesus ordered that they be filled with water to the brim), or between 120 and 180 gallons. That was after the original stock of wine had failed, giving some indication of the magnitude and likely social importance of the wedding party. Further, when the servants took some of the wine to the master of the feast, he told the bridegroom that it was the best wine served during the wedding festival (2:10). The miraculous wine was thus notable for its quantity and its vintage quality.

Remembering from John 1:4, 9 that the Word came into the world to give light and life to everyone, and looking forward to the meaning of "his hour had come" at the beginning of chapter 13 (in which "hour" Jesus would become the means of providing that life by offering his flesh and blood), we see that the first embedded layer of meaning to appear in this wedding miracle foreshadows Jesus's producing the divine wine of eternal life through the shedding of his blood on the cross, a tree of life. Even wedding feasts and wine cannot guarantee that life will not end—after all, the wine ran out, just as mortal life will end in death. Only Jesus through his atonement can offer the real promise of eternal life. The miracle at Cana illustrates the difference between the ephemeral and the eternal. The amount and quality of wine that Jesus produced, as well as the similarly great amount of food produced when he miraculously fed five thousand men, plus women and children (compare Matthew 14:21), portend the nature of the eternal life that Jesus can bestow. For example, in John 10:10, Jesus states: "I came that they might have life, and that they might have it in abundance." The miracle of the wine was real, but it was only for life in this world. The blood shed in Gethsemane and on the cross was also part of a real miracle, and it provides a rich life beyond the end of mortality, fulfilling with abundance the purposes for the creation of this earth.

Nicodemus

Another pair of symbols—darkness and light—point to Genesis 1–3 and the tree of life. Darkness represents sin and death in the Gospel of John and also, by extension, in the world since all who live in the world have sinned and all will die (e.g., Romans 3:23; 1 Corinthians 15:22). It is natural, therefore, for John to write of Jesus bringing both light and life into the world since both together signify his taking away the sin of the world and overcoming death. Following the account of the miracle at Cana, John presents this concept through successive encounters—one with a Pharisee named Nicodemus in Jerusalem and another with a Samaritan woman at the well of Jacob.

Nicodemus was a ruler of the Jews, placing him at the apex of Jewish society, and his pharisaism denotes his religious training and interest. He was well-disposed toward Jesus, primarily because of the miracles that Jesus performed among the Jews. John records that Nicodemus approached Jesus at night and declared him to be a teacher sent from God, as evidenced by his miraculous deeds (3:2). One may well speculate why he came "after hours," so to speak, but without an answer to that question, I shall propose an alternative suggestion after considering some details of their meeting.

The miracle of the wine at Cana had real and obvious physical benefits for those attending the festival, but few at the time could have fathomed the spiritual nature or significance attached to that sign.[3] Similarly, Nicodemus could see the physical aspects of Jesus's miracles, which piqued his curiosity, but he did not comprehend their spiritual meaning. In the dialogue that followed Nicodemus's declaration that Jesus was a teacher sent from God, Jesus twice invited him to be reborn spiritually and receive heavenly life and understanding. Nicodemus inexplicably demurred, attempting to keep the conversation on an earthly plane ("How can a man be born when he is old? Surely he is not able to enter the womb of his mother a second time and be born?" 3:4), and finally admitted that he did not understand what Jesus was saying (v. 9). Jesus asked him how he could be *the* teacher of Israel (the definite article may be significant here) and not know about spiritual matters, and then followed with the assertion that Nicodemus and his associates (the *you* is plural, including more than Nicodemus) would not receive the witness or testimony of Jesus and his disciples (vv. 11–12). After explaining that he came down from heaven to teach heavenly truths that would bestow eternal life on those who accepted them, Jesus summarized the critical issue facing Nicodemus and everyone else who hears the divine, life-giving message:

> This is the judgment [or test], that the Light came into the world, yet men loved the darkness rather than the Light, because their deeds were evil. For everyone who does base [wicked] things hates the Light and does not come to the light, lest his acts be exposed [reproved]. But the one who performs the truth comes to the Light, so that his deeds [acts] might be made manifest that they have been accomplished in God. (3:19–21)

Thus as we uncover a deeper layer of meaning in the text, we see that Nicodemus came to Jesus not only in the physical darkness of night but also in spiritual darkness. His reasons for not accepting Jesus's invitation to be reborn into light and life are not known to us,

---

3. John uses a term throughout his Gospel that is usually translated as "sign," rather than the word used in the other three Gospels that is usually translated as "miracle." For this reason, many commentators refer to the Fourth Gospel as the "Gospel of Signs."

for the accounting of one's life is a matter between that person and God and is not a matter for public scrutiny. Still, it must be said that Nicodemus came in the dark and unfortunately departed in the same condition despite his apparent religiosity and good reputation. When Jesus spoke of Moses lifting up the brazen serpent in the wilderness, he alluded to the cross upon which even the Son of Man must be raised (3:14). Being with Jesus is ultimately a matter of rising, ascending up to heaven and leaving behind one's sins and worldly concerns (3:13; 12:32). This idea points to a tree whereon Jesus was lifted up to die, only to move into greater light and life in the resurrection (3:14–15), and that tree of life is not accessible to those who choose to remain in the dark.

The Samaritan Woman at the Well

At some later time, Jesus and his disciples journeyed through Samaria on their way to the Galilee district. As he rested at the well of Jacob while the disciples went into the nearby town to buy food, a Samaritan woman arrived with a bucket to draw water from the deep well. When Jesus asked for a drink of water, she reacted with considerable surprise, for, as John informs us, Jews usually had nothing to do with Samaritans. But in this instance, Jesus offered to give the woman life through his living water (*hydōr zōn*).[4] She did not understand at first, limiting her side of the conversation to her world of wells, buckets, and drawing water. Finally, acknowledging that his living water that would quench thirst forever might save her the labor of returning every day to the well, she asked him to give her the living water. At that point, Jesus asked her to bring her husband, and we learn from her response that she had previously lived with five men and that she was not married to the sixth, her current companion. As in the brightness of noonday sun, her sinful life was exposed to Jesus (it was exposure only for her since he already knew). She recognized Jesus as a prophet and began to ask questions about God and worship, concluding with

4. This perhaps alludes to the river of water that came out of Eden to water the garden in which the tree of life was found in Genesis 2:10, and also to the waters issuing forth from the temple in Ezekiel 47:1.

a wistful statement: "I know that a Messiah is coming who is called Christ; when he comes, he will teach us all things" (4:25). One can imagine the thrill and joy she experienced when Jesus said, "I, the one speaking with you, am he" (v. 26).

The contrast between the reactions of Nicodemus and the Samaritan woman could not be clearer. He was educated, powerful, and religious, and he approached Jesus in darkness to discuss miracles and religion. She was none of those things. Whereas he was unwilling to be reborn into spiritual life, she accepted the invitation to receive eternal life in the brightness of the midday light, even though it meant the exposure and (assuredly, given the context) renunciation of her sins. These two examples provide great object lessons to anyone who reads the Gospel of John. Jesus offers life to all, but on his terms, not ours.

Feeding the Five Thousand

The miracle of the wine at Cana and John's account of Jesus miraculously feeding five thousand men[5] near Bethsaida have much in common. Whereas Mary made known the problem at Cana by stating that the hosts had run out of wine, Jesus introduced the problem of feeding the large crowd by asking Philip where they could buy food to feed the people. Since Philip was from Bethsaida, he might be expected to know where provisions could be purchased. Philip responded that not even with two-thirds of a year's wages for a skilled laborer could they buy enough food for everybody to have a bite.[6] Andrew brought a boy to Jesus who had five small barley loaves (not to be confused with the large loaves of bread available today) and two small fish (the word for fish used in John is the diminutive form, emphasizing the small size) and asked how such a small amount of food would help feed so many people. All of this seems to show the magnitude of the problem, not to suggest a solution, for John states that Jesus "knew what he was

5. Matthew 14:21 explicitly states that there were women and children in addition to the five thousand men.

6. The typical wage for a common laborer was one denarius per day, and so two hundred denarii would be about eight months' wages, assuming a six-day workweek. See John W. Betlyon, "Coinage," in *Anchor Bible Dictionary*, ed. David N. Freeman (New York: Doubleday, 1992), 1:1086.

about to do" (6:6). Just as at Cana, the need was great, and Jesus was willing and able to satisfy the need.

After having the disciples organize and seat the crowd on the large grassy area at hand, Jesus took the loaves and fish, gave thanks, and distributed the food. The text states that all ate as much as they wanted and were filled. Jesus then had the disciples collect the leftover food, and they gathered twelve basketfuls (one assumes one basket per apostle, although that is only a natural guess). There was much more food remaining after the meal than there was at the beginning. Again making a comparison to the miracle at Cana, we note that Jesus went beyond necessity to provide an overflowing abundance. The miracles bestowed physical benefits beyond measure upon recipients whose needs were real. The spiritual meaning underlying these miracles (keeping in mind that the giving of life suggested by the wine at Cana is repeated and even magnified in the feeding of the five thousand men and others) is clear: Jesus does not simply promise new life for all to whom death seems the inevitable end in this life, but his is a promise of a rich and abundant life. The new life is not merely a continuation but an enhancement of life as people know it on earth. Within this concept stands the view of the tree of life in the Fourth Gospel.

At least some people in the crowd recognized the miracle Jesus performed, for they proclaimed him to be the prophet who Moses prophesied would one day come as one like himself (Deuteronomy 18:15–18). When Jesus knew that the people were about to take him and declare him to be their king, he left them and went alone up a mountain.

On the following day, after walking on the sea to meet his disciples who were traveling to Capernaum by boat, Jesus was accosted by the crowd who had returned to Capernaum (not a very great distance from the area near Bethsaida). The people asked Jesus when he had arrived in Capernaum, a somewhat unexpected question since they knew he had not come by boat (they had observed that there were no boats save the one taken by the disciples on the previous evening). They might naturally have asked *how* he got there, but instead they asked, "When camest thou hither?" (6:25).

Rather than answer their question, Jesus responded that they were following him because he had fed them, and he exhorted them to work for food that would remain unto eternal life, which the Son of Man would give to them (6:27). Considering the miracle of the previous day, it seems strange that the people asked Jesus to show them a sign as a token that he was the one sent from God to give them the food of life (v. 30). It is ironic that, in their request for a sign, they made reference to the miracle of the manna in the time of Moses. The combination of dialogue and sermon in John 6 is known as the Bread of Life sermon, and it follows the pattern established in the meetings that Jesus had with Nicodemus and the Samaritan woman.

Jesus first clarified the ancient miracle by noting that it was not Moses who gave manna to the Israelites, but rather God who gives the true bread from heaven (6:32). As he earlier had attempted to raise Nicodemus's awareness of the heavenly origin of miracles (as opposed to a preoccupation with the physical miracles themselves), he now tried to elevate the thinking of the crowd to consider the true heavenly bread, which gives life to the world (v. 33). The people did at least express interest in receiving that bread every day (v. 34), just as the Samaritan woman finally requested Jesus to give her living water, even if neither they nor she initially comprehended the spiritual nature of that request.

Jesus earlier declared to Nicodemus that he had descended from heaven to give eternal life to all who would have faith in him (3:13–17), and he gave the same message in Capernaum, telling his audience that he is the Bread of Life, having been sent from heaven to give eternal sustenance to everyone who comes to him and has faith in him (6:35–38). His testimony that he is the Bread of Life and that he would give life to (literally raise up or resurrect) his faithful followers was not well received, and the Jewish audience began to argue what he meant by declaring himself to be bread from heaven (v. 41). Jesus answered their claim to know his earthly parentage by stating that only if they acknowledged God to be his Father could they come to him and have faith in him. Jesus reminded the people, who were determined to see everything in earthly terms (as Nicodemus earlier), that although their fathers had eaten the miraculous manna in the desert, they had all nevertheless died. He then assured them that the only way to overcome death and enjoy eternal life was to eat the Bread of Life, which he identified as his flesh (vv. 50–51).

That was more than the crowd could stand, and they erupted into a full-scale riot (6:52). Misunderstanding Jesus's meaning, they evidently thought he was advocating a kind of cannibalism, which was specifically forbidden in the law of Moses. Jesus then added that they must drink his blood as well as eat his flesh in order to be resurrected in the last day and have eternal life (vv. 53–54). He repeated the contrast between the Israelites who ate manna and died and those who would eat the true Bread from heaven and have eternal life (v. 58).

Although the phrase "tree of life" is not mentioned in the Bread of Life sermon, it is clear that partaking of Jesus's flesh and drinking his blood to obtain eternal life is functionally equivalent to partaking of the fruit of the tree of life in the Garden of Eden. Jesus's miracles of producing wine at Cana and bread near Bethsaida clearly foreshadow the sacrifice of his own flesh and blood to give eternal life to all who will partake of them in faith. One must leave behind the disputes and doubts of those in Capernaum and proceed to Gethsemane to find that fruit.

One cannot but feel some sympathy for those who found this sermon difficult to understand and accept. Even on a spiritual plane there is a natural reluctance to think of feasting on one who is beloved and whose blameless body should be honored rather than devoured. It is no small matter that even Jesus's disciples shrank from his request that they eat and drink of his essence. The sacrament of the Lord's Supper cannot be received without an awesome reverence—for by it he is in us, and we become one with him. Thus he prayed with those who supped with him prior to Gethsemane and the cross (John 17).

Raising Lazarus

As the miracles of the wine at Cana and the bread near Bethsaida foreshadowed Jesus's giving his blood and body to give life to the world, the raising of Lazarus from the grave at Bethany gave proof of his power over death itself. If the initial depletion of the wine at Cana symbolized the inevitability of death in the world, the restoring of life at Bethany betokened the ultimate rolling back of the finality of death that resulted from the fall within the Garden of Eden. John makes clear that Jesus's power to give life is greater than the power of darkness to destroy it.

At first it was a matter of Lazarus's illness. On numerous occasions Jesus had healed people suffering various maladies and diseases. The sisters of Lazarus, Mary and Martha, sent word to Jesus that Lazarus was ill, no doubt hoping that Jesus would bless his friend, described in the sisters' message as beloved of the Savior. When Jesus received their petition, he told his disciples that Lazarus's illness would not have death as its final result (this passage in Greek does not say that Lazarus would not die, only that the end result would not be death), but would redound to the glory of the Son of God. Jesus did not immediately go to Bethany but remained where he was for two days (11:6), after which he requested that the disciples go with him to Judea (v. 7). The disciples' fear that Jesus faced death by going to Judea shows that they did not yet understand that his authority and power concerning life and death were greater than that of his enemy and those in his enemy's service.

Jesus told his disciples that their friend Lazarus had fallen asleep and that he was going to awaken him (11:11). Having heard earlier that Lazarus's illness would not finally result in death, they naturally misunderstood the euphemism of speaking of death as a sleep. Knowing that sleep is normally an indication of healing rest, they responded that he must be on the mend, no doubt hoping that such an assurance would deter them from the dangerous journey to Bethany in Judea. Then, dispensing with veiled language, Jesus told them plainly that Lazarus had died (v. 14). The disciples must have wondered at Jesus's following statement: "I rejoice for your sake that I was not there, that you might have faith" (v. 15). They did not know that a greater miracle than healing an illness was about to occur. As a tribute to Thomas, usually identified with the epithet "the doubter," John records him saying in loyalty and boldness, "Let us also go, that we may die with him" (v. 16). John thus lets his audience know that in more than one sense this was to be a journey into the realm of death.

When the small group arrived at Bethany, Lazarus had already been entombed for four days (11:17). Significantly, an ancient Jewish belief held that the spirit of a deceased individual might hover about the body for three days, but it irrevocably departed after that. Throughout the ancient world (Egypt being a notable exception), the spirits of the dead were portrayed as leading a shadowy existence in a kind of half-life, neither really alive nor completely dead. So far as the body is concerned, however, death was final, with only decomposition and a return to the elements of the earth in its future. The reader begins to understand why Jesus delayed so long to make his way to Bethany: there was to be no question about simply reviving one whose death was so recent that recovery might theoretically be possible. When Martha met Jesus, she expressed her faith that had Jesus been present earlier, Lazarus would not have died (v. 21). When Mary arrived, she repeated Martha's declaration (v. 32). When they arrived at the tomb and Jesus commanded that the covering stone be removed, Martha said, "Lord, the odor is already terrible, for he has been dead four days" (v. 39).

The stone was removed, Jesus called Lazarus to come out, and he emerged (11:41–44)—undoubtedly with difficulty, for he was still shrouded with burial wrappings at his feet and hands and about his head (to keep the jaw in place). Having uncovered ancient burials in Egypt for more than a quarter of a century, I have some idea of and appreciation for the shocked—stunned—reaction of those present when witnessing that event. I wonder whether I would be rooted to the spot or would set a running record should a buried corpse at my excavation site stir and rise of its own accord. Jesus broke the frozen response of those present by telling them to remove the wrappings so Lazarus could walk about freely (v. 44).

The cosmic nature of the conflict between the light and life of Jesus and the world of darkness and death is exemplified by the counsel of the chief priests to kill Lazarus (12:10), as if his life or death would signify the victor in the battle between God and Satan. They had already decided that Jesus must be killed (11:50–53), claiming that it was for the good of the nation. John adds for his Christian audience that Jesus's death would not only benefit the Jewish people but would also be a blessing for all the children of God (v. 52). The Jewish leaders saw Christ's death as a temporal advantage for themselves; the testimony of John is that the death of Jesus brought about eternal blessings for all people. Out of his death would emerge life—life richer and more abundant than that temporarily interrupted by death.

Last Supper

Jesus's hour had come. It was time for him to return to his Father. Of course, the journey back would be by way of Gethsemane and the cross, where he would offer himself a perfect and willing sacrifice on behalf of the world. All who would accept his atonement through faith and repentance could then partake of his flesh and blood, the fruit of the tree of life that gives eternal light and life. Before his departure, Jesus taught his disciples how to prepare for their own journey back into the presence of their Father and his Son, their glorified Master. As he would go back to his Father through suffering and death, all can return to the Father only through Jesus. That instruction was given as Jesus celebrated his final earthly Passover with his disciples.

The importance John attaches to Jesus's teachings at the last supper can hardly be overstated. He devotes nearly a fourth of his Gospel to that occasion. It might seem strange to some that the synoptic Gospels (Matthew, Mark, and Luke) all present the introduction of the Eucharist, or sacrament, in their brief account of the last supper (Matthew 26:20–30; Mark 14:17–26; Luke 22:14–39), whereas John, whose last supper narrative covers five chapters, makes no mention of it. I offer a couple of reasons for this apparent omission. The synoptic Gospels were missionary tracts to different audiences, and it would be natural to introduce potential converts to principles and practices of the church through those writings. The earliest ancient commentators on John understood the Fourth Gospel to be written to people who were already church members as a guide into the sacred doctrines of their faith, making it less necessary to include items covered in the other Gospels. Indeed, as was seen in the account of Jesus restoring Lazarus to life from the grave, John presumed his readers' familiarity with the story by referring to Mary as the one who anointed and dried Christ's feet (11:2), although he did not relate the event until a chapter later. Church members would likewise have been familiar with the institution of the Eucharist, and its absence in an account focusing on other matters would not have occasioned surprise or concern. What one cannot say is that the symbols of bread and wine and their relationship to one's partaking of Jesus's body and blood are unimportant or lacking throughout this most sacramental of Gospels.

Before giving the sacred information that would prepare the disciples to return to the presence of God, Jesus washed their feet to cleanse them from the filth of the world. One properly associates baptism with becoming cleansed from sin, but if after bathing one went to a distant home for dinner, that person would pick up dust or dirt on the feet during the journey. Washing of a guest's feet by a slave usually took place before the meal, and it was therefore highly unusual for Jesus himself to wash feet and to do so during the meal. As Jesus moved from person to person, washing and drying their feet, all must have wondered why he was doing such a thing. When he came to Peter, that apostle surely voiced what others were thinking when he asked why Jesus was washing their feet. Jesus explained that it was necessary if they were to have a place with him (13:8). Typical of Peter's personality, he then extended his head and hands and said to give him a full wash (v. 9). Jesus responded that one who had already bathed (been baptized) had no further need except that his feet be washed in order to be completely clean (v. 10). He then stated that they were cleansed, but not all of them, for even though he had washed the feet of Judas Iscariot, that apostle would betray his Lord and thus was not cleansed spiritually. The others were now prepared to receive sacred teachings, and Judas was dismissed by Jesus before those things were given (vv. 27–30).

In the introduction to his Gospel, John said that the light shines in the darkness, yet the darkness did not seize or overtake it (1:5). Ever since Eden the conflict in this world has been between light and darkness, life and death. When Adam and Eve transgressed, they became subject to death and darkness, shut out from the sacred garden and its tree of life. When Jesus came to bring light and life into the world, it was inevitable that the deciding battle should take place between him and his enemy. As Judas left the dinner, it was to ensure that the cosmic duel would take place that night. Operating as the agent of Satan, Judas represented the power of darkness. There may be no more dramatic statement in literature than the one accompanying his departure: a three-word Greek sentence, *ēn de nux*, "and it was night" (13:30).

As if Judas took the darkness out with him, or more correctly, as soon as Jesus banished the darkness from his presence, the next two verses contain the word *glorify* five times, all in connection with God and Christ (13:31–32). The relationship between light and glory is obvious, and the light was shining more brightly once the darkness was dispelled. From John's perspective, Jesus had won the battle; and indeed, he will quote Jesus three chapters later saying, "But take courage, I have conquered [overcome] the world" (16:33). It was time to prepare the disciples to have life with God.

With the evil one dismissed, and sitting in the light without darkness, Jesus imparted instructions and preparations for the journey back to God in a classical manner of teaching—a dialogue. Some disciples are specifically named as participants, including Peter (13:36), Thomas (14:5), Philip (v. 8), and Judas—not Iscariot (v. 22). Elsewhere the disciples are mentioned together as asking or commenting during the course of the presentation (16:17, 29). It was a moment designed for all of them to enjoy learning in pure light.

Pertinent to our topic is Jesus's statement "I am the Way, the Truth, and the Life" (14:6). Amplifying this concept, Jesus compared himself to a vine and his disciples to branches (15:1–5). Remembering the miracle of the wine at Cana and the observations made concerning that miracle, one can see this comparison to a vine as specifically giving the promise of life. Jesus further explained that the branches could not bear fruit unless they were connected to and deriving life from the vine (v. 4). Clearly the vine of life is here equivalent to the tree of life, and without Jesus there is no fruit of the vine or tree. If the disciples remained in Jesus, they would bear much fruit and have such a fullness of life that every desire and request would be fulfilled for them (vv. 5–8).

John not only emphasizes the need for the disciples to be clean and pure before being prepared for the journey home to God, but he also records another necessary ingredient. Before the last supper narrative, John had written the noun and verb for *love* eight times (once for the noun and seven times for the verb), but in the meeting in the upper room he repeated them thirty times. Thus, in the presence of God, life and love are inseparable, and without love one cannot experience godly life. Partaking of the fruit of eternal life must be done in love. Even though Jesus is going to Gethsemane and Calvary, John records Jesus speaking the word for *joy* seven times in the last supper discourse, compared with only two times earlier in the Gospel (3:29). But love and joy are to be the distinguishing characteristics of those who approach and eat from the tree of life.

Gardens and Crucifixion

The synoptic Gospels all name Gethsemane as the place where Jesus went with the disciples after leaving the upper room, but only John specifically states that it was a garden (18:1, 20). He further states that the new and previously unused tomb in the place where Jesus was crucified was in a garden (19:41). When Jesus appeared to Mary Magdalene, she at first thought he was the gardener (20:15). The allusions to Genesis at the beginning of John's Gospel, coupled with the theme of the tree of life developed throughout it, make it natural to associate the two gardens of Jesus's suffering and crucifixion on a tree with the Garden of Eden and its tree of life. His suffering in the first garden made it possible for disciples to partake of the fruit of eternal life that was on the cross in the second garden. Thus, as Eden was the garden where Adam and Eve first lived and where death came into existence and deprived them of eternal life, so in these gardens in John the process was reversed, with death being first and eternal life coming into existence out of that death. Entry into the heavenly Eden has become possible through Jesus Christ.

In a related vein, there are a number of references to trees in the New Testament, but though there are two Greek words that mean "tree," one appears nearly half a dozen times in the New Testament for the cross (Greek *xylon*). That word is the same as the one written in the Septuagint for the tree of life (LXX Genesis 2:9). John employed the same word in the letter to the Ephesians in the book of Revelation: "To the one who overcomes I will give to eat from the Tree of Life, which is in the paradise of God" (Revelation 2:7).

John's narrative of the crucifixion contains yet another event that depicts Jesus as the fruit of the tree of life. After Jesus stated, "It is finished [has been completed or accomplished],"[7] he bowed his head and released his spirit from the body (19:30). While the body was still affixed to the cross, the soldiers attending the crucifixion pierced Jesus's side or chest[8] with a spear[9] to make certain Jesus was dead. John then states that "immediately blood and water poured out of the chest" (v. 34). The connections between water, blood, wine, and life have already been discussed, and I note here that Jesus also had referred more than once to "living water" in the Fourth Gospel (4:10–15; 7:38—"out of his abdomen will flow rivers of living water"). With the clear identification, therefore, between blood, water, and life, John bears eloquent testimony that through Jesus's suffering and death, life flows out from him into the world. The cross, usually recognized as a horrendous instrument of torture and death, in this one instance is miraculously transformed into a "tree of life," and Jesus becomes the fruit of that tree from whom the blood and water of life flow. As the

---

7. *Tetelestai*, the same root word as used in Genesis 2:1 to note the completion of the creation of heaven and earth. See Mary Coloe, "The Dwelling of God among Us: The Symbolic Function of the Temple in the Fourth Gospel" (master's thesis, Melbourne College of Divinity, Australia, 1998), 278; cited in Alan R. Kerr, *The Temple of Jesus' Body: The Temple Theme in the Gospel of John* (Sheffield, England: Sheffield Academic Press, 2002), 243.

8. *Pleuran*, the same word as in Genesis 2:21–22, where God takes one of Adam's ribs in order to form Eve.

9. *Romphaia*, the same word that appears in Genesis 3:25 to describe the sword that guards the tree of life.

Lamb of God has taken away the sin of the world (1:29), the fruit and life from the tree of life, inaccessible to God's children since the fall of Adam, has become available to all who have faith in Jesus Christ. The fruit of the tree, represented in the emblems of the sacrament, or Eucharist, bestow spiritual life now, with the promise of eternal life to come.

Conclusion

Threaded into John's Gospel is a tapestry of light and dark, of life and death, of thirst-quenching water and drying sin. All these images point more or less directly back to the tree of life planted in the Garden of Eden. What Adam and Eve started Jesus will complete; what they introduced he will perfect; what they closed he will open; what they were prevented from doing he will offer access to. His acts and words promise an abundance of life and derive their deepest meaning when we see him as the true representative of the tree of life.

Wilfred Griggs, professor of ancient scripture at Brigham Young University, studied history and Greek literature at BYU and received his PhD from the University of California, Berkeley, in ancient history and Mediterranean archaeology. He is field director for the BYU Egypt Excavation Project. His publications include Early Egyptian Christianity: From Its Origins to 451 C.E. *(2000) and numerous articles on the New Testament and early Christianity. Griggs's previous work on the tree of life has appeared in the* Ensign *(June 1988),* Book of Mormon Authorship: New Light on Ancient Origins *(1982), and* Book of Mormon Reference Companion *(2003).*

Plate 1. Apocalypse tapestry, Château d'Angers, Angers, France, 14th century. John the Revelator beholds Eden and the heavenly Jerusalem in vision.

Plate 2. World cross with tree of life below, apse mosaic, Basilica of San Giovanni Laterano, Rome, Italy, 4th–6th century (mosaic later restored).

Plate 3. Rohan Master, scene from the Book of Hours, 15th century. God plants a tree with people emerging from the trunk, echoing the biblical idea that the righteous are trees of life (see Isaiah 61:3).

Plate 4. Tree of Jesse window, ambulatory in the Basilica of St. Denis, Paris, France, depicting in abbreviated fashion the ascent of Christ from Jesse.

Plate 5. Ceiba Tree, Tikal, Guatemala. The towering ceiba is revered by the Maya as a manifestation of the World Tree, an *axis mundi* linking heaven, earth, and the underworld and marking the locus of creation.

Plate 6. Cemetery, Santiago Atitlán, Guatemala. In a number of traditional Maya cemeteries like this one, graves are planted with a tree, representing the rebirth of the interred individuals to new life.

Plate 7. Buddha Maitreya, or future Buddha, central Tibet, 13th century. Silk painting with embroidery. On the Buddha's left shoulder is a flower from an emerging alba tree, signifying that the next Buddha will experience a great awakening under that tree.

Plate 8. Borobudur Temple, Java, Indonesia, 8th century, representing sacred Mt. Meru of Hindu-Buddhist tradition. Pilgrims circumambulate the monument to learn sacred doctrines from wall reliefs, eventually reaching the stupa at the summit, symbolic center of the universe.

Plate 9. *Lehi's Vision of the Tree of Life,* by Robert Yellowhair. Oil on canvas. Lehi is seen as a Hopi priest offering glowing fruit to his family, who represent historical or cultural figures from surrounding tribes.

Plate 10. *Nephi's Vision of the Tree of Life,* by Gilbert Singh. Gouache on silk. Nephi's sweeping prophetic overview of spiritual history is depicted, culminating with the second coming of Christ (center).

Plate 11. The Genesis cupola of the Basilica of San Marco in Venice, Italy, is graced with 13th-century mosaics of the creation, such as this scene depicting the expulsion of Adam and Eve from Eden.

Plate 12. *Tree of the Cross,* refectory fresco by Taddeo Gaddi, Basilica of Santa Croce, Florence, Italy, ca. 1330. The cross has become a tree of life whose twelve branches representing the apostles are laden with the fruit of the Gospels.

Plate 13. *Tree of the Sacraments,* anonymous painting in the chancel of the parish church, Santa Cruz, Tlaxcala, Mexico, 1735.

Plate 14. In his night journey, Muhammad travels to the *sidrat al-muntaha,* or "lote-tree of the uttermost boundary," the farthest one can travel in his approach to Allah.

Plate 15. In his night journey on his noble steed Buraq, Muhammad ascends to paradise. The glorious being in the upper left is the angel Gabriel.

Plate 16. Tree of life floor mosaic in the audience chamber of the bathhouse at Khirbat al-Mafjar, in Jordan.

"I Have Dreamed a Dream": Lehi's Archetypal Vision of the Tree of Life

Charles Swift

At the heart of the Book of Mormon thrives the image of the tree of life—the perfect archetype for conveying the book's theme of coming to Christ and partaking of his divine love. This image, however, does not stand alone. It is the central element of a visionary dream graced with many archetypal images of good and evil that are rooted in the experiences of the prophet who saw the dream and that reach beyond his own time. As we study these various images and strive to see both the forest of archetypes and the tree, we come to realize that the vision is itself an archetype, offering an account of humankind's journey through a mortality plagued with temptations and dangers yet blessed with divine aid—a journey whose end is filled with ultimate joy.

Symbol as Ticket to the Other

In approaching the tree of life in the Book of Mormon as an archetype, we are considering it initially as a symbol. Therefore, to understand what we mean by *archetype*, we must first understand what we mean by *symbol*. In literature, a symbol is "a word or phrase that signifies an object or event which in its turn signifies something . . . beyond itself."[1] For example, the word *path* signifies a worn area of the ground that goes from one place to another, and the idea of a path can signify something beyond the worn area itself, such as a person's life. Symbolism is not linguistic adornment, words used poetically simply to

1. M. H. Abrams and Geoffrey Galt Harpham, *A Glossary of Literary Terms*, 9th ed. (Boston: Wadsworth Cengage Learning, 2009), 358.

enhance the beauty of a text. Though they certainly serve aesthetic purposes, more importantly symbols are essential to conveying meaning. "Originally, a symbol was a token or counter," the literary critic Northrop Frye writes, "like the stub of a theater ticket which is not the performance, but will take us to where the performance is. It still retains the sense of something that may be of limited interest or value in itself, but points in the direction of something that can be approached directly only with its help."[2] Just as we cannot attend the play without having the ticket in hand, we cannot directly approach the meaning that the symbol conveys if we do not have the symbol. The symbol is necessary for us to fully understand the meaning. This role for symbols may be greatly increased in the context of religion, which possesses, as Arnold Whittick points out, a "mysterious and abstract character" whose "expression flows naturally into various forms of symbolism."[3]

Keeping in mind the significance of symbol, we can now discuss archetypes as symbols that are repeated throughout literature. As Frye notes, archetypes are "images of things common to all men" that "therefore have a communicable power which is potentially unlimited."[4] An archetype is a "natural symbol imprinted in human consciousness by experience and literature, like dawn symbolizing hope or an awakening; night, death or repose; a mountain, aspiration or divinity; a cavern, the underworld or the depths of the mind; a flower, spring; a rose, beauty; the cycle of the seasons, the cycle of human life."[5] Simply put, archetypes are "universal symbols."[6] As I have written elsewhere,

2. Northrop Frye, *Words with Power: Being a Second Study of "The Bible and Literature"* (San Diego: Harcourt Brace Jovanovich, 1990), 109.

3. Arnold Whittick, *Symbols, Signs, and Their Meaning* (London: Leonard Hill, 1960), 307.

4. Northrop Frye, *Anatomy of Criticism* (Princeton: Princeton University Press, 1957), 118.

5. Northrop Frye et al., eds., *The Harper Handbook to Literature*, 2nd ed. (New York: Addison-Wesley Educational Publishers, 1997), 46.

6. Wilfred L. Guerin et al., eds., *A Handbook of Critical Approaches to Literature*, 4th ed. (New York: Oxford University Press, 1999), 160.

> At the risk of extending Frye's ticket metaphor an inch too far, if a symbol is a ticket, then an archetype is an unusual theater district pass. It is unusual in that, unlike a regular season pass that allows admission to all the plays performed at a given theater, this archetypal pass allows you to see the same play at all the theaters in which it is performed. Even though the play is the same, much is different. The actors portray their characters differently, the director interprets the play differently, the set design looks different, and the lights give a different feel. The performances are different but, since it is the same play, you see common threads of theme and dialogue and characters. This archetypal pass allows its possessor to see not just one play at one theater put on by one company but the richness of what the play offers as it is performed in many theaters by a variety of companies.[7]

The meaning of the play is both broadened and deepened as we see it in a variety of contexts. Similarly, an archetype grows and deepens in meaning because of the strength it gains through being used in other works. The repetition does not trivialize the symbol but rather enlivens it.

In speaking of archetypes, it is important to note that when we write the term we are not nodding toward the Jungian theory of the "collective unconscious"—a theory that Frye considered "an unnecessary hypothesis in literary criticism."[8] Other archetypal critics of literature have dropped the theory of the collective unconscious as well.[9] While the archetype finds at least part of its power in the fact that its meaning is not limited to a particular individual's response to it, that there is a commonality of meaning among different peoples, it

---

7. Charles Swift, "The Power of Symbol," in *Covenants, Prophecies, and Hymns of the Old Testament:* The 30th Annual Sidney B. Sperry Symposium (Salt Lake City: Deseret Book, 2001), 225–26.

8. Frye, *Anatomy of Criticism*, 112.

9. Abrams and Harpham, *Glossary of Literary Terms*, 15–17.

does not require a belief in Jungian psychology. Philip Wheelwright explains:

> My own discussions of archetypes are unaffected by the truth or falsity of Jung's special theories of the collective unconscious and of whether its "primordial images" are transmitted by inheritance. Jung is quite palpably right to this extent, that the primordial images are "as much feelings as thoughts" but that their strong feeling-tone does not by any means reduce them to the status of merely subjective occurrences. Their subjectivity has its origin somehow (unlike Jung I can't suggest how) beyond the confines of the individual. A genuine archetype shows itself to have a life of its own, far older and more comprehensive than ideas belonging to the individual consciousness or to the shared consciousness of particular communities.[10]

Lehi's Vision of the Tree of Life

According to the text in which the account of Lehi's vision occurs, the prophet Lehi and his family escape Jerusalem before its destruction in 587 BC and journey through the Arabian desert for many years. At one point, Lehi has a visionary dream. "The ancients recognized both dreams and visions but frequently used the terms interchangeably."[11] In fact, Lehi introduces it to his family with these words: "Behold, I have dreamed a dream; or, in other words, I have seen a vision" (1 Nephi 8:2). In that dream Lehi sees a dark wilderness. An unnamed guide in a white robe appears and asks the prophet to follow him. After Lehi travels for many hours in the darkness, he prays to the Lord and sees a large field before him and a tree with amazingly white fruit. He eats the white, sweet fruit and his soul is filled with "exceedingly great joy." As he looks for his family in hopes of inviting them to

10. Philip Wheelwright, *The Burning Fountain: A Study in the Language of Symbolism*, rev. ed. (Bloomington: Indiana University Press, 1968), 54–55.

11. Leland Ryken, James C. Wilhoit, and Tremper Longman III, eds. *Dictionary of Biblical Imagery* (Downers Grove, IL: InterVarsity Press, 1998), 217.

eat the fruit as well, he sees a river that runs near the tree. When Lehi sees his wife and two of his sons, Nephi and Sam, at the head of the river and invites them to partake of the fruit, they willingly come and partake. However, when he sees his other two sons, Laman and Lemuel, and extends the same invitation, they do not come and partake.

At this point in the dream, Lehi sees a rod of iron and a path that extend along the river and lead to the tree. He then sees a large group of people who begin along the path but wander off and are lost when a "mist of darkness" arises. Other people come and hold to the rod of iron, making it through the mist and eventually arriving at the tree and partaking of its fruit. They become ashamed, however, because onlookers in a "great and spacious building" whose "manner of dress was exceedingly fine" ridicule them for eating the fruit. Succumbing to their shame, they are lost in "forbidden paths." Lehi sees many other people in his vision: some hold to the rod, make it to the tree and partake of the fruit, and do not become lost; others feel[12] their way to the building; others drown in the river; and still others are lost, "wandering in strange roads."[13] As a result of his dream, Lehi admonishes his two rebellious sons to change their ways. Later, one of the prophet's obedient sons, Nephi, prays to see what his father saw and receives a grand vision, the account of which greatly expands the version we have of his father's dream (see 1 Nephi 11–14).

We now turn to the individual archetypes that play crucial roles in Lehi's dream. This approach will help us to better understand the significance of this dream as an archetypal symbol of life and its meaning.

A Dark and Dreary Wilderness or Waste

The first archetypal image Lehi sees in his vision is darkness. This image is the opposite of one of the most important symbols in the scriptures: light.

---

12. The original manuscript of the Book of Mormon uses the word *pressing* instead of *feeling*. See *The Book of Mormon: The Earliest Text*, ed. Royal Skousen (New Haven and London: Yale University Press, 2009), 23.

13. See 1 Nephi 8 for the entire account of Lehi's dream.

> Light is perhaps the most important of religious symbols. It has constantly been used as a symbol of the deity, and in some religions God is identified with light, as in the case of Ra in ancient Egypt, and in Christianity when John came to bear witness to the Light (John I, 4–9). By this association of light with God it has become symbolic of such qualities as knowledge, wisdom, truth and goodness, while darkness is associated with the opposites of these qualities, folly, ignorance and evil.[14]

Darkness is part of the world of archetypes. Leland Ryken, in one of his several books on the Bible as literature, writes that the "archetypes of literature . . . fall into a dialectical pattern of opposites. The two categories of archetypes form a pattern of ideal and unideal experience, wish and nightmare, tragedy and comedy. Together they are a vision of the world that people want and do not want."[15] While light is part of the ideal world, darkness is an element of the "unideal" world.[16]

Darkness is not simply the absence of light, however. It can also refer to "mythic nothingness"; it is "the Great Void." It can represent "misfortune," "spiritual need," or "ignorance,"[17] as well as "chaos, mystery, [and] the unknown."[18] In religious terms, it is "a silencing of prophetic revelation" and "the state of the human mind unilluminated by God's revelation."[19]

The place Lehi sees is not simply dark and dreary; it is a wilderness—an archetypal location that is part of the "unideal" world. Since at this point in the narrative the desert is the wilderness that Lehi and his family have experienced, it is likely that the wilderness he sees in the vision is itself a desert. If so, the desert

---

14. Whittick, *Symbols, Signs, and Their Meaning*, 310.

15. Leland Ryken, *Words of Delight: A Literary Introduction to the Bible*, 2nd ed. (Grand Rapids, MI: Baker Book House, 1992), 26.

16. Ryken, *Words of Delight*, 26–27.

17. Ad de Vries, *Dictionary of Symbols and Imagery* (Amsterdam: North-Holland, 1974), 129, s.v. "darkness."

18. Guerin et al., *Critical Approaches to Literature*, 161.

19. Ryken, Wilhoit, and Longman, *Dictionary of Biblical Imagery*, 192.

is another archetype in the vision. Symbolic of "spiritual aridity," "death," "nihilism," and "hopelessness,"[20] the desert is not a place of spiritual sustenance. However, despite the negative imagery of the desert wilderness, there is an element of potential goodness about it. This can be the place where people must prove themselves and draw nearer to God. As Hugh Nibley explains,

> The desert has two faces: it is a place both of death and of refuge, of defeat and victory, a grim coming down from Eden and yet a sure escape from the wicked world, the asylum alike of the righteous and the rascal. The pilgrims' way leads through sand and desolation, but it is the way back to paradise; in the desert we lose ourselves to find ourselves.[21]

The description "dark and dreary" indicates that the wilderness that Lehi sees is a place of spiritual need, though it also plays a role in his eventual communion with the tree of life. At this point in the vision, however, Lehi is not aware of what lies ahead, and so he likely views the wilderness as bleak and uninviting, in direct contrast to the world of the tree of life.

Later in the vision, Lehi will find himself in a "dark and dreary waste" (1 Nephi 8:7), which can be read as another unideal archetype, one similar to the "wasteland" archetype identified by Ryken.[22] All that we have said about wilderness applies to this image as well. In fact, we find that *waste* bears a meaning that is remarkably appropriate for Lehi's vision: "A desolate or uncultivated country. The plains of Arabia are mostly a wide *waste*."[23]

---

20. Guerin et al., *A Handbook of Critical Approaches to Literature*, 165.

21. Hugh Nibley, *An Approach to the Book of Mormon*, 3rd ed. (Salt Lake City: Deseret Book and FARMS, 1988), 148.

22. Ryken, *Words of Delight*, 26.

23. Noah Webster, *An American Dictionary of the English Language, 1828, Facsimile First Edition*, 6th ed. (San Francisco: The Foundation for American Christian Education, 1989), s.v. "waste" under noun list. It is the third definition.

A Man in a White Robe

The darkness of the wilderness at the beginning of the vision contrasts with the whiteness of the guide's robe, white being a symbol of "purity, chastity, innocence, spotlessness, and, to a less[er] extent, of peace."[24] Interestingly, in biblical symbolism white is not set opposite to black but rather to darkness.[25] More than any other color, white "has been associated with religious devotion since the days of ancient Egypt," representing "spiritual purity and chastity of thought."[26] And the robe is itself archetypal, representing righteousness.[27] It is the symbol of a "godly, upright character."[28] As a "stately garment symbolizing legitimate position or success," it is an archetype of the ideal world.[29] Lehi finds himself in darkness, and the man in the white robe represents what he desperately needs: deliverance.

Large and Spacious Field

After Lehi prays to the Lord, he sees "a large and spacious field," an obviously green place amidst the wilderness. As an archetype, a field can represent "space, freedom from restraint, unlimited possibilities of action."[30] The field in the vision most closely fits in the category of the ideal world, which includes such similar settings as pastoral scenes and fertile valleys.[31] After Lehi wanders for hours alone in a dark and dreary waste, this field certainly represents a release for him from the fear and oppression that would logically accompany his situation. It is significant that this field does not appear to the prophet until he finally prays to the Lord for mercy. It did not appear at the beginning of the vision, nor was it associated with the man in the white robe. The prophet had to turn to the Divine before he could begin to see

24. Whittick, *Symbols, Signs, and Their Meaning*, 293.
25. Ryken, Wilhoit, and Longman, *Dictionary of Biblical Imagery*, 944.
26. Whittick, *Symbols, Signs, and Their Meaning*, 293.
27. De Vries, *Dictionary of Symbols and Imagery*, 388, s.v. "robe."
28. Walter Lewis Wilson, *Wilson's Dictionary of Bible Types* (Grand Rapids, MI: Eerdmans Publishing, 1957), 382.
29. Ryken, *Words of Delight*, 27.
30. De Vries, *Dictionary of Symbols and Imagery*, 182, s.v. "field."
31. Ryken, *Words of Delight*, 26.

what the vision was fundamentally about. This image of the field sets the stage for the remarkable focus of Lehi's vision, for its very most important and significant archetype: the tree of life.

Tree of Life

At its simplest level in literature, the tree can represent immortality.[32] But there is much more to the archetype than that. "The sacredness of trees and plants is so firmly and deeply rooted in almost every phase and aspect of religious and magico-religious phenomena," E. O. James writes, "that it has become an integral and a recurrent feature in one form or another at all times and in most states of culture."[33] So important was the tree to different cultures that many made it the object of worship.[34] Trees were considered sacred because they possessed, along with plant life in general, "the gifts of immortality and health. The subject enters into every form of religion, and its ramifications are traceable in different aspects and degrees from the tree of life to the May-pole. It rests on the earliest conceptions of the unity of life in nature, in the sense of communion and fellowship with the divine centre and source of life."[35]

The tree represents "cosmic life." It "connects the three worlds: its roots are in the underworld, its trunk on earth, and its foliage in heaven"; and it stands for "perpetual regeneration, victory over death, immortality."[36] The symbol of the tree of life is the embodiment of the life principle, and "the wide range of meanings which may accrue to this symbol results from a fundamental insight into the unity of all nature and a sense of communion and fellowship with the divine center and source of life."[37] This symbol is the point at which all things come together, tied as it is to sacred space or the temple. Because of "its

32. Guerin et al., *Critical Approaches to Literature*, 165.

33. E. O. James, *The Tree of Life: An Archaeological Study* (Leiden: Brill, 1966), 1.

34. Whittick, *Symbols, Signs, and Their Meaning*, 276.

35. Thomas Barns, "Trees and Plants," in *Encyclopaedia of Religion and Ethics*, ed. James Hastings (New York: Charles Scribner's Sons, 1924), 11:448.

36. De Vries, *Dictionary of Symbols and Imagery*, 473, s.v. "tree."

37. Stephen Jerome Reno, *The Sacred Tree as an Early Christian Literary Symbol: A Phenomenological Study* (Saarbrücken, Germany: Homo et Religio, 1978), 54.

situation at the center of the cosmos," Mircea Eliade tells us, "the temple or the sacred city [with its tree] is always the meeting point of the three cosmic regions: heaven, earth, and hell."[38] Thus, the tree plays an archetypal role similar to that of the temple. Trees were considered one of the abodes of the gods or the embodiment of supernatural power. E. O. James notes:

> In the first instance the sacredness of trees arises from their being regarded as the embodiment of the life principle and the bearers of supra-mundane power manifest especially in the regeneration of vegetation, the seasonal sequence celestial phenomena and potencies (e.g. cloud, rain, the sun, moon and stars), and in association with mountains, stones, plants and trees regarded as the abode of a god, spirit, or inherent sacredness rendering it transcendentally unapproachable and tabu, or an object of veneration and worship as the embodiment of supernatural power and cosmic potentialities, equated sometimes with the creative principle in the universe, variously personified and symbolized as the World-Tree, like the Scandinavian Yggdrasil, or as a primeval pair of deities, the Earth and the Sky, as by the Egyptians and the Greeks, while in Mesopotamia the Cosmic Tree was brought into relation with the primal waters as the source of all life.[39]

Based on "the many and varied forms and meanings of tree worship and symbolism among widely distributed peoples," the tree represents not only life, regeneration, and immortality but also "knowledge and wisdom" and "the world or universe." It is "the most widespread of symbols, and in considering Christian architecture it can be regarded as second only to the cross."[40]

Another reason the tree came to be such a significant symbol for many different peoples is the very practical fact that, in their daily

38. Mircea Eliade, *The Myth of the Eternal Return*, trans. Willard R. Trask (London: Routledge & Kegan Paul, 1955), 15.

39. E. O. James, *Tree of Life*, 245.

40. Whittick, *Symbols, Signs, and Their Meaning*, 275, 276.

lives, it fed them and kept them alive. "The sacred tree was the source and the sustenance of life."[41] The importance of the tree is amplified when we consider that primitive people had to invest such a tremendous amount of time and effort in obtaining food and staying alive. While the tree in the world produces food for people, the tree of life "sustains all things by its life-force, it is the judgment seat of the gods, it produces the food of immortality, and it typifies the year's cycle and expansion in all six directions."[42]

The tree of life "has long been recognized by historians of religion and students of folklore as one of the most widely-distributed and recurrent motifs of mythology and religious iconography." The tree is "regarded as the source of life and as the embodiment of life everlasting. By means of this symbol there is expressed one of religious man's most profound nostalgias, namely, the desire to be situated at the very source of life and vitality."[43] This is exactly the role that the tree plays in Lehi's dream: it is the source of life and vitality. People who come to it and partake of its fruit live, and those who refuse to partake of it, or who fall away once they have partaken of the fruit, spiritually die.

When Nephi seeks to understand what the tree of life means, he is immediately shown Mary and the birth of the Son of God (see 1 Nephi 11:9–22). Nephi understands by what he sees that the tree represents the love of God, but it is also clear that the love of God is personified in the Savior. The fact that Nephi's vision continues with a preview of the Savior's mortal ministry and death supports the idea that the tree of life is a symbol for the Savior.

It is not surprising that the tree of life as a type of Christ is not limited to the Book of Mormon. Early church writers, such as Eusebius of Caesarea and Methodius, wrote that the tree of life represented the Son of God.[44] "If the Garden of Eden is a type of heaven, then the tree

41. Barns, "Trees and Plants," 454.

42. De Vries, *Dictionary of Symbols and Imagery*, 473, s.v. "tree," subentry "the Tree of Life."

43. Reno, *Sacred Tree*, 7.

44. Reno, *Sacred Tree*, 102, 103.

of life is a type of Christ through whom eternal life may be gained."[45] "Paradise is the type, as well as the eschatological goal, of the Church. The Tree of Life in it is the type of Christ as source of the Church's life, with reference both to the Eucharist and to the sacraments involving anointing, especially the pre-baptismal 'signing.'"[46] So readily identified is the tree of life in the Garden of Eden with the Lord that some believe the reason Adam and Eve were denied partaking of the fruit of the tree of life is that they were sinners, having eaten the forbidden fruit from the tree of knowledge of good and evil. According to those who hold this view, Adam and Eve could not partake of the tree of life for the same reason that some churches deny unbelievers the chance to partake of the Lord's supper.[47]

The image of the tree of life, like any archetype, helps us to better understand that which it symbolizes. There are a number of ways to understand how the Savior is like the tree of life:

> When we clear ourselves of the mists of darkness that precede the tree of life, we may see beyond the symbol more clearly. With or without branches, the tree bears fruit and is adorned beautifully. It extends through the center of the universe, connecting heaven, earth, and the underworld. It is associated with eternal life and has great curative value to all who partake; its fruit is most desirable and delicious above all. The tree grows near the edge of the water and its roots extend down into the chaotic waters to control them. The waters that emerge from it possess life-giving virtues.
>
> Thus we see that each of these features may be applied to Christ. His love and influence is over all, he is found in the temple, he is the "Way" which leads to eternal life. He is the foundation of the world, the firstfruits of the resurrection.

45. Geoffrey W. Bromiley, ed., *The International Standard Bible Encyclopedia* (Grand Rapids, MI: Eerdmans, 1982), 4:902, s.v. "Tree of Knowledge."

46. Robert Murray, *Symbols of Church and Kingdom: A Study in Early Syriac Tradition* (London: Cambridge University Press, 1975), 125.

47. Bromiley, *International Standard Bible Encyclopedia*, 4:902.

> He offers healing power to the souls of all who will believe in him. He is the king of kings and the last and final sacrifice.[48]

As discussed above, with all that the tree symbolizes—immortality, the divine center and source of life, cosmic life, sustenance of life, life everlasting, the abode of the gods—it is clear that the tree of life can be a powerful type of the Savior.

This role of the tree of life as a type of the Savior leads to another image that also becomes a type of him: the cross.[49] The cross as a symbol of the Savior is yet another use of the tree of life as a type. For example, "Aphrahat, Ephrem and Cyrillona agree in seeing Christ, hanging on the tree of the Cross and pierced by the lance, as the Tree of Life bearing its fruits."[50]

> Clement [of Alexandria] carries the symbolism of the tree beyond a simple identification with Christ. To be sure, this motif is well represented in the development of the tree of life which is planted in paradise to that of the Logos which is the tree of life planted in the world. But the further association of the tree and the crucified Christ, made stronger by identifying the tree as the means of the knowledge of Christ, introduces a new theme: the tree of life symbolizes the cross of Christ, owing to the fact that both bear fruit.[51]

Others also saw the tree of life as connected to the cross. The connection was so pronounced that "by the seventh century the Cross itself was called 'the Tree of Life.'"[52] A tree can also symbolize "sacrifice and redemption, or punishment," which appears related to the fact that "in Christian art the Cross is often represented as a living tree."[53] The tree

48. Jeanette W. Miller, "The Tree of Life, a Personification of Christ," *Journal of Book of Mormon Studies* 2/1 (1993): 106.

49. Reno, *Sacred Tree*, 106.

50. Murray, *Symbols of Church and Kingdom*, 320.

51. Reno, *Sacred Tree*, 107–8.

52. E. A. S. Butterworth, *The Tree at the Navel of the Earth* (Berlin: Walter de Gruyter, 1970), 214.

53. De Vries, *Dictionary of Symbols and Imagery*, 473, s.v. "tree."

of life is even physically a type of the cross, in that the "vertical line of the cross, which represents the axis[,] becomes, in the tree, the trunk; whereas the horizontal line (or lines, in the case of tree dimensions) forms its branches."[54]

The Fruit

After Lehi approaches the tree of life, he partakes of its fruit. Eating is a way of taking something inside of us; it is a way of becoming one with something. The feast, meal, and supper are part of the ideal world,[55] and eating is how we invite this aspect of the ideal into ourselves. The sweet taste of the fruit is closely related to the symbol of the tree of life:

> The fruit of the tree of life has great sweetness; [earlier] we saw that the tree is on occasion spoken of as oozing honey from its boughs. Such a tree reappears as a wood (as the tree of life often does) in 1 *Samuel* 14, 25–28; in it honey dropped upon the ground, and Jonathan, putting the rod which was in his hand into the honey (let us not forget Aaron's rod, which both blossomed and became a serpent), tasted of it 'and his eyes were enlightened'. In verse 29 Jonathan attributes the enlightenment of his eyes to the tasting of the honey.[56]

Not only does the sweetness of the fruit indicate something that is good and prized, but so does its whiteness as an archetype of purity and peace.

While the tree of life may represent immortality, it has little to do with the immortality *of people* unless they eat its fruit. The fruit, then, symbolizes how the meaning of the tree of life could become part of the fulfilling of the person. The fruit is the means by which the tree of life changes the person's life. When Lehi eats the fruit, he does not say that it fills his stomach, but that it fills his soul. The fruit of the tree

54. Reno, *Sacred Tree*, 136.
55. Ryken, *Words of Delight*, 27.
56. Butterworth, *Tree at the Navel of the Earth*, 78.

of life feeds his soul, that immortal part of him that transcends the physical.

Water

In the ideal world, water as an archetype is frequently portrayed as "a river or stream" or "a spring or fountain."[57] Lehi sees a "river of water" that runs along the tree of life and at the head of which members of his family stood (see 1 Nephi 8:13–14). Later, he mentions that the path leading to the tree of life also "led by the head of the fountain, unto a large and spacious field" (v. 20). In Nephi's account of the vision, he equates the tree of life with "the fountain of living waters" and notes that the "waters are a representation of the love of God" (11:25). The use of the word *fountain* is significant, supporting the idea that the water bubbles from a spring. Moreover, water that comes from the earth conveys the idea of the source of life more than water that merely flows on top of it. The fountain is one of the chief ways in which water symbolism appears in literature.[58] Water is often associated with the tree of life; for example, in "Mesopotamia the Cosmic Tree was brought into relation with the primal waters as the source of all life."[59]

The image of water also appears in the vision as a negative archetype. Towards the end of the vision, Lehi sees that many people who did not follow the path to the tree of life were "drowned in the depths of the fountain" (1 Nephi 8:32). And Nephi sees in his vision a "fountain of filthy water," which represented the "depths of hell" (12:16). Unlike the fountain of living waters, this dangerous water is part of the unideal world. Nibley sees this image as relating to "a typical desert sayl, a raging torrent of liquid filth that sweeps whole camps to destruction." He also notes that one "of the worst places for these gully-washing torrents of liquid mud" is "the very region through which Lehi traveled on his great trek."[60]

57. Ryken, *Words of Delight*, 26.
58. Frye, *Anatomy of Criticism*, 153.
59. E. O. James, *Tree of Life*, 245.
60. Nibley, *Approach to the Book of Mormon*, 262.

The Rod of Iron

Although we know that Nephi understood the rod of iron to be the word of God (see 1 Nephi 11:25), we can gain a deeper understanding of the symbol if we look at some of the different meanings of the words. Iron "symbolizes great power and persistence,"[61] as well as "hardness, durability, constancy."[62] While the rod in Lehi's vision is a kind of railing, usually the word *rod* connotes in the scriptures a staff, such as a shepherd's staff. Such a rod can be used to discipline others, but it can also be an image of "comfort, protection and security."[63] Hence, Lehi's rod of iron may be seen as a strong, powerful instrument of both correction and protection.

Even Nephi's idea that the rod of iron represents the word of God can be interpreted on different levels. Taken at the most apparent level, the rod of iron represents the scriptures and other words from God. However, it is also possible that the rod of iron is a type of Christ, who, in other sources, embodies the Word of God (see John 1:1–5). In fact, Nephi determines that the rod of iron is the word of God after seeing in his vision the ministry of Christ (see 1 Nephi 11:25). He receives what could be considered a prophetic interpretation of the symbol of the rod of iron, which includes an account of Christ's mortal ministry (see v. 28), his choosing of the twelve apostles (see v. 29), and his healing of the sick (see v. 31), culminating with the Savior's being "lifted up upon the cross and slain for the sins of the world" (v. 33).

The Path

The path that leads to the tree of life, as a "safe pathway," belongs to the archetypal ideal world.[64] While there are dangers in Lehi's vision, they are external to the path. The mist is dangerous, as are the great and spacious building, the filthy water, and the forbidden paths. But the path itself is not dangerous or evil in and of itself. If the

61. Ryken, Wilhoit, and Longman, *Dictionary of Biblical Imagery*, 427.
62. De Vries, *Dictionary of Symbols and Imagery*, 271, s.v. "iron."
63. Ryken, Wilhoit, and Longman, *Dictionary of Biblical Imagery*, 734.
64. Ryken, *Words of Delight*, 26.

travelers along the path stay on it, ignoring the external dangers, then they will be safe.

A path can represent "life, experience, learning"[65] and is part of the archetypal world in scripture and secular literature. "The human use of the inorganic world involves the highway or road as well as the city with its streets," Frye writes, "and the metaphor of the 'way' is inseparable from all quest-literature, whether explicitly Christian as in *The Pilgrim's Progress* or not."[66] Though many do not succeed, the people on the path in Lehi's dream are on a quest for the tree of life. Each is a pilgrim—a "human being on earth, travelling towards the Mystic Centre."[67] The relationship between the path and the tree of life adds to the archetypal quality of the vision. As Eliade writes:

> The center . . . is pre-eminently the zone of the sacred, the zone of absolute reality. Similarly, all the other symbols of absolute reality (trees of life and immortality, Fountain of Youth, etc.) are also situated at a center. . . . The road [leading to the center] is arduous, fraught with perils, because it is, in fact, a rite of the passage from the profane to the sacred, from the ephemeral and illusory to reality and eternity, from death to life, from man to the divinity. Attaining the center is equivalent to a consecration, an initiation; yesterday's profane and illusory existence gives place to a new, to a life that is real, enduring, and effective.[68]

The tree of life is at the center of Lehi's dream. Though we cannot discern whether it is at the center geographically, it is without a doubt at the center thematically and symbolically. All effort and purpose in the vision center around the tree of life and the desire to either partake of its fruit or reject it. The people who desire to partake of the tree are, in effect, pilgrims along the path whose promised land is the tree of life.

65. De Vries, *Dictionary of Symbols and Imagery*, 359, s.v. "path."
66. Frye, *Anatomy of Criticism*, 144.
67. De Vries, *Dictionary of Symbols and Imagery*, 366, s.v. "pilgrim."
68. Eliade, *Myth of the Eternal Return*, 17–18.

One obstacle that the people on the path encounter is the mist of darkness. A mist can represent a "state of indetermination: between formal and informal, between air and water."[69] This mist is a symbol with roots in the reality of the Arabian landscape:

> In the many passages of Arabic poetry in which the hero boasts that he has traveled long distances through dark and dreary wastes all alone, the main source of terror (the heat and glare of the day, though nearly always mentioned, are given second place), and the culminating horror is almost always a "mist of darkness," a depressing mixture of dust, and clammy fog, which, added to the night, completes the confusion of any who wander in the waste.[70]

While we know from the text that the mist of darkness symbolizes the temptations of the devil (see 1 Nephi 12:17), Lehi's people would most likely understand—either by personal experience or hearing accounts from others—the dangerous circumstances such a mist creates. We know how mists cling to our skin, how they cover us so completely that avoidance is futile. The image of a mist of darkness suggests a blackness that clings to us, that prevents us from seeing and does not allow our escape. This is a very visual, even tactile symbol for the temptations of the devil.

Later in the vision are forbidden paths that belong to the unideal world of types.[71] Each is an example of the path that symbolizes "the perilous path to the land of the dead."[72] These paths help create an image of "the labyrinth or maze, the image of lost direction, often with a monster at its heart."[73] In Lehi's vision the monster at the heart of these strange paths is spiritual death. The image of being lost in a desert wilderness would be a powerful image for Lehi and his family.

---

69. De Vries, *Dictionary of Symbols and Imagery*, 323, s.v. "mist."
70. Nibley, *Approach to the Book of Mormon*, 256–57.
71. Ryken, *Words of Delight*, 27.
72. De Vries, *Dictionary of Symbols and Imagery*, 359, s.v. "path."
73. Frye, *Anatomy of Criticism*, 150.

"Need we say," Nibley writes, "that to get lost in the desert is the chief waking dread and most common nightmare of the Arab?"[74]

The Building and Its People

This building fits in the archetypal world of the unideal.[75] It is also a feature of ancient south Arabian architecture. There is evidence that ancient Arab houses "built after the Babylonian design of Lehi's day" were ten and twelve stories high, with their windows starting twenty to fifty feet above the ground for purposes of defense. "At night these lighted windows would certainly give the effect of being suspended above the earth." Early castles of Arabia looked like they stood in the air, high above the earth.[76] "In Arabic parlance the prime index of elegance and ease in any house or dwelling (including tents) is always 'spaciousness.'"[77]

The building also relates to the city, a symbol of evil. The closer desert people are to a town, the more corrupt they risk becoming. When the nomadic family is out in the desert, alone from the influences of the world, they can honor their family and religious traditions without interference. However, when they have to go into the city for supplies, they are mocked by the city dwellers. The people of the city secretly envy the people of the desert yet mock them as inferiors.[78] "Bitter experience has taught the desert people that the world envies and resents their hard-bought freedom. The mass and inertia

---

74. Nibley, *Approach to the Book of Mormon*, 260.

75. Ryken, *Words of Delight*, 28.

76. Nibley, *Approach to the Book of Mormon*, 257. This is not to imply that the building in Lehi's vision was like one of these castles in that it actually had a foundation (one Lehi did not see). The building in Lehi's vision apparently had no foundation. The significance of the allusion in Lehi's vision to the Arabic castles is that it would have possessed additional power if Lehi and his family were familiar with the image from their experiences in the physical world—namely, south Arabia. On this point, see "The Queen of Sheba, Skyscraper Architecture, and Lehi's Dream," *Journal of Book of Mormon Studies* 11 (2002): 102–3.

77. Nibley, *Approach to the Book of Mormon*, 258.

78. Nibley, *Approach to the Book of Mormon*, 258–59.

of a city civilization is a terrible thing: since none can stand against it, the only hope of opposing it lies in escaping from its reach."[79]

The group of people in the great and spacious building, as their "exceedingly fine" clothes (1 Nephi 8:27) indicate, belong to the archetypal unideal world.[80] Symbolically, clothes can represent different ranks or stations in life,[81] and the clothes of this group clearly represent the prideful, materialistic group that so often serves as an archetype of people who are spiritually dead.

Lehi's Vision of the Tree of Life as Archetype

It is significant that Lehi does not speak of seeing the tree in the physical world, but rather in a dream. Dreams themselves are archetypes, part of the ideal world.[82] The scriptures and other literatures often describe them as communications from God. They are journeys to other worlds—worlds that may have ethereal, even visionary qualities. As we revisit Lehi's dream of the tree of life by replacing the archetypal images with what they represent, we can better see at least one approach to the entire dream itself as an archetype.

We begin with a man. Though we know him as Lehi from the context in which the account of the dream appears, in the dream itself he has no name, no particular position. He is not called a prophet; we only know him as a man who has a family. He is, in a sense, *everyman*. He sees a dark, chaotic state of ignorance. He does not know where he is or to where he is going. Without any light or knowledge, he is motionless and stagnant. This is the state of humankind without the Divine, before beginning the journey towards light and knowledge. In fact, it may be this feeling of nothingness that helps humankind feel the need to begin the journey—this recognition that there is a void in life and a yearning for something better.

The man comes to understand that he must turn to purity and righteousness if he is to be delivered from his darkened state. His

79. Nibley, *Approach to the Book of Mormon*, 149.
80. Ryken, *Words of Delight*, 28.
81. De Vries, *Dictionary of Symbols and Imagery*, 102, s.v. "clothes."
82. Ryken, *Words of Delight*, 27.

deliverance is not immediate, however; it takes much effort on his part, and he is not successful at first. But when he finally turns to God, he begins to find the light, knowledge, and help that he so desperately needs. He is free from the burden of his own darkness, his ignorance and lack of vision.

Now that he is free, he can experience true love in its purest, sweetest form. Partaking of this love fills his soul with great joy. This love is the very center of existence. It is cosmic life, bringing together earth, heaven, and hell. It is knowledge and wisdom, and it brings the man immortality. It sustains him in this life and through the next. Ultimately, this love is not in the abstract, but rather personified in Christ. Upon tasting of this love, the man immediately wishes to share it with those whom he loves the most, his family.

Though he has tasted the freedom of this love and personally knows the joy that can be his, he also comes to know that not everyone chooses to come to that love as he did. Some hold on to the word of God and stay true to it, but others, as lost souls worse off than the man was when he wandered in darkness, succumb to temptation and sapping influences and end up without the love he cherishes.

As we study Lehi's vision of the tree of life in terms of its archetypes, we see that it is an allegory for what we must do to gain eternal life. It is an intensely Christian story of a journey, conveyed through a visionary dream that comes to a prophet during his own perilous journey with his family. While they all struggle against the dangers of a desert wilderness, the prophet experiences the heartache of seeing members of his own family reject the God he worships in favor of following their own ways. Ultimately, it is a story of love and how that love changes people forever.

Charles Swift is an associate professor of ancient scripture at Brigham Young University. His doctoral dissertation dealt with archetypal images in Lehi's vision of the tree of life, and in 2005 he published an article about the vision as an example of visionary literature ("Lehi's Vision of the Tree of Life: Understanding the Dream as Visionary Literature," Journal of Book of Mormon Studies*). His research interests focus on scripture as sacred literature and on Christianity and literature.*

The World Tree and Maya Theology

Allen J. Christenson

The Maya believed that carved stone monuments, painted walls, and woven textiles were far more than mere decoration. They were living objects, each bearing a soul. Maya art, therefore, did not mimic reality; it was a sacred reality in itself, a kind of frozen ceremonial act created and given life by the artist in much the same way that the gods themselves created the world. The Maya conceived of their gods as artists. A beautiful incised bone from the royal tomb of Jasaw Chan K'awil I at Tikal (see fig. 16) depicts a delicate hand reaching out from the open maw of a vision serpent (symbolic of the portal leading to the otherworld, where sacred ancestors and gods live). The hand is holding a paintbrush, suggesting that sacred beings paint the world into existence, just as mortal artists paint or sculpt their art. The painted or carved images, with their accompanying hieroglyphic texts, perpetually carry out their part as if they were actually the thing they represent. Most often these are deities, rulers, or members of the nobility engaged in life-renewing rituals aimed at rebirthing the world

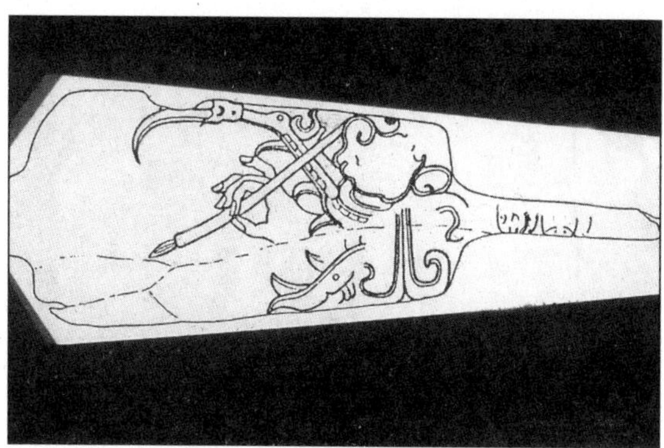

Fig. 16. Incised bone from the royal tomb of Jasaw Chan K'awil I, Tikal, Guatemala.

or some aspect of its power. One of the principal symbols for this life-renewing power is the World Tree, conceived by the Maya as the first living thing to emerge from the waters of the primordial sea at the dawn of creation.

The World Tree at Palenque, Mexico

A spectacular example of this kind of "ensouled" art from the Classic Maya world is found on the sarcophagus and surrounding tomb chamber of another powerful Classic Maya king, K'inich Janab' Pakal I of Palenque (a major site in Chiapas, Mexico), who lived from AD 603 to 683. Palenque was a major city, one of the largest in the Maya world. A long hieroglyphic text from the site claims that its dynasty of kings extends back as far as 967 BC with the accession of a king named U K'ix Chan. There is no archaeological evidence that Palenque's history dated back nearly that far into the past. Its first known historic king was likely K'uk' B'alam I, who reigned from AD 431 to 435.[1] Nevertheless, the very fact that Palenque's rulers claimed descent from a powerful ruler or deity from the distant past attests their confidence in the sanctity of the dynasty's royal bloodline. The year 967 BC would fall well within Olmec times, the Olmec being the first great culture in Mesoamerica to have practiced a form of divine kingship. It is likely that the kings of Palenque saw themselves as the rightful heirs of Olmec power, which by the Classic Period (AD 250–900) had attained mythic status as the foundation of royal legitimacy. A number of Olmec jade objects have been found with the portraits or inscriptions of later Maya rulers. These were likely worn by the Maya as a token of their power long after the Olmec dynasties had died out in the fourth century BC. As late as AD 794, the last ruler of a site called Piedras Negras erected a massive stone monument, Stela 12, commemorating a short-lived victory over the nearby site of Pomona. The king, whose name is thus far unknown, is shown seated above a group of captives and wearing an Olmec jade deity around his neck. Even near the end of the Classic Period, the Maya continued to revere

1. Simon Martin and Nikolai Grube, *Chronicle of the Maya Kings and Queens* (London: Thames and Hudson, 2000), 156.

Fig. 17. Stucco skull from Temple XII, Palenque, southern Mexico.

their Olmec predecessors nearly twelve hundred years after the last Olmec king had died.

The name *Palenque* is derived from Spanish, but we now know from hieroglyphic inscriptions at the site that its ancient name was B'aakal (Bone), perhaps because it is situated at the extreme western periphery of the Maya world, a direction associated with the death of the sun. Skull and bone imagery are fairly common at the site (see fig. 17). Yet this is not to say that bones are associated only with death. In Maya art and theology, bones also represent seeds of potential new life. In most Mayan languages a grain of maize is also called "bone" or "skull" because it is the dry and seemingly dead remnant of the once-living maize plant. The sowing of this seed is associated with burial, and its subsequent germination and sprouting is considered a type of resurrection. Thus Palenque not only is situated in a place of death but also occupies sacred ground where life is potentially reborn.

K'inich Janab' Pakal became king at the young age of twelve in AD 615. He led a remarkably long life for a Maya ruler—ultimately

Fig. 18 Temple of Inscriptions, Palenque.

dying at eighty years old on the undoubtedly hot tropical day of August 31, 683. Pakal's building of his own funerary pyramid-temple was somewhat unique because this was a task usually carried out by the king's son. Today it is known as the Temple of Inscriptions (see fig. 18), the name referring to the long hieroglyphic text within its sanctuary, one of the longest known from the Maya world. The three panels of this text give a detailed dynastic history of Pakal's predecessors, establishing Pakal's right to rule and asserting his divine royal lineage (see fig. 19). The Temple of Inscriptions is one of the largest buildings at the site, located immediately adjacent to the massive palace complex. The elaborate nature of the tomb and the complexity of its theologic message likely reflect the king's own heartfelt desire for regeneration after death—a task perhaps best done himself rather than left to one of his sons.

Although the site of Palenque has been known by non-Maya since at least the 1700s, it was not until after World War II that the inner tomb chamber was discovered by Mexican archaeologist Alberto Ruz Lhuillier. In 1949 he noticed that the rear wall of the temple's upper sanctuary extended below the flagstones, somewhat unusual for

Fig. 19. East Inscription Panel, Temple of Inscriptions, Palenque.

Maya construction. In addition, he noticed a number of plugged holes carved into one of the flagstones. His workmen joked that perhaps they were finger holes for a trapdoor—unlikely for a slab of limestone weighing several hundred pounds. Nonetheless, the stone intrigued him, and he succeeded in lifting it, revealing the upper tiers of a stairway that led deep into the pyramid's interior. After four seasons of digging out the tons of rubble that the ancient Maya had placed to seal the passage, Ruz and his workmen were able to clear an upper flight of forty-five steps (see fig. 20), as well as another flight of twenty-one steps that doubled back toward the center of the pyramid's ground-level base. The actual crypt at the base of the stairway was opened on June 13, 1952. The archaeologists discovered an elaborate tomb chamber whose walls were adorned by stuccoed images of Pakal's ancestors dressed in full royal regalia. The crypt is dominated by a massive sarcophagus covered by a fifteen-ton slab of intricately carved limestone (see fig. 21). This monument is so well preserved that one can still see the slight incidental scratches and tool marks of its carvers. In some ways it is as if it had been carved only the day before. The sculptors of Palenque were masters, among the finest anywhere in the Maya world,

Fig. 20. Upper flight of steps, Temple of Inscriptions, Palenque.

and the sarcophagus lid of Pakal is a masterwork justly ranked as one of the most beautiful Maya carvings to have survived from antiquity. It is also one of the most theologically rich in its depiction of the cycle of royal death and rebirth, particularly as it is expressed through the metaphor of the World Tree that occupies much of the lid's surface.

The lid itself is oriented to the four cardinal directions, the east being marked with the four-leaf clover–shaped glyph for *k'in* (sun, day) in the center of the right-hand edge, and west marked with the crescent-shaped moon glyph in the same position on the left. In Maya theology the direction south is linked with the entrance into the underworld, and, indeed, the open jaws of the underworld are seen at the south-oriented base of the lid. The north is associated with the sky and rebirth, and the tree grows upward in this direction on the panel with a sacred bird nestled in its upper branch. Thus the reclined figure of the king and the cross-shaped tree above him occupy the center position, the place where the four cardinal directions meet.

The central panel of the sarcophagus lid is dominated by the World Tree itself, similar to examples found in the sanctuary tablets of the nearby Temple of the Cross and the Temple of the Foliated

Cross, which were constructed soon after Pakal's death by his son K'inich Kan B'alam II. The tree on the sarcophagus lid is no ordinary tree. It is marked with the profile head of God C, seen on the lower left corner of the trunk, a symbol that the Maya use to identify objects that are profoundly sacred. At first glance the tree looks like a cross, leading early Spanish priests who saw similar trees in the monumental art at the site to conclude that they were Christian crosses. But the Maya were careful to identify the motif as a tree. The trunk and each of the three branches are marked with curving double lines with two attached beads, the glyphic sign for *te* (tree); they are also marked with shining mirror signs, the triple-lined motif with cross-hatchings, indicating that the tree shines with reflective light, analogous to the bright surface of highly polished jade, obsidian, or hematite mirrors. Such mirrors were used for at least three thousand years in pre-Hispanic Mesoamerica as a means of prophecy and divination. In Maya art such signs distinguish objects and deities as divine, precious, or the means of passage to the world of the sacred. At the ends of each of the branches of the tree are jeweled serpent heads with squared snouts that curl back on themselves. These represent sacred flowers, likely the flower of the ceiba tree, whose stamens and pollen cores double back in a similar manner.

Fig. 21. Tomb Chamber of K'inich Janab' Pakal, Temple of Inscriptions, Palenque.

Fig. 22. Ceiba Tree, Tikal, Guatemala.

In Mesoamerican theology the World Tree grew at the locus of creation, all things flowing out from that spot toward the four directions. The tree thus forms part of what Mircea Eliade refers to as the "symbolism of the center." The center is, first and foremost, the point of absolute beginning, where the latent energies of the sacred world first came into being.[2] This source of all creation was often depicted by the Maya as a tree or maize plant, forming a vertical axis, or *axis mundi*, that stands at the center of the cosmos and passes through each of the three major layers of existence—underworld, terrestrial plane, and sky. As the symbolic expression of this *axis mundi*, the World Tree at once connected and supported heaven and earth while firmly fixed in the world below. In addition to serving as the vertical pivot point of the cosmos, the World Tree also oriented the horizontal plane of the world by extending its branches outward toward the four cardinal directions. In ancient Maya inscriptions the human soul was sometimes called the *sak nik' nal* (white-flower-thing), referring to the white flowers of the ceiba tree.[3] The implication is that the soul first came into being as a sacred flower on the branches of the World Tree, thence to be clothed with flesh at birth.

2. Mircea Eliade, *The Sacred and the Profane: The Nature of Religion*, trans. Willard R. Trask (New York: Harcourt, Brace & World, 1959), 36–42 (quotation on p. 39).

3. David Freidel, Linda Schele, and Joy Parker, *Maya Cosmos: Three Thousand Years on the Shaman's Path* (New York: William Morrow and Co., 1993), 183, 395–96.

The ceiba is an ideal symbol for this conception of the World Tree. It is one of the tallest of trees indigenous to southern Mesoamerica (see fig. 22). In areas of dense tropical rain forest, such as Chiapas (where Palenque is located), or the Petén region of northeastern Guatemala, the ceiba soars to the very top of the jungle canopy, attaining heights of 175 feet or more. The trunk is remarkably straight, and its branches extend at nearly right angles high above the ground, reminiscent of the cross-shaped trees seen in the art of Palenque (see fig. 23, also pl. 5).

Fig. 23. Ceiba Tree, upper branches. See plate 5.

The ceiba tree is still revered by the modern Maya as one of the principal manifestations of the World Tree. Many towns and villages have a carefully tended ceiba tree growing in their main plazas. This tree marks their homeland as the center place of the world. The Maya often refer to their communities as *ri u muxux kaj, u muxux ulew* (the navel of the sky, navel of the earth) because of the presence of such trees or other sacred objects that center their community in relation to the rest of the world. The Maya name for the tree reflects the importance it holds. The K'iche' Maya of the highlands call it *räx che'*, while the Yucatek Maya call it the *yax che'*. Both mean "first, green, new, or preeminent tree." The souls of the dead are said to follow its roots into the underworld, while ancestors may return in the same way to visit the living on special occasions.

The presence of the ceiba in the underworld is a very ancient concept throughout the Maya world. In the sixteenth century, Father Diego de Landa, first bishop of Yucatán, recorded that the souls of the benevolent dead entered a place dominated by this tree:

> The delights which they said they were to obtain, if they were good, were to go to a delightful place, where nothing would give them pain and where they would have an abundance of foods and drinks of great sweetness, and a tree which they call there *yaxche*, very cool and giving great shade, which is the ceiba, under the branches and the shadow of which they would rest and forever cease from labor.[4]

Such World Trees appear in the mythic traditions of a number of world cultures, including the various indigenous nations of North America. The shaman-chief Black Elk of the Oglala Sioux described it while in a visionary trance:

> I was seeing in a sacred manner the shapes of all things in the spirit, and the shape of all shapes as they must live together like one being. And I saw the sacred hoop of my people was one of the many hoops that made one circle, wide as daylight and as starlight, and in the centre grew one mighty flowering tree to shelter all the children of one mother and one father. And I saw that it was holy.[5]

Atop the World Tree on Pakal's sarcophagus lid is an odd-looking bird wearing a jeweled pectoral and bearing sacred mirror markings on its forehead and tail. The cut shell on his head and other deity markers identify him as Itzam Ye, the avian form of Itzamna, a sky god and one of the gods who participated in the creation of the world. His name is derived from the word *itz*, a Maya concept that is difficult to translate into English. *Itz* is a kind of life-generating power that permeates the fluids of all living things. It may be found in blood, tears, milk, semen, rain, tree sap, honey, and even candle wax. The great Mayanist Linda Schele liked to refer to it as "cosmic ooze, the

---

4. Diego de Landa, *Relación de las cosas de Yucatán*, trans. Alfred M. Tozzer (Cambridge, MA: Peabody Museum of American Archaeology and Ethnology, 1941), 131.

5. Roger Cook, *The Tree of Life: Image for the Cosmos* (New York: Avon, 1974), 7–8.

magical stuff of the universe."[6] Itzam Ye was believed to wield the means to channel this supernatural power so as to give order to the cosmos and set the stage for creation. His presence atop the World Tree, as depicted on the sarcophagus lid of Pakal, indicates that the tree is alive with sacred, life-giving power.

On the sarcophagus lid of Pakal, all around the tree's branches are symbols for flowers, cut shells (the glyph that in Maya reads *yax*, meaning "first, new, preeminent"), chains of three jade beads, and the glyphic sign for zero (expressing the idea of completion or wholeness in Maya belief rather than nothingness). These glyphic symbols all express the Maya concept of *k'ulel* (sacredness), indicating that the tree is surrounded by an ambient atmosphere of sacred space.

Winding through the branches of the tree is a great double-headed serpent with glyphs for "jade" all along its body. This is a "vision serpent," a being that symbolized the pathway by which sacred beings pass from one world to another. The ancient Maya believed that sacred persons such as kings and other members of the royal family carry within them the divine spark of godhood. By drawing blood from their bodies, they released a portion of their divine nature, thereby giving birth to the gods. The symbolic representation of this birth was the opening of the maw of the great vision serpent, through which sacred beings emerged to bestow on the world tokens of power and life. For non-Maya the metaphor for such a portal between worlds would be a veil. For the Maya it was the open jaws of the serpent. Numerous inscriptions and carved panels show royal individuals letting their blood onto fragments of bark paper. This paper was then burned in offertory bowls, sometimes combined with aromatic incense or rubber to accentuate the scent, color, or volume of smoke rising from the flames. The Maya believed that within the smoke of such offerings could be seen manifestations of the World Tree as well as undulating vision serpents, with supernatural beings issuing from them.

6. Linda Schele, seminar lecture on the topic "Maya Iconography of Death," University of Texas, Austin, 1996 (copy in possession of author); Freidel, Schele, and Parker, *Maya Cosmos*, 411.

Fig. 24. Yaxchilan Lintel 25, Chiapas, Mexico.

A beautiful example of this concept may be seen on Yaxchilan Lintel 25, in which a royal woman, Lady K'ab'al Xook, has just completed a bloodletting ritual (see fig. 24). She may be seen looking upward in the lower right-hand corner of the panel. She holds in her left hand the offertory bowl with the blood-spattered bark paper and instruments of bloodletting visible within it. Immediately to the left is the same bowl with an immense vision serpent rising above it. From the open jaws of the serpent emerges a sacred royal ancestor bearing the tokens of divine warfare—a round shield and spear. This particular bloodletting was conducted in order to empower Lady K'ab'al Xook's husband, Itzamnaaj B'alam II, to accede as king in AD 681, two years prior to the death of Pakal in nearby Palenque.

Returning to Pakal's sarcophagus lid, emerging from the jaws of the left-facing serpent's head is a god named K'awil, the embodiment of divine power inherent in royal blood. From the right-facing serpent's jaws the god Sak Hunal, the patron deity of the royal family and divine kingship, emerges. Upon accession, Maya kings had a white cloth band tied around their heads with one or three jade images of this deity set over the brow. The god of royal blood thus emerges on the left (western) side of the sarcophagus lid as a token of the sacrifice of Pakal. Sak Hunal emerges on the right (eastern) side as a sign of the dawn or restoration of kingship. This may refer to the rebirth of Pakal himself or to the rebirth of kingship in the guise of his son and successor, K'inich Kan B'alam II.

Also on the sarcophagus lid is a sacrificial bowl (like those used for offertory blood) resting on a head at the base of the tree. The bowl is marked with a large, four-leaf clover–shaped *k'in* (day, sun) glyphic sign, identifying the head as the sun. The upper portion of the head is fleshed, with the curled pupils in the eyes characteristic of the sun deity. The lower half of the head is skeletal, however. The bony lower jaw bears the tiny holes, or foramina, where nerves and blood vessels once entered the mandible in life. The fleshed upper portion of the sun and the bony lower half indicate that the sun is in transition, half above and half below the horizon. This occurs at both dawn and dusk. This begs the question of which is implied here—sunrise (rebirth, resurrection) or sunset (death and sacrifice)? From the standpoint of Maya theology, it is likely that both are implied simultaneously. The motif suggests that the sun is in transition, the critical moment when life and death are in balance. Death and rebirth are instantaneous, one flowing naturally into the other in endless cycles.

Within the bowl resting atop the sun are four articles associated with blood sacrifice as well as the regeneration of life. The central element is an upright stingray spine, the principal instrument used by the Maya to draw their own blood in ritual offerings. On the left is a sectioned spondylus shell, a bright red spiny seashell that marks the bowl's contents as holy or precious. It is also symbolic of the entryway into the watery environment of the otherworld. The cut shell is one of the versions of the *yax* glyph, representing the concept of "first, new, preeminent." Thus this sacrifice is not just associated with Pakal; it is the first sacrifice carried out at the time of creation. In the Maya world nearly all major rituals are associated with creation and rebirth. Such actions have the power to fold time back upon itself, to transport its participants back to the moment of first beginnings when these actions were first performed. The sacrifice of Pakal is thus linked to the sacrificial acts of the gods themselves, carried out so that the world and life itself could be set in motion.

On the right is a glyph similar to a percent sign. This is the *cimi* (death) sign, indicating that Pakal's sacrifice is not one of simple bloodletting, but of his life. Growing from the death sign are three leaflike motifs, a glyphic collocation that together reads *way* (transformation), attesting that death allows the sun, and by extension the king, to pass from one state of being to another. Maize leaves growing from the sides of the offering bowl indicate that the sacrifice engenders abundance and new life.

Pakal himself lies across the sacrificial bowl, indicating that it is the symbolic sacrifice of his body in death that invests the entire scene with its life-giving power. Both he and the bowl are set within the immense jaws of a dragon (with both serpent and centipede characteristics) that rears upward to swallow both the sun and Pakal into the underworld. The lower teeth of the great beast are seen at the base of the composition, while its upper jaws and eyes frame both sides of the lid as they curve upward and inward toward the left knee and neck of the king. Again, it is somewhat irrelevant to try to determine whether Pakal is descending into the underworld jaws in death or whether he is being reborn upward. It is the idea of transition that is important. A small bone may be seen on Pakal's nose. As mentioned previously, bones are not only associated with death but also conceived as human "seeds" bearing the potential for new life.

Pakal wears a net skirt, tonsured hairstyle, and jade ornaments that identify him as the embodiment of the great creator god Jun Ixim, the Maize God, who had also descended into the underworld, ultimately to rise again to new life as a creator god. A fiery torch is set into Pakal's brow, a symbol of deification that appears only on images of gods or deceased kings. A similar torch is seen in the forehead of K'awil, the god of royal blood and sacrifice who is seen emerging from the left head of the serpent winding through the World Tree. In death the king has become the principal god of life and the organizer of the cosmos. Across his chest is a turtle pectoral, symbolic of the earth through whose cleft surface Jun Ixim emerged at the dawn of creation.

Within the sarcophagus the adorned skeletal remains of Pakal repeat this imagery in physical terms. Over seven hundred pieces of fine jade adorn the body, including a heavy mosaic mask that completely covered his face, delicately carved rings on each of his fingers, and heavy necklaces, bracelets, and anklets. A jade Sak Hunal god was found next to the head, originally worn affixed to the royal headband as a sign of Pakal's office as king. Two large jade pieces, one carved into a sphere and held in the king's left hand and the other a cube in the right hand, remain an intriguing mystery. This interest in dichotomous geometric shapes is unprecedented in known Maya royal burials, and its significance is still unexplained, although the sphere may represent the curved dome of the heavens and the cube the quadrilateral earth with its four cardinal directions.

The arrangement of jade pieces about the waist and thigh bones indicates that the king once likely wore a net skirt similar to the one seen carved on the lid. Thus the king was dressed as Jun Ixim (the Maize God) himself, the principal god of creation. Jade earflares with pearl counterweights, carved in the shape of ceiba tree flowers, were found about the head of the king. At his feet was the carved jade image of the Pax God, the anthropomorphic personification of the World Tree. The body of Pakal was thus adorned as if he were not only the creator god Jun Ixim but also the symbolic embodiment of the precious jade World Tree itself.

The overall theme of the king's burial goods and the carved sarcophagus lid powerfully express the instant of transformation from death and mortality to new life and godhood in the midst of the sacred World Tree at the center of creation. In ancient Mesoamerica, kingship was an eternal office that, once held in life, persisted beyond the grave. Particularly in agricultural societies like that of the Maya, survival was dependent on the rhythmic flow of one aspect of nature into its complementary opposite. Life could not exist in the absence of death. The sun must rise in its time to bestow its light and warmth on the crops. The rains must fall in their season and in sufficient amounts or the crops will not grow to maturity and the community will die. The dry, seemingly lifeless maize seed must be buried in the earth before it can sprout anew. The king represented the hope that these forces could be controlled and ensured through ritual. It was his responsibility to conduct sacred ceremonies, particularly the sacrifice of his own blood, to empower the world to regenerate itself. He was the guarantor that the cycles of the universe would continue to be predictable and benevolent. From their tombs, the dead royal ancestors continued to preside over and assist the ritual acts of their living successors.

Fig. 25. Cemetery in Santiago Atitlán, Guatemala. See plate 6.

The tomb of K'inich Janab' Pakal was oriented as the central axis point of the universe, the place where worlds drew closest to one another. Sacred and precious things were placed in the king's tomb, where they would come into contact with the life-sustaining power of the otherworld. The most precious offering was the blood and body of the divine king, who, like the World Tree, carried within him the seed of new life. Burial of the king's body within the bowels of his sacred pyramid-temple symbolically returned him to the place of creation in the hope that proximity to its regenerative power would assist his rebirth into godhood. The appearance of the sacred World Tree growing from the underworld on the sarcophagus lid of Pakal was the symbolic expression of this concept.

It is evident that this journey was recapitulated at death by each ruler of Palenque. The sides of Pakal's sarcophagus are decorated with the images of ten individuals, identified by their hieroglyphic name signs as ancestral men and women who preceded Pakal in the office of king. All are depicted in a similar fashion, emerging from a cleft in the ground line marked with *kab'an* (earth) signs. Behind each of them a fruit-bearing tree grows, indicating that they are rising from their graves in parallel fashion to the sprouting of World Trees. In a number of traditional Maya cemeteries today, graves are planted with a tree, representing the rebirth of the interred individuals to new life. In the Santiago Atitlán cemetery, there are long rows of graves bearing trees, giving the place the appearance of a great orchard or grove (see fig. 25, also pl. 6). Ximénez described a similar practice in highland Guatemala at the beginning of the eighteenth century and noted that persons were frequently buried in the maize fields, an indication that the dead were reborn as maize.[7]

Other Maya World Trees

These ideas regarding the World Tree were not limited to the site of Palenque. Throughout the Maya world, kings were eager to identify themselves with the power of the World Tree to bestow life and abundance on their people:

> On public monuments, the oldest and most frequent manner in which the [Maya] king was displayed was in the guise of the World Tree. . . . This Tree was the conduit of communication between the supernatural world and the human world: The souls of the dead fell into [the underworld] along its path; the daily journeys of the sun, moon, planets, and stars followed its trunk. The Vision Serpent symbolizing communion with the world of the ancestors and the gods emerged into our world along it. The king was this axis and pivot made flesh. He was the Tree of Life.[8]

By portraying themselves wearing tokens of the World Tree, rulers declared themselves to be the intermediaries between worlds at the center point of creation. An early example is Stela 11 from Kaminaljuyu, Guatemala, dated stylistically to approximately the time of Christ, give or take a century (see fig. 26). This stone monument depicts a standing ruler with a leafy World Tree growing from his headdress. His ear jewels display crossed bands, a centering device implying that the ruler stands at the pivotal juncture where the world was first created.

At Quirigua in Guatemala and Copan in Honduras, great plazas were set aside for the erection of immense limestone stelae bearing

---

7. Francisco Ximénez, *Historia de la Provincia de San Vicente de Chiapa y Guatemala de la Orden de Predicadores*, 3 vols. (Guatemala: Biblioteca "Goathemala," 1929–31), 1:100.

8. Linda Schele and David A. Freidel, *A Forest of Kings: The Untold Story of the Ancient Maya* (New York: Morrow, 1990), 90.

Fig. 26. Kaminaljuyu Stela 11, Guatemala.

the images of kings wearing the heavy tokens of godhood. The same elements seen on Pakal's sarcophagus lid are abstracted and incorporated into the vestments of the king in many of these royal portraits. Copan Stela H depicts the king Waxaklajun Ub'aj K'awil (reigned AD 695–738) wearing the net skirt also worn by Pakal on his sarcophagus lid, in token of the Maize God (see fig. 27). On the back of this stela, the sun god is seen wearing his sacrificial bowl, and the sacred bird Itzam Ye is perched above it (see fig. 28). On Quirigua Stela F (see fig. 29), King K'ak' Tiliw Chan Yoat (reigned AD 724–785) wears the image of Itzam Ye as a headdress, with three panaches of feathers representing the bird's wings and tail feathers cascading elegantly about the king's head. A personified tree appears on his loincloth, while ear jewels in the shape of ceiba tree flowers appear on either side of his head. The king holds in his arms the coils of the double-headed vision serpent, which winds about the branches of the World Tree, just as it is depicted on Pakal's sarcophagus. Deities emerge from both of the serpent's open jaws. The stone portrait thus depicts the king as a personified World Tree.

Fig. 27 (top left). King Waxaklajun Ub'aj K'awil, Copan Stela H, Honduras.

Fig. 28 (top right). Sun god and sacred bird Itzam Ye, Copan Stela H (back).

Fig. 29 (bottom left). King K'ak' Tiliw Chan Yoat, Quirigua Stela F (north and south faces), Guatemala.

Conclusion

In the Maya world death was a crisis. It was the victory of unseen and little-understood forces over a member of the community. When death took a king—particularly one considered to be a divine being, as were Maya rulers—the crisis took on universal proportions, threatening the very existence of the world and life itself. Royal tombs were constructed by the Maya as a desperate attempt to forestall this horror by ritually ensuring the king's triumph over death and darkness. At Palenque, and in numerous other Maya centers, the ultimate expression of this ability to escape the harrowing of the underworld was the World Tree. It was the central focus of the Maya's journey into the afterlife and the principal token of the power to overcome death. Its blossoms symbolized the purity of the human soul. In ancient Maya art this tree could be represented as a ceiba tree, a cacao tree, a calabash tree, any number of other trees, or a stalk of maize. The actual species of tree makes little difference since each is a metaphor, representing the sacred power inherent in the fabric of the cosmos to allow kings, the sun, and all other mortal things to emerge from death to new life.

Allen J. Christenson has worked as an ethnographer and linguist in highland Guatemala since 1978, working principally with the K'iche'-Maya and Tz'utujil-Maya. His MA and PhD degrees are in Precolumbian art history and literature from the University of Texas, Austin. He has written numerous journal articles and book chapters as well as three books on the Maya, including Art and Society in a Highland Maya Community *(2001) and a new translation and critical edition of the* Popol Vuh *(2000), an important ancient Maya text containing detailed descriptions of ancient theology, creation, and history. He is currently an associate professor in the Department of Humanities, Classics, and Comparative Literature at Brigham Young University, where his research and teaching focus on the art and culture of the Maya.*

The Tree of Life in the Catholic Religious and Liturgical Imagination

Jaime Lara

> Catholics live in an enchanted world, a world of statues and holy water, stained glass and votive candles, saints and religious medals, rosary beads and holy pictures. But these Catholic paraphernalia are mere hints of a deeper and more pervasive religious sensibility which inclines Catholics to see the Holy lurking in creation. As Catholics, we find our houses and our world haunted by a sense that the objects, events, and persons of daily life are revelations of grace.[1]

So begins a book by Father Andrew Greeley entitled *The Catholic Imagination*. Greeley is a priest and sociologist at the University of Chicago, and in the book he asks the question, What makes Catholics different from Protestants? In doing so, Greeley does not imply either a Catholic superiority or a Protestant inferiority; he simply asks, What is unique about Catholics? In this paper, I too ask what makes Catholics different from Protestants, and I invite the reader to ask and answer the correlative question, How do Latter-day Saints imagine religiously?

I submit that what is special about Catholicism is not so much its ecclesial structure, nor the papacy or hierarchy, nor even its particular doctrines, but rather something much more basic. I submit that it is the Catholic imagination. Catholics imagine the world in a way different from Protestants, and probably also different from Latter-day

1. Andrew Greeley, *The Catholic Imagination* (Berkeley, CA: University of California Press, 2000), 1.

Saints. By using the word *imagination*, I do not mean fantasy or make-believe but rather the God-given faculty of the soul by which we humans create mental images of what is not perceived by the senses.[2]

Most scholars agree that the classic works of Catholic theologians and artists (writers, painters, musicians) tend to emphasize the *presence* of God in the world, while the classic works of Protestant theologians tend to emphasize the *absence* of God from the world. Put another way, Catholic writers stress the nearness of God to creation (the immanence of God), while Protestants emphasize the distance between God and creation (the transcendence of God).[3] But this difference is a matter of emphasis and not an absolute either-or distinction.

Furthermore, the Catholic imagination tends to accentuate the metaphorical nature of reality, and this has much to do with the topic at hand: the tree of life. The Catholic imagination loves metaphors. For Catholics, the objects, events, and persons of ordinary existence hint at the nature of God and indeed make God present to us. God is sufficiently similar to creation that creation tells us something about its Creator. And for Catholics, the metaphors that most reveal God's presence in the world and God's nearness are human flesh and human relationships, as well as tactile and sensorial elements like water, wine, oil, bread, light, aroma, and even trees.

Certainly an important part of the Catholic imagination has been its two-thousand-year models of biblical interpretation. Catholics are not biblical fundamentalists or literalists who stay at the letter of the text and never advance further. Catholics know well that God uses metaphors, poetry, and symbols because these are the most common means of human communication, as well as the most profound. This, then, leads us to consider the tree of life in the Catholic biblical tradition.

The Four Senses of Scripture

From the second to the nineteenth centuries, theologians and preachers read biblical passages on four levels, which, by coincidence,

2. On this topic, see Paul Avis, *God and the Creative Imagination: Metaphor, Symbol and Myth in Religion and Theology* (London and New York: Routledge, 1999).

3. David Tracy, *The Analogical Imagination* (New York: Crossroad, 1981).

were always diagrammed as treelike (see fig. 30). The four senses of scripture were history, allegory, morality, and anagogy. The first and root sense was *history*, the literal meaning of the reality, to which were added three senses that gave it higher spiritual meanings (like tree branches) in the here and now or in the hereafter. The second sense, *allegory*, signified the fulfillment of the image or symbol in the New Testament; it was an explanation in terms of foreshadowing Christ, the church, or the sacraments in the lives of living believers. The third sense of scripture, called tropological or *moral* sense, provided an ethical meaning applied to men and women here and now and to the salvation of the individual soul. The fourth sense, *anagogy*, provided an eschatological explanation that elevated the thoughts of the exegete or the reader from visible to invisible things—to a higher truth and an eternal fulfillment in heaven.[4]

For example, the Hebrew scriptures begin the drama of sacred history in a garden called Eden or paradise, while the Christian scriptures end the cosmic drama in a garden-city, a sacred metropolis—the heavenly Jerusalem.[5] The word *Jerusalem* has always meant much more than just a municipality in Israel or Roman Palestine. In the interpretation of the Middle Ages, it too could be explained on four levels.[6] Jerusalem was historically the city situated in the Holy Land, allegorically the church as a body of living believers, *morally* the soul of the individual, and anagogically the heavenly city mentioned in the biblical book of Revelation, also known as the Apocalypse.

The same could be said of the tree of life in Eden. Historically or literally it could be presumed to have been a botanical plant; morally it could be understood as the human soul growing into God-likeness by grace; allegorically or Christologically it could be the sign and symbol

4. Henri de Lubac, *Exégèse médiéval: Les quatre sens de l'escriture*, 4 vols. (Paris: Aubier, 1959–1964).

5. For the notion of the "vision of peace," see the medieval hymn "Urbs Beata Hierusalem Vision Dicta Pacis," translated in the nineteenth century by John Mason Neale as "Christ Is Made the Sure Foundation."

6. De Lubac, *Exégèse médiéval*, esp. 1:129–38. For a discussion of the role of this formula in medieval exegesis, see Beryl Smalley, *The Study of the Bible in the Middle Ages*, 2nd ed. (Notre Dame, IN: University of Notre Dame Press, 1964), 28.

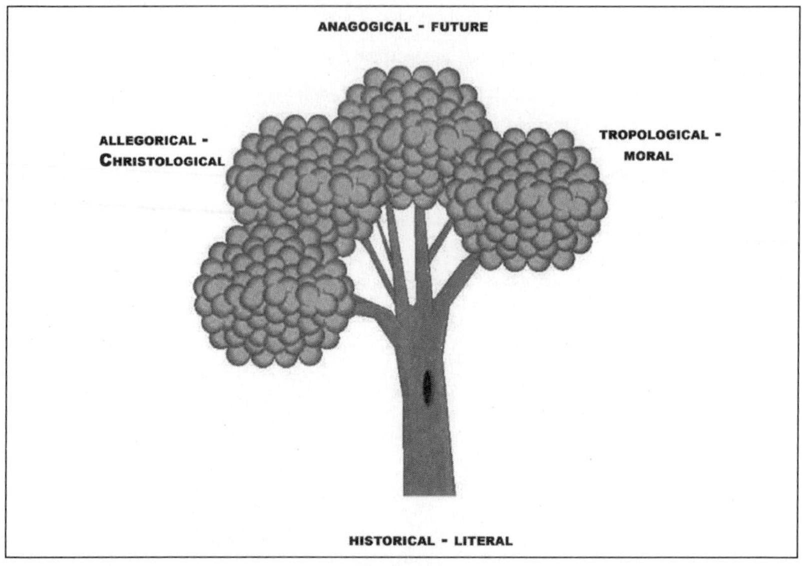

Fig. 30. Tree of the classic four senses of scripture.

for the central event of salvation history: the life, death, and resurrection of Jesus Christ, which was encoded in the triumphant, glorious, victorious, and risen cross of Christ; and anagogically it could be the fruitful abundance of future life in the heavenly Jerusalem. Thus, when medieval Christians read a Bible passage, they read it looking, so to speak, backward to the past and forward to the future and simultaneously saw it as relevant to the here and now of the present.

We see evidence of this fourfold sense of scripture in the biblical text itself: Historically we know that the tree of life is based on the Eden story in Genesis, where God provided a tree of life in the midst of the garden. But it is clear that biblical authors, like the writer of the book of Proverbs, understood the tree as a moral metaphor comparable to wisdom or peaceful conduct. "Wisdom is a tree of life to those who lay hold of her" (Proverbs 3:18). "The fruit of the just man is a tree of life and he who gains souls is wise" (11:30). "Hope that is deferred afflicts the soul; desire when it comes is a tree of life" (13:12). "A peaceable tongue is a tree of life" (15:4).[7]

7. Douay-Rheims translation.

Saint Paul hinted at an allegorical or Christological interpretation of the tree of life by using the metaphor of being grafted onto the tree, which is Christ himself.[8] In his letter to the Romans, he compares the recent converts to wild olive shoots grafted onto the refined olive tree: "If the root is holy, so are the branches. If some of the branches have fallen off, and you [Gentiles], though a wild olive shoot, have been grafted in among the others and now share in the nourishing sap [Christ] from the olive root, do not boast over those branches. If you do so, consider this: You do not support the root, but the root supports you" (Romans 11:16–18).

We will see that this grafting tree became a popular image for the Christianized Aztecs in the New World who, by baptism, were grafted onto the Christian tree of life. That New World of the Americas was understood as having been prophesied in the book of Revelation, or the Apocalypse. In the Apocalypse, John the Seer uses the tree of life as a poetic description of the indescribable life of the blessed in the anagogical celestial Jerusalem: "Then the angel showed me the river of life-giving water, sparkling like crystal, flowing from the throne of God and of the Lamb down the middle of the city's street. On either side of the river grew the Tree of Life that produces fruit twelve times a year. . . . The leaves serve for the healing of the nations" (22:1–2).

The Catholic imagination has always understood this tree of life pictorially in hundreds of ways. One of the best images is found in the splendid thirteenth-century mosaics in the Basilica of San Marco, Venice. Around the year 1250, mosaics were added to a dome where

8. "Letter to Diognetus," in *Early Christian Fathers*, ed. Cyril Richardson (Philadelphia: Westminster Press, 1953), 205–24, written ca. AD 150 to a new convert: "If you read this, and listen to it earnestly, you will discover what God has prepared for those who love him as they ought, and have become a Paradise of delight, cultivating in themselves a flourishing tree, rich with all kinds of fruit, while they themselves are decked out with a variety of fruits; for in this Garden a tree of knowledge and a tree of life have been planted. . . . Indeed, there is a deep meaning in the passage of Scripture which tells how God in the beginning planted a tree of knowledge and a tree of life in the midst of Paradise, to show that life is attained through knowledge. . . . If you bear the tree of this teaching and pluck its fruit, you will always be gathering in the things that are desirable in the sight of God, things that the serpent cannot touch and deceit cannot defile."

Fig. 31. Narthex mosaic of the creation, Basilica of San Marco, Venice, Italy, mid-13th century. See plate 11.

they relate the story of the creation of man and woman, the fall, and the promise of redemption in Christ (see fig. 31, also pl. 11). We can see that the artist made the tree of life into a prophet who announces two future moments in salvation history: the giving of the old covenant to Moses at the burning bush and the establishment of the new covenant in the glorious, risen cross of Jesus Christ.[9]

Fig. 32. Apse mosaic featuring Christ as the tree of life, Basilica of San Clemente, Rome, Italy, 12th century.

A century earlier, in the Roman Basilica of San Clemente (AD 1120–1130), a very subtle theology of life budding forth from Christ's atoning death and resurrection was depicted with the cross blossoming from a great acanthus plant (see fig. 32). Birds, representing Christian souls, are feeding on the spiritual fruit of this plant, which is at one and the same time the cross of Calvary and the new tree of life.

9. Antonio Niero, "The Genesis Mosaics of the Narthex," in *St Mark's: The Art and Architecture of Church and State in Venice*, ed. Ettore Vio (New York: Riverside, 2004), 248–81.

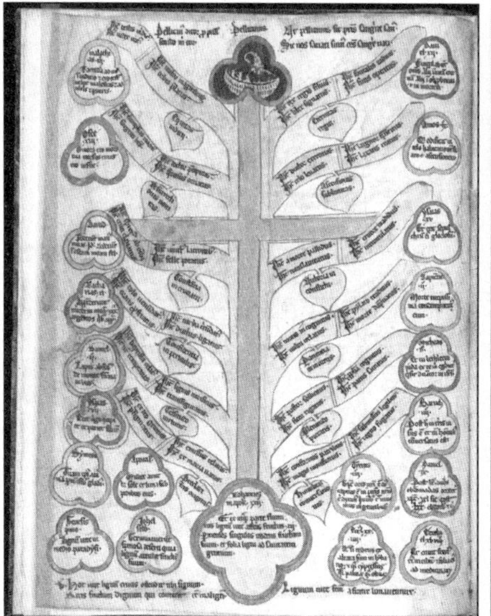

Fig. 33 (left). "St. Bonaventure's Tree of Life" in *Speculum Theologicae,* depicting Christ as a tree bearing fruit in the lives of holy individuals. German manuscript of unknown authorship, ca. 1300.

Fig. 34 (right). *Tree of the Cross,* refectory fresco by Taddeo Gaddi, ca. 1330, Basilica of Santa Croce, Florence, Italy. See plate 12.

In the thirteenth century, Saint Bonaventure (d. 1274) wrote a series of meditations on the life of Christ entitled *The Tree of Life,* in which he demonstrated that Christ bears fruit in the present moment in the lives of holy individuals (see fig. 33). The Italian painter Taddeo Gaddi (1300–1366) illustrated this theme in the refectory of the Franciscan friary of Santa Croce in Florence. The outgrowth of Christ's resurrected life is shown as blossoming into the twelve apostles and gospel fruit (see fig. 34, also pl. 12). The tree is being tended by Saint Francis of Assisi, who was considered by his Franciscan followers to be an eschatological saint of the latter days.[10]

To this fourfold interpretation of the tree of life must be added a notion that the Catholic imagination has had since the second century—the eschatological tree of the cross.

10. See Jaime Lara, *City, Temple, Stage: Eschatological Architecture and Liturgical Theatrics in New Spain* (Notre Dame, IN: University of Notre Dame Press, 2004), 53–59.

The Eschatological Cross

Both in the scriptures and in the poetic imagination of the Christian Apocrypha, the cross is a personified actor in the cosmic drama. The second-century *Gospel of Peter* and *Apocalypse of Peter* relate a story of the cross: on Easter Sunday when Christ rose from the tomb, his cross also rose from "the dead"; and when Christ ascended to heaven, his cross also left the earth with him from the Mount of Olives.[11]

> When those soldiers saw this [the sepulchre opening and two angels entering it], they awakened the centurion and the elders, for they also were there to mount guard. And while they were narrating what they had seen, they saw three men come out from the sepulchre, two of them supporting the other and a cross following after them. . . . And they heard a voice out of the heavens crying, 'Have you preached to those who sleep?', and from the cross there was heard the answer, 'Yes.'[12]

> As the lightning that shines from the east to the west, so will I come upon the clouds of heaven with a great host in my majesty; with my cross going before my face will I come in my majesty; shining seven times brighter than the sun will I come in my majesty with all my saints, my angels.[13]

These texts are typical of a vast literature from the first millennium concerning the victorious cross of Christ. Indeed, the legend of the resurrected and ascended cross (the cross that goes up to heaven with Christ) was such a familiar theme in the Middle Ages that it was

11. Bellarmino Bagatti, *Il Golgota e la croce: ricerche storico-archeologiche*, Studium Biblicum Franciscanum: Collectio minor, n. 21 (Jerusalem: Franciscan Press, 1978), 73–75.

12. *Gospel of Peter* 10.38–42, in *The Apocryphal New Testament: A Collection of Apocryphal Christian Literature in an English Translation*, ed. J. K. Elliott (Oxford: Clarendon, 1993), 156–57.

13. *Apocalypse of Peter* (Ethiopic text), in Elliott, *Apocryphal New Testament*, 600.

frequently depicted in mosaic art, sculpture, liturgical manuscripts, and objects.[14] How should we understand this imaginative story?

We need to go back and look at a detail in the Gospel of Matthew:

> Immediately after the tribulation of those days the sun will be darkened and the moon will not give its light, and the stars will fall from the sky . . . and then the **sign** of the Son of Man will appear in the heavens, and all the tribes of the earth will mourn, and they will see the Son of Man coming upon the clouds of heaven with power and great glory. And he will send out his angels with a trumpet blast, and they will gather the elect from the four winds. (24:29–31, emphasis added)[15]

The biblical "sign of the Son of Man" has always been understood to mean the cross. But in the Catholic imagination and Catholic doctrine, the cross is never separated from resurrection and victory, which is to say that when Catholics contemplate or imagine Good Friday, they always see it in relation to Easter Sunday.[16] Additionally, because of his victory over death, Christ is now invested with eternal sovereignty. At judgment day, the cross will be not only his weapon and symbol of victory but also his scepter as cosmic magistrate: its appearance legitimates the right of the Lord Jesus to judge all humankind, and it will be the sign for the resurrected that their sentence is now decided.[17] As Christ will return again one day, so will the celestial cross return, preceding Christ at the Second Coming as his precursor; it acts in his stead as a sort of stand-in or understudy. This is the origin and meaning of all those wonderful Christian objects and mosaics in

14. Yves Christe, *La Vision de Matthieu (Matth. XXIV-XXV), Origines et developpement d'une image de la Seconde Parousie* (Paris: Bibliothéque des Cahiers Archeologiques, 1973), 80–88.

15. New American Bible translation.

16. For example, at a Catholic mass the congregation's acclamation after the consecration of the bread and wine is "Christ has died, Christ is risen, Christ will come again!"

17. The great silver-encrusted cross in the Holy Sepulchre complex at Jerusalem, the *Staurotheca*, donated by the Emperor Constantine, was regarded as the likeness of the heavenly cross, that is, the gleaming cross that legend had declared to have both risen and ascended with Christ to heaven.

Fig. 35. Apse mosaic of the transfiguration with the eschatological cross, Basilica of San Apollinare-in-Classe, Ravenna, Italy, sixth century.

which the jeweled cross—no gallows tree here!—shines proudly among the stars of a blue heaven (see fig. 35).

At the turn of the first millennium, the symbols of Christ's Passion began to appear in art together with the victorious cross. One can see the nails, the crown of thorns, the ladder, the lance, and so forth; they are not presented as instruments of torture and defeat, but rather as victory emblems or trophies.

In addition to being expressed in art, this theology of the victorious tree of the cross was expressed in liturgy. Catholics do not sing the Baptist hymn "The Old Rugged Cross" (1913) because of its theology of defeat:

> On a hill far away stood an old rugged cross,
> The emblem of suffering and shame;
> And I love that old cross where the Dearest and Best
> For a world of lost sinners was slain.

On the contrary, since about the year AD 600, on every Good Friday, Catholics throughout the world sing some translation of the ancient victory hymn "Pange lingua gloriosi":

> Sing, my tongue, the Savior's glory;
> tell His triumph far and wide;
> tell aloud the famous story
> of His body crucified;

how upon the cross a victim,
vanquishing in death, He died.

Eating of the Tree forbidden,
man had sunk in Satan's snare,
when our pitying Creator did
this second Tree prepare;
destined, many ages later,
that first evil to repair.

Faithful Cross, above all other,
one and only noble Tree!
None in foliage, none in blossom,
none in fruit thy peers may be;
sweetest wood and sweetest iron!
Sweetest weight is hung on thee!

Lofty Tree, bend down thy branches,
to embrace thy sacred load;
oh, relax the native tension
of that all too rigid wood;
gently, gently bear the members
of thy rising King and God.[18]

The Tree of Life in Mexico

All of this rich, imaginative, and deeply theological symbolism blossomed and flowered in the sixteenth century upon the discovery and evangelization of Mesoamerica. A sense of being proximate to the end of the world was certainly one element that motivated the mendicant friars to travel to Mesoamerica, similar in some ways to nineteenth-century Latter-day Saints who crossed the ocean or the continent to settle in the

18. Composed by Venantius Fortunatus in the sixth century and translated into English by John Mason Neale in the nineteenth century. There are several versions; see J. M. Neale, *Medieval Hymns and Sequences* (London: Joseph Masters, 1867) 1–5.

promised land of Utah.[19] Beginning in 1524, the Franciscans arrived in Mexico, followed soon by the Dominicans and the Augustinians. For them the discovery of the New World was an eschatological event—the beginning of the end of the world. The Franciscans and Dominicans arrived in New Spain in groups of twelve, like the twelve apostles of the New Testament and the future twelve apostles of the latter days as prophesied in the eleventh century by the abbot Joachim of Fiore (ca. 1135–1202), who had a tremendous influence on the friars, especially on the Franciscans. While the Franciscans and Dominicans arrived in groups of twelve, it appears that the Augustinian friars had a slightly different idea of themselves. They arrived in New Spain not in groups of twelve but of seven, like the seven angels of the Apocalypse who announce the end of history.[20]

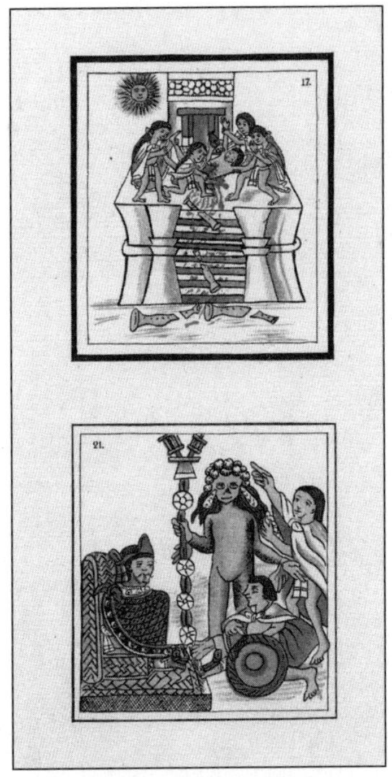

Fig. 36. Images of Aztec human sacrifice. Above: human heart extraction. Below: deity impersonator wearing flayed human skin.

In the New World, the friars encountered undreamed-of tribes and civilizations, one being the Mexica, commonly known to us as the Aztecs. While the missionaries were delighted to come upon millions of new souls to Christianize, they were also shocked by the human sacrifice and ritual cannibalism that they witnessed, rituals in which the heart of the victim was extracted live (see fig. 36). The friars even theorized

19. Compare, for example, John Leddy Phelan, *The Millennial Kingdom of the Franciscans in the New World*, 2nd ed. (Berkeley, CA: University of California Press, 1970), with Laurel B. Andrew, *The Early Temples of the Mormons: The Architecture of the Millennial Kingdom in the American West* (Albany: State University of New York Press, 1978), and Lara, *City, Temple, Stage*, 41–90.

20. Lara, *City, Temple, Stage*, 59–69.

that the natives were the descendants of the lost tribes of Israel, who in ancient times had practiced animal sacrifice and who must have fallen into a perversion of those ancient sacrifices, converting them to human sacrifice (see fig. 37).

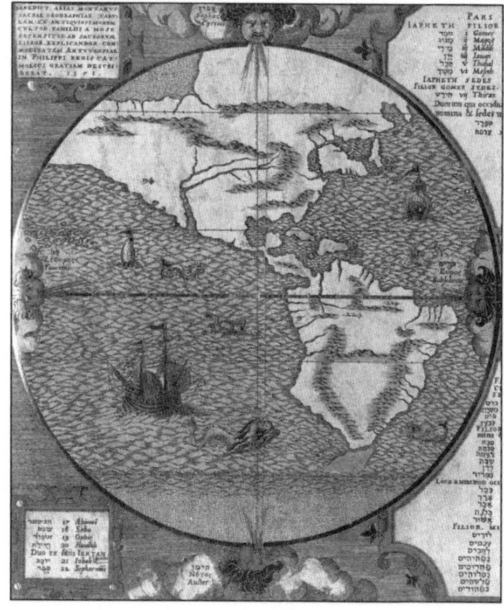

Fig. 37. Sixteenth-century world map depicting the dispersal of the Hebrew tribes.

The first task of the missionaries was to understand the many native languages and to compile dictionaries, pictographic catechisms, pictographic prayer books, and lists of Aztec metaphors, both verbal and visual. They sought out a "symbolic proximity," that is, similarities between Aztec beliefs and practices that were near enough to Christian theology and sacraments that an easy transition might be possible. Simultaneously, the native peoples were noticing similarities between their paraphernalia and practices and the Catholic religious objects and sacred personages. The Amerindians would eventually come to equate many elements of Catholicism—like the tree of life or the tree of the cross—with particulars in their own religion. This, the friars hoped, would eventually lead the neophytes to a more thorough and orthodox Christianity as their own religious systems would begin to recede and Christianity would become more thoroughly internalized.

One of those common elements was the paradise garden. The representation of heaven as a paradisiacal garden appears in sixteenth-century mural art made by and for the new Aztec Christians. The frescoes of the Augustinian cloister of Malinalco, for example, are a type of cosmic paradigm relating to the Eden of the first man and woman, to the earthly utopia that the mendicants wished to establish in the

Fig. 38. Cloister frescoes, Augustinian conversion center of San Salvador, Malinalco, Morelos, Mexico, ca. 1565.

latter days, as well as to an anticipation of the celestial hereafter of the blessed[21] (see fig. 38). The murals, painted in the 1570s, cover the four walls and barrel vaults of the cloister and are a rich and accurately represented world of flora and fauna.

Flowering gardens as symbols of terrestrial and celestial bliss have a long history in Christian art, and there was abundant medieval literature concerning imaginary journeys to paradise and its descriptions.[22] In the fourfold biblical exegesis, paradise could be associated with the atria and porticoes of Solomon's temple where the apostolic church taught and met for communal prayer.[23] It is no coincidence that the first European architecture constructed in Mesoamerica, the open-air conversion centers, were copied from late-medieval illustrated Bibles and modeled on the temple of Jerusalem as seen in the visions of the prophet Ezekiel (chaps. 40–44). The Christian temple in sixteenth-century Mexico consists of an atrium with four corner-stational chapels for dance processions, a monumental altar cross mounted on a pedestal at the atrium's center, an outdoor apse and pulpit, and a tripartite single-nave church designed to replicate the Jerusalem temple-house[24] (see fig. 39).

21. Jeanette Favrot Peterson, *The Paradise Garden Murals of Malinalco: Utopia and Empire in Sixteenth-Century Mexico* (Austin: University of Texas Press, 1993).

22. Mircea Eliade, "Paradise and Utopia: Mythical Geography and Eschatology," in *The Quest: History and Meaning in Religion* (Chicago: University of Chicago Press, 1969).

23. George Williams, *Wilderness and Paradise in Christian Thought* (New York: Harper, 1962), 48.

24. Lara, *City, Temple, Stage*, 111–50.

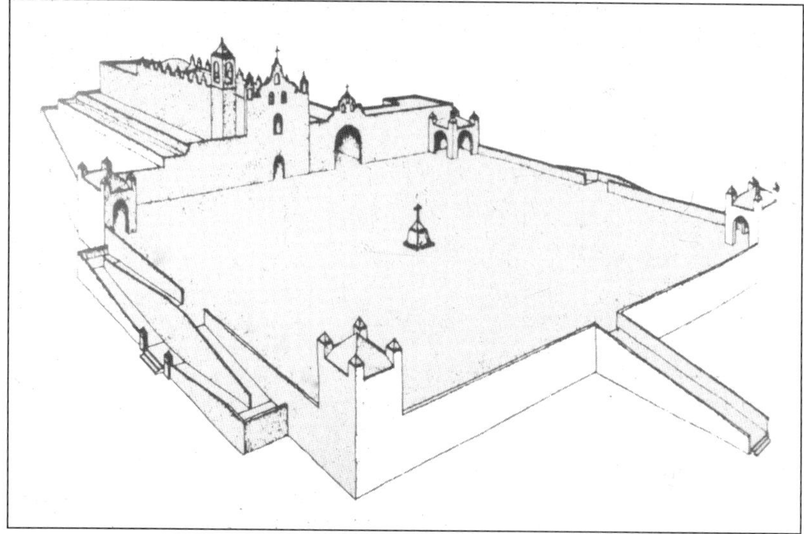

Fig. 39. Drawing of a generic 16th-century conversion center in Mexico.

In the classic four senses of scripture, the courts of the Jerusalem temple corresponded anagogically to the paradise-garden of the blessed; and for monks, both Jerusalem and paradise were already experienced tropologically in the here and now of the monks' cloister, which was, of course, a walled garden with a fountain at its center.[25] Pre-Columbian peoples seem to have made similar associations by arranging luxurious gardens on temple property. Indeed, in Aztec mythology the highest level of the afterlife, *Omeyocan*, was a garden, green and fertile.[26] It appears that the friars were aware of these native beliefs. The site of Malinalco was chosen for a conversion center because of the medicinal herb garden that the indigenous population had established there in the pre-Conquest period. At the center of Malinalco's cloister there was a fruit tree and a fountain with four water outlets, symbols respectively of the tree of life and the four rivers

25. Jean Daniélou, "Terre et paradis chez les pères de l'église," *Eranos Jahrbuch* 22 (1954): 433–72, esp. 454; Peter Raedts, "St. Bernard of Clairvaux and Jerusalem," in *Prophecy and Eschatology*, ed. Michael Wilks (Oxford: Blackwell, 1994), 169–82.

26. Peterson, *The Paradise Garden Murals of Malinalco*, 132–33. Tlalocan, the rainy paradise of the deity Tlaloc, was also envisioned as exceptionally fertile and green.

Fig. 40. Detail of cloister frescoes with the name of Jesus abbreviated as "IHS." Malinalco, Morelos, Mexico.

Fig. 41. Cross-shaped Mesoamerican images.

of paradise feeding the four continents of the then-known world. There are two visual references to the primeval Eden: the presence of the tree and the serpent. But as one can see, all the plants are blooming into a person represented by his name; it is the holy name *Jesus* written as an abbreviated monogram[27] (see fig. 40).

Another tree of life element that would have been familiar to the Mexica was the cruciform. The cruciform was a commonly shared cosmic symbol. Mesoamericans had cross-shaped images,[28] actually *axis mundi* or totems, and Spanish explorers encountered them as soon as they arrived (see fig. 41). When asked about the origin of one cruciform, the Indians replied that a "most beautiful man had left them as relics." Others claimed that on it "a man more radiant than the sun had died."[29] Likewise, the Christian cross was the first foreign icon that the

27. Richard Phillips, "La participación de los indígenas en las processiones por los claustros del siglo XVI en México," *Relaciones: Estudios de Historia y Sociedad* 78 (1999): 225–50.

28. G. Raynaud, "Les nombres sacrés et les signes cruciformes dans la Moyenne Amérique precolombienne," *Revue de l'historie des religions* 44 (1901): 235–61.

29. Both statements are suspiciously similar to early Christian legends surrounding the cross; see below. The "most beautiful man" was interpreted by Peter Martyr d'Anghiera to be St. Thomas the Apostle. See Frank Graziano, *The Millennial New World* (Oxford: Oxford University Press, 1999), 185.

native population encountered at the moment of European contact. The friars even whitewashed pagan altars of human sacrifice, preserving them and using them as pedestals for the eschatological cross.[30]

The iconography of the carved motifs on the cross is based on the instruments of the Passion that, as we already saw, were not so much means of torture as much as Christ's weapons or trophies by which he won universal salvation[31] (see fig. 42). Just before doomsday, the cross, gleaming and shining, will reappear in the sky to herald Christ's return, and with it the trophies of his triumph.

Fig. 42. Atrium cross with the instruments of Christ's Passion, Huandacareo, Michoacán, Mexico.

Pre-Columbian beliefs aided in this arboreal connection, and a convergence of metaphors took place for both Mesoamericans and missionaries.[32] The Aztec heaven of Tamoanchan—"the home from which we descend"—had both celestial and terrestrial features of a paradise of origins. Tamoanchan was often represented by an anthropomorphic tree, sometimes broken and bleeding.[33]

For the Christianized Aztecs, a particularly sacred tree was the two-hundred-foot tall cypress cross, erected in the atrium of the Franciscan

30. Antonio Ybot León, *La Iglesia y los eclesiásticos españoles en la empresa de Indias* (Barcelona: Salvat, 1954-63), 1:435.

31. Lara, *City, Temple, Stage*, 151–76.

32. Louise Burkhart, "Flowery Heaven: The Aesthetic of Paradise in Náhuatl Devotional Literature," *Res* 21 (1992): 89–109.

33. Kay Read, "The Fleeting Moment: Cosmogony, Eschatology, and Ethics in Aztec Religion and Society," *Journal of Religious Ethics* 14 (1986): 113–38, informs us that trees acted as a sort of indigenous Limbo: Aztec children who died in infancy were thought to return to inhabit them. Burr Cartwright Brundage, *The Fifth Sun: Aztec Gods, Aztec World* (Austin: University of Texas, 1979), 46–47, posits the possibility that this Aztec myth was early "contaminated" by the friars' story of the biblical Garden of Eden.

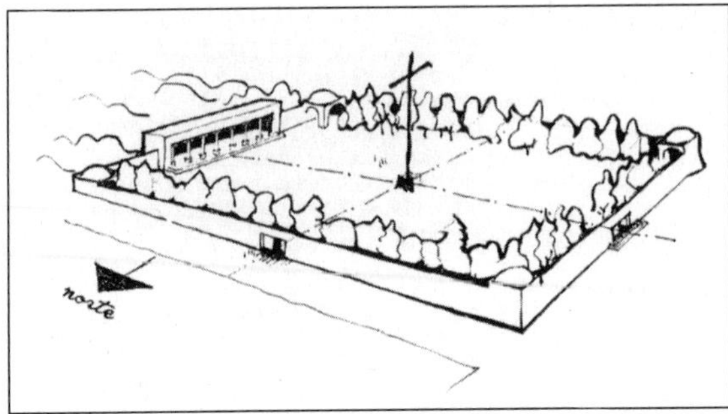

Fig. 43. Reconstruction of the Franciscan conversion center of San José de los Naturales, Mexico City, as seen ca. 1550 with the 200-foot-tall tree cross.

chapel at Mexico City. The natives had made it from the tallest of the trees of Moctezuma's garden. It towered over everything else in Mexico City and could be seen for miles around (see fig. 43). Liturgical dancing circumambulated the cross, especially during the processions.

The native Christians of Tlaxcala incensed and venerated their Christian cross as *Tonacaquahuitl*, "the tree that sustains our life." At Huejotzingo the cross is a bare stone tree with lopped-off branches (see fig. 44). This cross is one example of the grafting cross symbol, which, as noted earlier, was an image taken from Saint Paul's epistle and often used to represent the cross that would return on judgment day or the cross as the new tree of life.[34] The cross shown in fig. 44 is surrounded by the four processional chapels (see fig. 45) on whose facades are sculpted apocalyptic angels bearing the trophies of the passion in their hands.[35] Notice the movement of the angels' robes, as if these angels have just alighted from heaven or else are still hovering around the eschatological cross soon to descend to earth.

The natives of Huejotzingo would dance around this cross in cross formation themselves and sing the aforementioned ancient victory hymn, "Pange lingua gloriosi." One of the earliest hymns composed

34. Antoni Noguera, *El Pantocràtor Romànic de les Terres Gironines* (Barcelona: Terra Nostra, 1986), 86–88. Anna Esmeijer, *Divina Quaternitas: A Preliminary Study in the Method and Application of Visual Exegesis* (Assen: Gorcum, 1978), 105, indicates that the purpose of lopping off the branches is to "graft" Christ's body onto the Cosmic Tree. The grafting cross was also an emblem of the penitential and flagellant confraternities of the Passion.

35. In recent times the cross has been moved out of the atrium and relocated to the town plaza.

Fig. 44 (left). This cross at the Franciscan conversion center of San Miguel Archangel, Huejotzingo, Puebla, Mexico, was originally located at the center of the atrium.

Fig. 45 (right). One of four stational processional chapels in the atrium, with reliefs of alighting angels, ca. 1560. San Miguel Archangel, Huejotzingo, Puebla, Mexico.

locally in Nahuatl, the Aztec language, also speaks of this new Christian tree in very native metaphors:

> The Tree of Life grows
> In the Land of Mystery:
> There we were created;
> There we were born.
> There He-by-whom-all-things-live
> Spins the thread of our lives. . . .
>
> You have become the Tree of Life.
> Dying, you have been born again.
> Swaying, you spread your branches
> And stand before the Giver-of-all-life.
> In your boughs our home shall be:
> We will be your flowers.[36]

36. Translated for me by John Bierhorst from Ángel María Garibay, *La literatura de los aztecas* (Mexico City: J. Mortiz, 1964), 55, and *Historia de la literatura náhuatl* (Mexico City: Porrua, 1953), 1:212.

Fig. 46. A typical "May Cross" from contemporary central Mexico is made to be decorated with flowers.

Fig. 47. *Tree of the Sacraments*, anonymous painting in parish church's chancel, Santa Cruz, Tlaxcala, Mexico, 1735. See plate 13.

Decorating the cross with flowers as a living tree—or using instead a green cross, as if it were verdant and alive—is a practice that has continued since colonial times (see fig. 46). Here is a compact visual theology, not one of defeat and death but rather one that stands the gallows tree on its head, and the judgment of the world as well. For the Christian, Good Friday is never the end but rather the link between Gethsemane and Easter. For Catholics, this fruitfulness of life-in-Christ is experienced in the present moment in the seven sacraments, which are represented in a delightful eighteenth-century painting in Santa Cruz, Tlaxcala (see fig. 47, also pl. 13). The sacraments are depicted as a fruit-laden tree of life, and Christ is the tree, which is being hoed and watered by the apostles. In each of the blossoms, Aztec Indians are receiving one of the seven sacraments, like baptism or matrimony, each of which is described in their language.

At the discovery and evangelization of the New World, a convergence of metaphor, symbol, and religious imagination made possible the conversion of thousands of souls to Christianity—a Christianity with its own rhythms, colors, tastes, and aromas. Both cultures, Catholic and Mexica, had sacred

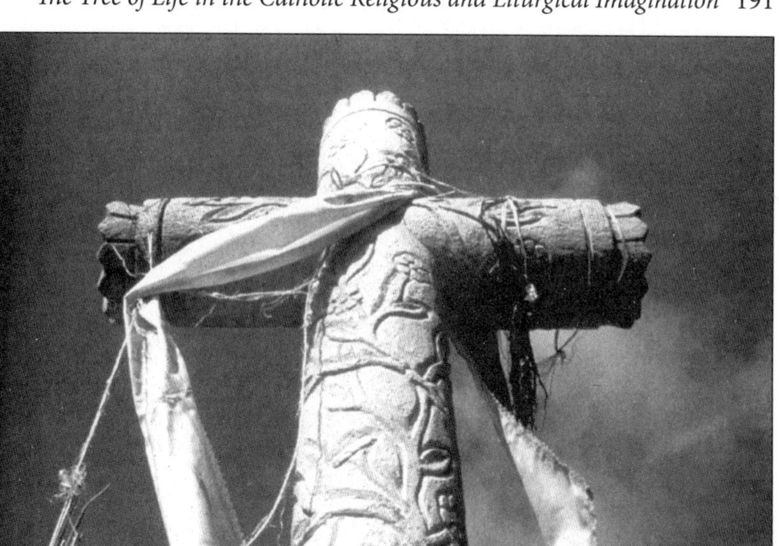

Fig. 48. Atrium cross as the tree of life, Franciscan conversion center of San Juan Bautista, Huitzilac, Morelos, Mexico, mid-16th century.

trees. Christ as the new tree of life of Aztec Christianity was the result of a convergence of root metaphors common to natives and Europeans alike. We know now that the friars' worldview and symbols were much closer to the native imagination and metaphors (and vice versa) than has previously been thought. It was precisely this religious similarity or compatibility that eventually made the synthesis and convergence of the sixteenth century possible. It created what we today call Mexico and Mexican Catholicism, and there the fruit of Christian faith blossomed from the tree of life (see fig. 48).

Jaime Lara has degrees and interest in art, architecture, liturgics, and anthropology. He earned an MDiv from Immaculate Conception Seminary, an MA from City University of New York, an STM (master of sacred theology) from Yale University, and a PhD from Graduate Theological Union and the University of California, Berkeley. His studies have focused on early Christianity, the Spanish Middle Ages, and the colonial era of Latin America. His most recent publications include The Flowering Cross: Holy Week in an Andean Village

(2010); Christian Texts for Aztecs: Art and Liturgy in Colonial Mexico *(2008);* City, Temple, Stage: Eschatological Architecture and Liturgical Theatrics in New Spain *(2004); and "Christian Cannibalism and Human(e) Sacrifice: The Passion of Christ in the Conversion of the Aztecs," in* Perspectives on the Passion *(2008). His book on volcanoes, Inca myths, and the book of Revelation in the Andean countries will appear in 2011. He is currently a senior fellow at the Center for the Study of Visual Arts at the National Gallery of Art, Washington, DC.*

The Qurʾanic Tree of Life

Daniel C. Peterson

The Qurʾan, the sacred book of Islam, is a 114-chapter collection of revelations received by the Arabian prophet Muhammad during the roughly twenty-two years that elapsed between his call in approximately AD 610 and his death in AD 632. The revelations were committed to writing sometime between their initial reception and the middle of the 600s—there is some scholarly dispute on this point (I myself lean toward the earliest date)—and have constituted the fundamental basis of Muslim faith ever since.

Unlike the Bible, the Qurʾan is not a library of different literary genres. Nor is it a single narrative, whether about Muhammad or about any prior prophet or community. Muhammad is named in the Qurʾan, but he does not speak. In fact, he is *addressed*. The speaker throughout is God (using the first-person plural), although some other speakers—prophets and infidels alike—are quoted in what God says. If I were to compare the Qurʾan to any scriptural text familiar to Latter-day Saints, I would say that it somewhat resembles the Doctrine and Covenants, in that the revelations are organized on a roughly chronological principle, according to the date of their reception, rather than according to theme. Just as a section of the Doctrine and Covenants need have no particular relationship of topic with the sections that precede and succeed it, the contents of the Qurʾan are not grouped by theme.

For many centuries, the chapters of the Qurʾan, known as *surahs*, have been divided between those received at Makka (Mecca), where Muhammad was a preacher with a relatively small flock of followers, and those received at al-Madina (Medina), where he became not merely a prophet but a political leader. The Makkan revelations tend to be quite short, with short poetic verses, and to concentrate on apocalyptic warnings, ethical criticisms of pagan Arabian practices, and, above all, the denunciation of polytheism and heedlessness and the repeated summons to recognize the lordship of the one true God. But Muhammad's role and responsibilities changed dramatically when he went to al-Madina in AD 622; this *hijra*, or "emigration" or "flight," marks AD 622 as the base year of the Muslim calendar. The Madinan surahs are distinctly longer, with longer verses, and more prosaic. Not unexpectedly, they focus to a much greater extent on issues that would confront the leader of a state or community, such as rules for inheritance and the conduct of war. But they also feature more extended narratives.

The Qurʾan is a relatively short book, approximately the length of the New Testament. Very early, therefore, devout Muslims felt the need to supplement it by gathering up reports of the teachings and practices of the earliest Islamic community, and preeminently those of the Prophet Muhammad. These are known as *hadith*. While their authority is plainly, at least in theory, subordinate to that of the Qurʾan itself, in practice they fill in gaps where the Qurʾan is silent and provide much of the lens through which the Qurʾan itself is interpreted.

One problem with the hadith is that, just as an economist would predict, surging and ardent demand for such accounts of the Prophet's teachings and practices encouraged the growth of supply. Even the early gatherers of hadith reports recognized this, and many thousands of tendentious and spurious hadith were rejected. But skeptical Western scholars still often view large portions of the canonical hadith collections as only dubiously Muhammadan in origin, while acknowledging that they provide us invaluable if sometimes inscrutable glimpses of the issues and controversies that dominated the first centuries of theological development among Muhammad's followers.

In what follows, I will concentrate heavily upon the text of the Qur'an itself.[1] The hadith materials as they appear in the literature of Qur'anic commentary (*tafsir*) and in the biography of the Prophet (*sira*), to say nothing of the canonical hadith collections themselves, are a vast sea and, plainly, exceed the dimensions of this paper.

The tree of life is a very ancient and well-nigh universal motif that can be identified in regions as disparate as early Mesopotamia, Viking Age Scandinavia, and pre-Columbian Mesoamerica.[2] "Hercules found a tree of life in the garden of the gods, at the end of the world," wrote the Dutch scholar of comparative religions G. van der Leeuw. "Adam found it in paradise, at its beginning. The concept was also known to the Egyptians and the Babylonians."[3] It clearly enters the Islamic tradition in something like its biblical form. My paper will attempt to clarify what the Qur'an takes over from earlier tradition and what it omits and will also suggest reasons for those choices.

God's command to Adam and Eve that they not approach "this tree lest you be among the wrongdoers" appears twice in the Qur'an (2:35; 7:19), much as it appears in the biblical book of Genesis. In the second surah, for example, which dates to the Madinan period, the account reads:

> 35. And We said, "O Adam, dwell, you and your wife, in the Garden, and eat comfortably from it wherever you will. But do not approach this tree lest you be among the wrongdoers."
>
> 36. Then Satan caused them to slip from it [the Garden] and expelled them from the state in which they had been. And We said, "Go down, at enmity with one another. There will be

1. Unless otherwise indicated, all translations are mine.

2. For an interesting treatment of sacred trees in general, see G. van der Leeuw, *Phänomenologie der Religion*, 4th ed. (Tübingen, Germany: J. C. B. Mohr [Paul Siebeck], 1977), 42–46 (§5.3). I have examined one occurrence of what seems to be the tree of life in Daniel C. Peterson, "Nephi and His Asherah: A Note on 1 Nephi 11:8–23," in *Mormons, Scripture, and the Ancient World: Studies in Honor of John L. Sorenson*, ed. Davis Bitton (Provo, UT: Foundation for Ancient Research and Mormon Studies, 1998), 191–243. A much-condensed version of this article appeared as Daniel C. Peterson, "Nephi and His Asherah," *Journal of Book of Mormon Studies* 9/2 (2000): 15–25, 80–81.

3. Van der Leeuw, *Phänomenologie der Religion*, 45.

Fig. 49. *The Temptation of Adam and Eve,* Tabriz, Iran, 1307. In the Qurʾan, the tree whose forbidden fruit Adam and Eve partake of is called the "Tree of Eternity."

> a place of residence for you and the necessities of life on the earth, for a time."[4]

It is important to note here that the "fall" in the Qurʾan appears to involve literal descent from a high place to the earth. I have argued, in an as-yet-unpublished paper, that the ancient concept of the cosmic mountain occurs in the Qurʾan and that, among other things, the fall of Adam and Eve appears to involve descent from a garden atop that mountain to the earth. The great Swedish comparative religionist Geo Widengren observes that, in Mesopotamia too, the tree of life grew on "the mountain of the gods" (*auf dem Götterberge*) and that this notion

4. Qurʾan 2:35–36. Interestingly, the dual Arabic verbs in 2:35, addressed to Adam and Eve, are followed by plural verbs and plural pronouns in 2:36, referring, evidently, to a larger group.

lived on in Christian art, where the tree of life is commonly depicted on a hill with the rivers of paradise flowing from its foot.[5]

The account given in the seventh surah, also Madinan, is very similar and even, at some points, identical:

> 19. "O Adam, dwell, you and your wife, in the Garden, and eat comfortably from it wherever you will. But do not approach this tree lest you be among the wrongdoers."
>
> 20. Then Satan whispered to them, to call to their attention their shame that had been concealed from them. And he said, "Your Lord only forbade this tree to you lest you be a pair of angels or among the immortals."
>
> 21. And he swore an oath to them: "Truly, I am a well-intentioned counselor to you."
>
> 22. Thus, by deception, he caused them to fall. And when they tasted of the tree, their shame became apparent to them, and they began to sew upon themselves leaves from the Garden. And their Lord called to them, "Did I not forbid that tree to you and tell you that Satan is a manifest enemy to you?"
>
> 23. They said, "Our Lord! We have wronged our own souls. Truly, if you do not forgive us and have mercy upon us, we will be lost."
>
> 24. He [God] said, "Go down, at enmity with one another. There will be a place of residence for you and the necessities of life on the earth, for a time."
>
> 25. He [God] said, "You shall live in it, and you shall die in it, and from it you will be taken out."[6]

5. Geo Widengren, *Religionsphänomenologie* (Berlin: Walter de Gruyter, 1969), 384. The classic treatment of the cosmic mountain in the ancient Near East is Richard J. Clifford, *The Cosmic Mountain in Canaan and the Old Testament* (Cambridge, MA: Harvard University Press, 1972).

6. Qurʾan 7:19–25. Once again, there is a shift from the Arabic dual verbs of 7:19–23 to plural verbs and pronouns in 7:24–25, and there seems to be a literal descent from the garden.

Fig. 50. Tree of life stone screen, Sidi Sayyid Mosque, Ahmadabad, India.

They were barred from that tree, says the Qurʾan, "lest you be a pair of angels or among the immortals" (7:20). The suggestion of immortality by means of the tree is consistent not only with biblical materials but with standard notions about the tree of life from elsewhere. Widengren noted years ago, for instance, that the Mesopotamian tree of life "possesses the power to renew life" and that, in the widespread ideology that, he says, surrounded ancient and medieval monarchs in various cultures, the royal scepter represented a life-giving branch of the tree of life.[7] When they tasted of the tree, they became conscious of their nakedness, just as in Genesis, and sewed leaves together in order to cover themselves (7:22; 20:121).

Although the similarities between the biblical account and the Qurʾanic account are obvious, there are also significant differences between the narratives. The tree that Adam and Eve are advised to avoid, but from which they partake of the fruit, is called, in the

7. Widengren, *Religionsphänomenologie*, 331, 376, 383–84; Geo Widengren, *The King and the Tree of Life in Ancient Near Eastern Religion* (Uppsala, Sweden: A.-B. Lundequistska Bokhandeln, 1951).

Qurʾan, the "Tree of Eternity" (*shajarat al-khuld*, 20:120). Here is the relevant passage from Surah 20, a Makkan chapter:

> 116. When We said to the angels, "Prostrate yourselves to Adam," they prostrated themselves except for Iblis, who refused.[8]
>
> 117. Then We said, "O Adam! Truly this is an enemy to you and to your wife. Don't let him cause you to be expelled from the Garden and be miserable.
>
> 118. "Truly, there is, in it, [enough] for you that you neither go hungry nor naked,
>
> 119. "And that you not go thirsty in it nor suffer from the sun."
>
> 120. But Satan whispered to him and said, "O Adam! Shall I lead you to the Tree of Eternity and a kingdom that does not decay?"
>
> 121. So they ate of it and their shame became apparent to them, and they began to sew upon themselves from the leaves of the Garden. And Adam rebelled against his Lord and went astray. . . .
>
> 123. He [God] said, "Go down from it [the Garden], all of you, at enmity with one another."[9]

The term that I've translated as "Eternity" in the phrase "Tree of Eternity," *khuld*, is cognate with the word *khalidun*, which I've rendered "immortals" in the previous passage (7:20), where Adam and Eve are barred from partaking of the tree "lest you be a pair of angels or among the immortals." Both share the root *kh-l-d*.

The Tree of Eternity is, as already noted, a tree that confers angelic status and immortality upon those who eat of its fruit. Having eaten

8. Iblis is the devil, and like the word *devil*, the name *Iblis* derives from the Greek *diabolos*.

9. Qurʾan 20:116–21, 123. This passage features dual verbs throughout, including the "Go down" of 20:123. But the "all of you" (*jamʿian*) and the "at enmity with one another" (*baʿdukum li-baʿdin ʿaduwwun*) that follow "Go down" nonetheless seem to suggest plurality again, rather than mere duality.

from it, Adam and Eve became aware of their "shame" (the word can also implicitly refer to the sexual organs, and in this context it manifestly does); immediately thereafter they began to sew for themselves coverings of leaves. Satan had promised them that if they partook of its fruit, they would become immortal. But they did not become immortal. Clearly, Satan was lying to them, and the Tree of Eternity did not in fact possess the power to make them deathless—not, at least, through a single eating. Yet it is called the "Tree of Eternity," and the Qur'an explains their expulsion from the garden as necessary in order to prevent their joining "the immortals." So, perhaps, repeated consumption of the fruit of the tree might have guaranteed immortality, while a single partaking was not enough to accomplish that. In Zoroastrianism, the tree of life "is called the white haoma (homa), and its fruit is used to nourish the blessed spirits in heaven."[10]

The Genesis account in the Bible differs significantly in this respect from that of the Qur'an. Among other things, it features two trees with differentiated functions, rather than just one:

> The Lord God planted a garden in Eden, in the east, and placed there the man whom He had formed. And from the ground the Lord God caused to grow every tree that was pleasing to the sight and good for food, with the tree of life in the middle of the garden, and the tree of knowledge of good and bad. . . .
>
> The Lord God took the man and placed him in the garden of Eden, to till it and tend it. And the Lord God commanded the man, saying, "Of every tree of the garden you are free to eat; but as for the tree of knowledge of good and bad, you must not eat of it; for as soon as you eat of it, you shall die."[11]

10. George Lechler, "The Tree of Life in Indo-European and Islamic Cultures," *Ars Islamica* IV (1937): 369. In the Avesta, the principal collection of the sacred texts of Zoroastrianism, the beverage made from the fruit of the homa plant bears the same name, which is related to the soma of the ancient Indian Vedas (and, for that matter, of Aldous Huxley's *Brave New World*).

11. Genesis 2:8–9, 15–17. As rendered in *Tanakh: The Holy Scriptures: The New JPS Translation According to the Traditional Hebrew Text* (Philadelphia: Jewish Publication

After the creation of Eve,

> the two of them were naked, the man and his wife, yet they felt no shame. Now the serpent was the shrewdest of all the wild beasts that the Lord God had made. He said to the woman, "Did God really say: You shall not eat of any tree of the garden?" The woman replied to the serpent, "We may eat of the fruit of the other trees of the garden. It is only about fruit of the tree in the middle of the garden that God said: 'You shall not eat of it or touch it, lest you die.'" And the serpent said to the woman, "You are not going to die, but God knows that as soon as you eat of it your eyes will be opened and you will be like divine beings who know good and bad." When the woman saw that the tree was good for eating and a delight to the eyes, and that the tree was desirable as a source of wisdom, she took of its fruit and ate. She also gave some to her husband, and he ate. Then the eyes of both of them were opened and they perceived that they were naked; and they sewed together fig leaves and made themselves loincloths.[12]

In Genesis it is the "tree of knowledge of good and bad," or of "good and evil"—seemingly absent (at least as a separate plant) from the Qurʾan—that Adam and Eve are admonished to avoid, the eating of whose fruit brings about their awareness of their nakedness and, eventually, their fall from Eden. The tree of life (or, Qurʾanically, the Tree of Eternity) is a distinct object, whose fruit would have caused those who ate it to "live forever." But, unlike the account in the Qurʾan, the Genesis narrative says that Adam and Eve did *not* partake of the fruit of the tree of life:

> And the Lord God said, "Now that the man has become like one of us, knowing good and bad, what if he should stretch out his hand and take also from the tree of life and eat, and

---

Society, 1988), hereafter referred to as the "Jewish Publication Society translation."

12. Genesis 2:25–3:7 (Jewish Publication Society translation).

> live forever!" So the Lord God banished him from the garden of Eden, to till the soil from which he was taken. He drove the man out, and stationed east of the garden of Eden the cherubim and the fiery ever-turning sword, to guard the way to the tree of life.[13]

John Kselman, writing in a one-volume biblical commentary produced by the Society of Biblical Literature and responding to the story of the fall of Adam and Eve, remarks that

> nakedness in the OT suggests weakness, neediness, and the like (Deut. 28:48; Job 1:21; Isa. 58:7). The unawareness of their nakedness on the part of the man and the woman suggests their unawareness of their dependence on God who provides in the garden for all their needs. . . .
>
> Ironically, what the man and woman discover is not that they are gods but that they are naked—weak, vulnerable, and helpless, having rejected their dependence upon God.[14]

He is surely right, as far as he goes. But he seems to have missed, or at least to have underemphasized, an important aspect of the story. Satan had told the woman that partaking of the fruit of the tree would make her and Adam "like divine beings [*ke-elohim* in the Hebrew text, ως θεοι in the Septuagint Greek] who know good and bad."[15] And though he is not wholly to be trusted, it appears that, in this respect at least, Satan told the truth, since God himself subsequently comments that "the man has become like one of us, knowing good and bad."[16] This

13. Genesis 3:22–24 (Jewish Publication Society translation).

14. John S. Kselman, "Genesis," in *Harper's Bible Commentary*, ed. James L. Mays et al. (San Francisco: Harper & Row, 1988), 88.

15. Genesis 3:5 (Jewish Publication Society translation). The word *elohim* is a sound masculine plural but is also commonly translated by the English singular *God*. This is the preference, probably for theological reasons, of the evangelical Protestant commentary supplied by H. L. Ellison and D. F. Payne, "Genesis," in *The International Bible Commentary with the New International Version*, ed. F. F. Bruce (Grand Rapids, MI: Zondervan, 1986), 117. However, the Septuagint Greek renders the term with the plural θεοι, which demonstrates that the translators of the Septuagint took it in its plural sense.

16. Genesis 3:22 (Jewish Publication Society translation).

contrasts with the upshot of the Qur᾿anic narrative: By eating the fruit of the tree of knowledge of good and evil, the biblical Adam and Eve appear to have become mortal, but they have also become not like the angels but like God or the gods.

In the Qur᾿an, when Adam and Eve partake of the fruit of the *shajarat al-khuld*, have they indeed, as Satan had predicted, taken upon themselves the nature of angels? It seems that they have not. His promise was false, as had been his promise that eating from the tree would grant them immortality.

To summarize, while the Genesis biblical account features two trees with divided functions, the Qur᾿an mentions only one tree that, with a trio of very notable exceptions, combines the functions of the two biblical trees and, in fact, assumes the role in the story largely played by the biblical tree of knowledge of good and evil rather than that of the biblical tree of life. The biblical tree of life genuinely does confer—or, at least, could have conferred—immortality upon partakers of its fruit, but its Qur᾿anic equivalent, the Tree of Eternity, did not confer immortality upon Adam and Eve when they ate from it despite Satan's misleading promise that it would (though, again, perhaps repeated consumption of the fruit of that tree might have done the job). In the Bible, the primordial pair eat from the tree of knowledge of good and evil but are barred from eating from the tree of life. In the Qur᾿an, by contrast, Adam and Eve partake of the tree of life (there being no other tree of note in the Garden). The biblical tree of knowledge of good and evil conferred something like godhood upon Adam and Eve, consisting, precisely, in that knowledge, whereas the Qur᾿anic Tree of Eternity, according to Satan, would have conferred angelic status—something a little lower than the gods—but, in fact, did not.

I mentioned a trio of functions played by the combined two biblical trees that are not, in fact, assumed by the Qur᾿anic Tree of Eternity. Two of these I have already mentioned: First, the Qur᾿anic tree does not bestow immortality upon those who eat its fruit—not, anyway, at first partaking. Second, the Qur᾿anic tree does not deify those who partake of it. Nor, as it turns out, does it even make them angels.

The third function that belongs to the biblical tree of knowledge of good and evil is, precisely, the conveying of such knowledge. As the Catholic commentator Bruce Vawter observes,

> *Knowledge* to the Semite is never anything abstract or extrinsic to the knower: knowledge is experience. A man "knows" his wife; to "know" the Lord is to live the life ordained by the Lord, even, in a true sense, to live the Lord's life (cf. Jn 14:7, 15–17). What experiential knowledge is signified by eating of this tree? *Good and evil* is not disjunctive in sense but cumulative: just as "going and coming" to the Hebrew meant movement in general, "good and evil" involves the entire moral order. Without the experience of sin, man could not be said to know good and evil, that is, to experience the entire moral order.[17]

John Kselman makes much the same point when he comments:

> "Good and evil" is [an] instance of merism; the "knowledge of good and evil" is thus the unlimited knowledge appropriate to divinity, as the serpent suggests in v. 5 ("You shall be like gods").[18]

Note the implications of deification in these comments and in the verses to which they refer: "To 'know' the Lord," says Vawter, "is . . . in a true sense, to live the Lord's life." The biblical "knowledge of good and evil," says Kselman, is "the unlimited knowledge appropriate to divinity."[19]

---

17. Bruce Vawter, "Genesis," in *A New Catholic Commentary on Holy Scripture*, ed. Reginald C. Fuller, Leonard Johnston, and Conleth Kearns (Nashville and New York: Thomas Nelson, 1975), 178 (151f). Compare Eugene H. Maly, "Genesis," in *The Jerome Biblical Commentary*, ed. Raymond E. Brown, Joseph A. Fitzmyer, and Roland E. Murphy (Englewood Cliffs, NJ: Prentice-Hall, 1968). 1:12 (paragraph 25): "For the Semites, 'to know' means to experience in any way. 'Good' and 'evil' are terms of polarity and can signify totality (cf. Nm 24:13), hence a total experience, not necessarily in a moral sense."

18. Kselman, "Genesis," 88.

19. Kselman, "Genesis," 88.

Not only is the tree of knowledge of good and evil absent from the Qur'anic accounts, however, but that godlike knowledge is never mentioned. It is the third function of the biblical trees that is not picked up in the Qur'an's narrative of the fall of Adam and Eve from the Garden of Eden.

Why the differences? One can only speculate, of course. But the differences between the two narratives seem to me to reflect and to illustrate broader differences between the Qur'anic/Islamic view of the relationship between God and humanity and that found in the biblical tradition.

The most salient difference is this: In the Judeo-Christian tradition, God is seen as being somehow related to humanity and humanity as in some sense related to God. This is arguably the case for the Hebrew Bible—in which human beings are "intrinsically theomorphic" and "humanity appears as an earthly extension of God's divine council of deities"—and it is explicitly so in the New Testament.[20] (One need look no further than the *Pater noster*, the "Our Father," taught by Jesus to his disciples as part of the Sermon on the Mount.)[21] As the apostle Paul tells his Athenian audience in Acts 17, humans are the "offspring," the *genos* or "kin," of God.[22] In the Qur'an, however, and in the Islamic tradition generally, humans are regarded as creatures of God, but never as God's children, and God is never described as our Father. Whereas deification might be viewed as the natural destiny of children of deity, there is no obvious reason to expect, as a matter of natural course, that Pinocchio will assume the human nature of

20. The quotations are from an interesting recent paper (unpublished) by David E. Bokovoy, a doctoral student in Hebrew Bible at Brandeis University in Massachusetts, entitled "The Image of God: The Biblical Doctrine of Deification." For a sustained discussion of the evidence, see Daniel C. Peterson, "'Ye are Gods': Psalm 82 and John 10 as Witnesses to the Divine Nature of Humankind," in *The Disciple as Scholar: Essays on Scripture and the Ancient World in Honor of Richard Lloyd Anderson*, ed. Stephen D. Ricks, Donald W. Parry, and Andrew H. Hedges (Provo, UT: Foundation for Ancient Research and Mormon Studies, 2000), 471–594.

21. Matthew 6:9–13.

22. Acts 17:28–29.

his creator, Gepetto. Children grow up to become like their parents; Thomas Edison's light bulb will never become a man.[23]

The biblical story of the Garden of Eden seems to represent Adam as having been placed there as a divine king, responsible, as Near Eastern kings appear, ritually speaking, to have been, for tending the garden. Such gardening was the responsibility of lesser members of the divine council.[24] On the other hand, the Qurʾan never mentions any responsibility on the part of Adam and/or Eve for the maintenance of the garden, thus clearly omitting one of the characteristics, common both to the biblical narrative and to Mesopotamian tradition, that seem to identify the primordial pair as, in some sense, divine.

It will be recalled that, in the Qurʾanic narratives of the fall of Adam and Eve, their fall appears to have been a literal one, from a high place to a lower. In this context, it is worth noticing the extraordinarily interesting twenty-eighth chapter of Ezekiel, which expressly draws upon the Eden story to make its point regarding the king of Tyre:

> The word of the Lord came to me: O mortal, say to the prince of Tyre: Thus said the Lord God:
>
> Because you have been so haughty and have said, "I am a god; I sit enthroned like a god in the heart of the seas," whereas you are not a god but a man, though you deemed your mind equal to a god's. . . .
>
> Assuredly, thus said the Lord God: Because you have deemed your mind equal to a god's,
>
> I swear I will bring against you
> Strangers, the most ruthless of nations. . . .
> They shall bring you down to the Pit;
> In the heart of the sea you shall die

23. There are, of course, a few exceptions or near exceptions to this rule over the long course of Islamic history. Certain extreme Sufis (such as al-Hallaj) appear to have flirted with a kind of human deification, for example. For another such instance, see Daniel C. Peterson, "Cosmogony and the Ten Separated Intellects in the *Rahat al-ʿAql* of Hamid al-Din al-Kirmani" (unpublished PhD diss., University of California at Los Angeles, 1990).

24. For the notion of the god or divine king as sanctuary-gardener, see Widengren, *The King and the Tree of Life*, 15–19. Bokovoy, "The Image of God," also discusses this topic.

The death of the slain.
Will you still say, "I am a god"
Before your slayers,
When you are proved a man, not a god,
At the hands of those who strike you down? . . .

The word of the Lord came to me: O mortal, intone a dirge over the king of Tyre and say to him: Thus said the Lord God:

You were the seal of perfection,
Full of wisdom and flawless in beauty.
You were in Eden, the garden of God;
Every precious stone was your adornment:
Carnelian, chrysolite, and amethyst;
Beryl, lapis lazuli, and jasper;
Sapphire, turquoise, and emerald;
And gold beautifully wrought for you,
Mined for you, prepared the day you were created.
I created you as a cherub
With outstretched shielding wings;
And you resided on God's holy mountain;
You walked among stones of fire.
You were blameless in your ways,
From the day you were created
Until wrongdoing was found in you. . . .
You were filled with lawlessness
And you sinned.
So I have struck you down
From the mountain of God,
And I have destroyed you, O shielding cherub,
From among the stones of fire.
You grew haughty because of your beauty,
You debased your wisdom for the sake of your splendor;
I have cast you to the ground.[25]

25. Ezekiel 28:1–2, 6–9, 11–17 (Jewish Publication Society translation).

Here, quite clearly, we have a literal casting down from a high place, which is identified with "Eden, the garden of God." Its references to a cherub certainly echo the Genesis narrative, as well as, it would seem, does the king of Tyre's apparent grasping after divinity, blurring the distinction between human and god—a blurring whose absence from the Qur᾿an, I have argued, represents the principal theological difference between the biblical and the Qur᾿anic Eden stories.

In this context, it is appropriate to mention the famous tree mentioned in the Qur᾿anic "light verse," as it is called, one of the most beloved passages in the Muslim scriptural book:

> God is the light of the heavens and the earth. The likeness of his light is that of a niche, in which is a lamp, the lamp enclosed in a glass, the glass as if it were a brilliant star lit from a blessed olive tree neither of the east nor of the west, whose oil would almost shine forth even if fire never touched it. Light upon light. God guides to his light whomever he wills.[26]

In the first-century-AD *Life of Adam and Eve*, the tree of life is an olive tree.[27] Moreover, one of the elements, according to Widengren, of the standard image of the tree of life is that its oil is used for anointings. One might argue, accordingly, that the Qur᾿an's "blessed olive tree" is yet another instance of the tree of life.

Interestingly, in the description of Tyre given by the Greek poet Nonnus of Panopolis in his fifth-century *Dionysiaca*, there is a reference to a "double rock" in the ocean, called the "ambrosiac one." (The Greek *ambrotos*, from which our word *ambrosia* derives, means "immortal.") In the center of that rock (*mesomphalon*)—that is, in the midst of the "omphalos," the navel, with all of the associations of that concept with temples, sanctuaries, and creation, and thus perhaps also to be described as "neither of the east nor of the west"—there is said to be an olive tree that automatically emits fire (*automaton pur*),

26. Qur᾿an 24:35.

27. *Life of Adam and Eve*, 36:2; 40ff. Compare *2 Enoch* 8:5 (A), in which an olive tree is *near* the tree of life, flowing with oil continuously.

leaving it in a state of perpetual flame.[28]

However, it is not necessarily to this tree that another passage of the Qurʾan refers:

Fig. 51. *Sidra* tree fruit, Muscat, Oman.

> 24. Do you not see how God coins a likeness, a goodly word like a goodly tree, whose root is firmly fixed and whose branches reach into the sky?
>
> 25. It brings forth its fruit all the time by the leave of its Lord, and God coins likenesses for the people so that perhaps they might remember.
>
> 26. And the likeness of an evil word is that of an evil tree, uprooted from the surface of the earth. It has no stability.[29]

Here we do indeed have two trees, but the second certainly does not appear to be the tree of knowledge of good and evil.[30]

One might assume that this is all purely metaphorical. But, in fact, the righteous in paradise are depicted, Qurʾanically, as reposing among gardens and springs, surrounded by lotus and other heavily laden trees, where they partake of every kind of fruit; and there seems no reason not to take this as intended entirely literally.[31] By contrast, however, the unrighteous are condemned to hellish punishments, including an "accursed tree."[32]

To the damned in hell, the Qurʾan says:

---

28. Nonnus, *Dionysiaca*, xl: 467ff. Philostratos also identifies this tree as an olive tree. My attention was called to this by Wensinck, "Tree and Bird."

29. Qurʾan 14:24–26. It's difficult, in this context, not to think of the biblical Psalm 1.

30. Wensinck, "Tree and Bird," 11–12, however, tries to link the biblical tree of knowledge with death. I am not persuaded. For another instance of two opposed trees, see Lechler, "Tree of Life," 373.

31. See, for example, Qurʾan 44:51–57; 56:12–38.

32. The phrase "accursed tree" (*al-shajara al-malʿuna*) occurs at Qurʾan 17:60 and plainly refers to the "tree of Zaqqum."

52. You will eat of the tree of Zaqqum,
53. Filling your bellies from it.
54. And you will drink scalding water on top of that.
55. Truly, you will drink greedily.[33]

And in another passage:

43. Truly, the tree of Zaqqum
44. Will be the food of the sinful,
45. Like molten brass boiling in their bellies,
46. Like the boiling of scalding water.[34]

And, finally, in yet another:

63. We have truly made it a trial for the wrong-doers.
64. Truly, it is a tree that emerges at the root of hell.
65. Its shoots are like the heads of devils.
66. Truly, they will eat of it and fill their bellies from it.
67. Then, truly, on top of that, they will have a contaminated mixture of scalding water.[35]

The *zaqqum* is, in fact, a real tree (see fig. 52), known both in and beyond the Arabian Peninsula. It bears an intensely bitter almondlike fruit, and it has thorns up to eight centimeters long.

But let's accentuate the positive rather than dwelling upon the negative. Let's return to paradise.

I am interested, now, in the notion that the paradise of our primordial parents was conceived as being in an elevated position, in order to argue that, according to this view, after death and even occasionally during mortal life, the righteous were thought to reascend to that paradise and to the presence of God. I will be unable to develop this idea here, but I would nonetheless like to mention the fact that the sacred tree is very commonly associated with a sanctuary and,

33. Qurʾan 56:52–55.
34. Qurʾan 44:43–46.
35. Qurʾan 37:63–67.

Fig. 52. The *Zaqqum* tree has intensely bitter almondlike fruit. According to the Qurʾan, the damned souls in hell will eat of this "accursed tree," setting their bellies to boil.

likewise, with the divine throne.[36] We are, in other words, dealing not only with the paradisiacal garden but also with its ritual representation. And the two are not always easily distinguished.

"Many times," reports the famous Dutch comparative Semitist A. J. Wensinck, "we find paradise . . . situated on a high mountain or the highest mountain in the East."[37] "An Altaic folk song relates of the tree of life: 'In the center of the earth there is an iron mountain and on this iron mountain a white seven-branched birch.'"[38] Widengren points out that the Mesopotamian tree of life stood "at the confluence of the rivers" and that such a tree was depicted in early and medieval Christian art on a hill from the foot of which flow the rivers of paradise.[39] It is difficult not to think, in this context, not only of the paradisiacal trees and rivers of Genesis but of the recurrent Qurʾanic description of the paradise in the world to come as "a garden under which rivers flow" (*al-janna tahtaha al-anhar*).[40] As a matter of fact, the tree of life is typically connected in

36. On this topic, see, among others, Wensinck, "Tree and Bird," 33; Widengren, "The King and the Tree of Life," 9, 10, 59; and Donald W. Parry, "The Garden of Eden: Sacred Space, Sanctuary, Temple of God," *Explorations: A Journal for Adventurous Thought* 5/4 (1987): 83–107.

37. Wensinck, "Tree and Bird," 5 (compare p. 41); see Widengren, "The King and the Tree of Life," 11, 44 n. 2.

38. Lechler, "Tree of Life," 380. Compare the seven-branched candelabra in the Hebrew tabernacle.

39. Widengren, *Religionsphänomenologie*, 331–32, 384.

40. Recurrrent throughout the Qurʾan.

ancient Mesopotamia and among the western Semites with water, and specifically with what might be called "the Water of Life."[41] This probably lies behind the comparison made in the First Psalm:

> Happy is the man who has not followed the counsel
> of the wicked,
> or taken the path of sinners,
> or joined the company of the insolent;
> rather, the teaching of the Lord is his delight,
> and he studies that teaching day and night.
> He is like a tree planted beside streams of water,
> which yields its fruit in season,
> whose foliage never fades,
> and whatever it produces thrives.[42]

Even more apropos, however, is the heavenly Jerusalem described in Revelation 22:

> Then the angel showed me the river of life, rising from the throne of God and of the Lamb and flowing crystal-clear. Down the middle of the city street, on either bank of the river were the trees of life, which bear twelve crops of fruit in a year, one in each month, and the leaves of which are the cure for the nations.[43]

The Qurʾan makes nothing of the rivers of Eden, but it repeatedly mentions the rivers of the garden of the next life. Moreover, it knows of a tree that it calls the "lotus tree" or "lote-tree of the uttermost boundary," the *sidrat al-muntaha*. Speaking of Muhammad, it asks,

> Will you dispute with him concerning what he saw?
> For he saw him [Gabriel or, perhaps, God] at a
> second descent,

41. Lechler, "Tree of Life," 371; and Widengren, "The King and the Tree of Life," 5, 19, 36, 42, 59.

42. Psalm 1:1–3 (Jewish Publication Society translation).

43. Revelation 22:1–2 (New Jerusalem Bible).

Fig. 53. *Sidra* tree, Wadi Bani Awf, Oman. The *sidra* is the earthly counterpart of the Qurʾanic "lote-tree of the uttermost boundary" in the sixth or seventh heaven.

> At the lote-tree of the uttermost boundary.
> Near it is the garden of abode. . . .
> Truly, he saw the greatest of the signs of his Lord.[44]

There is a real *sidra* tree on earth, the *Ziziphus jujuba*, a kind of wild plum that grows in Arabia and India (see fig. 53). It occupies a special place among some Muslims, who customarily throw its leaves into the water that they use to cleanse a corpse during a burial ceremony.[45]

But this is clearly not that tree. For the Qurʾan's reference to what Muhammad saw appears to refer—certainly it is traditionally *taken* to refer—to the Prophet's *miʿraj*, or ascent to heaven, during which he saw "the Heavens and the Lote Tree, the Divine Throne and [the] Divine Court."[46] This *sidra* tree is not an earthly plant. Certain accounts of

---

44. Qurʾan 53:12–15, 18.

45. Lechler, "Tree of Life," 369.

46. Hajjah Amina Adil, *Muhammad, the Messenger of Islam: His Life and Prophecy* (Washington, DC: Islamic Supreme Council of America, 2002), 155.

Fig. 54. In his night journey, Muhammad traveled to the *sidrat al-muntaha*, or "lote-tree of the uttermost boundary," the farthest one can travel in his approach to Allah. See plate 14.

the ascension place it in the sixth heaven, while others put it in the seventh.

According to some of the classical commentators, "It is called 'Sidratul Muntaha' (the lotus tree of the extreme limit) because it is the end of all that is knowable, and nobody can know what is beyond it." (In a sense, then, the *sidra* represents the extremity of possible knowledge and thus may be related to the biblical tree of knowledge of good and evil.) Certain other commentators have explained that "whoever comes from above, arrives here and cannot pass on further down. Whoever comes from below, reaches this point and cannot ascend further. Therefore it is called by this name." Yet others suggest that "the world of spirits ends at this point, therefore it is called the Lote tree of the extreme limit."[47]

The late George Lechler maintained that the ancient Canaanite tree symbolism of the asherah appears on Muslim prayer rugs and that "the Sidra in the niche [of the mosque indicating the direction of prayer] reminded the praying man of the desired goal in heaven."[48]

I suspect that he is right. Consistent with the principle that eschatology (or "last things") often recapitulates protology (or "first things"), I think we may, in the lotus tree of the boundary, be seeing the Edenic

47. The quotations in this paragraph are from Adil, *Muhammad*, 219.

48. Lechler, "Tree of Life," 396. On the asherah, see Peterson, "Nephi and His Asherah: A Note on 1 Nephi 11:8–23."

Fig. 55. Mounted on his noble steed Buraq, Muhammad ascends to paradise. The glorious being in the upper left is the angel Gabriel. See plate 15.

tree of life yet again. Muhammad ascended to the garden from which Adam and Eve fell. It is the same garden to which the righteous may aspire. In the words of T. S. Eliot's *Four Quartets*, we can hope that

> We shall not cease from exploration
> And the end of all our exploring
> Will be to arrive where we started
> And know the place for the first time.[49]

Daniel C. Peterson earned a PhD in Near Eastern languages and cultures from the University of California at Los Angeles. He is a professor of Islamic studies and Arabic at Brigham Young University, where he also serves as editor in chief of the Middle Eastern Texts Initiative.

49. T. S. Eliot, "Little Gidding," *Four Quartets*, lines 239–42.

The Tree of Life in Asian Art, Religion, and Folklore: A Sampling of the Evidence

John M. Lundquist

The tree of life motif in Asian art has been studied to an exhaustive extent over the past 150 years or more. The vast literature that has accumulated on this topic, in all of its variety and subcategories, has not been superseded but has rather retained its value, and it rewards repeated returns to its riches.[1]

In all world religion and art where it appears, this motif relates to and derives from cosmology or cosmogony, that is, the views of ancient peoples about the nature and origins of the world. Thus the tree of life is culturally conditioned and culturally specific. It is *cosmic* in that it relates to the cosmos, specifically the world as we know it, as it came into being at the time of creation. The tree of life possesses a kind of "cosmic botanical logic" in that it grows up "naturally" as a central part of the processes by which the world came into being. And since the primary place where we can observe this cosmological process in antiquity is the temple—which incorporates all aspects of the

1. Chief among the works on this topic are James Fergusson, *Tree and Serpent Worship; or, Illustrations of Mythology and Art in India in the First and Fourth Centuries after Christ, from the Sculptures of the Buddhist Topes at Sanchi and Amravati* (Delhi: Oriental, 1971); Uno Holmberg, *Der Baum des Lebens* (Helsinski: Suomalainen tiedeakatemla, 1922); and Edric A. S. Butterworth, *The Tree at the Navel of the Earth* (Berlin: Walter de Gruyter, 1970). In preparing this paper I have benefited enormously from Frederik D. K. Bosch, *The Golden Germ: An Introduction to Indian Symbolism* (The Hague: Mouton, 1960); and from Ananda K. Coomaraswamy, *Elements of Buddhist Iconography*, 3rd ed. (New Delhi: Munshiram Manoharlal, 1979). Also of great value are several works by Mircea Eliade, primarily *Patterns in Comparative Religion*, trans. Rosemary Sheed (New York: World, 1958); and *Shamanism: Archaic Techniques of Ecstasy*, trans. Willard R. Trask (Princeton, NJ: Princeton University Press, 1964).

cosmology into its architecture, ritual, and symbolism—the tree of life motif becomes a central feature of what I refer to as "temple ideology" or, less broadly, "temple symbolism" or "temple typology."

The Tree and Temple Ideology

Regarding the primordial creative process and how it is assimilated into temple typology, I earlier concluded the following: "[1] The temple is the architectural embodiment of the cosmic mountain. . . . [2] The cosmic mountain represents the primordial hillock, the place which first emerged from the waters that covered the earth during the creative process. In Egypt, for example, all temples are seen as representing [in their holy of holies] the primeval hillock. . . . [3] The temple is often associated with the waters of life which flow forth from a spring within the building itself—or rather the temple is viewed as incorporating within itself or as having been built upon such a spring. The reason such springs exist in temples is that they are perceived as the primeval waters of creation, Nun in Egypt, Abzu in Mesopotamia. The temple is thus founded on and stands in contact with the primeval waters."[2] I later added to this list "The temple is associated with the

2. I have published this "temple typology" in a number of different articles, each with a somewhat expanded and revised list: John M. Lundquist, "What Is a Temple? A Preliminary Typology," in *The Quest for the Kingdom of God: Studies in Honor of George E. Mendenhall*, ed. H. B. Huffmon, F. A. Spina, and A. R. W. Green (Winona Lake, IN: Eisenbrauns, 1983), 205–19; "The Legitimizing Role of the Temple in the Origin of the State," in *Society of Biblical Literature 1982 Seminar Papers*, ed. Kent H. Richards (Chico, CA: Scholars Press, 1982), 271–97; "The Common Temple Ideology of the Ancient Near East," in *The Temple in Antiquity: Ancient Records and Modern Perspectives*, ed. Truman G. Madsen (Provo, UT: BYU Religious Studies Center, 1984), 53–76; and "New Light on the Temple Ideology," *East and West* 50/1–4 (December 2000): 9–42. These articles and the "temple typology" are being referenced in a wide range of scholarly disciplines as a means of better understanding the theory of the temple. See, for example, Robert Karl Gnuse, *Dreams and Dream Reports in the Writings of Josephus: A Tradition-Historical Analysis* (Leiden: Brill, 1996), 48 (referring to my study "What Is a Temple?"); John W. O'Malley et al., eds., *The Jesuits: Cultures, Sciences and the Arts, 1540–1773* (Toronto: University of Toronto Press, 1999), 520 (referring to my book *The Temple: Meeting Place of Heaven and Earth* [London: Thames and Hudson, 1993]); Gregory Stevenson, *Power and Place: Temple and Identity in the Book of Revelation* (Berlin: Walter de Gruyter, 2001), 48 (referring to my study "Common Temple Ideology"); Alan R. Kerr, *The Temple of Jesus' Body: The Temple Theme in the Gospel of John* (London: Sheffield Academic Press, 2002),

tree of life"[3] and went on to combine all these features (cosmic mountain, primordial hillock, waters of life, tree of life) into what I refer to as "'the primordial landscape,' which we can expect to see reproduced architecturally and ritually in ancient Near Eastern [and, I would now add, Asian] temple traditions."[4]

Since the tree of life emerges from the primal creative waters, its fruit possesses life-giving qualities. The clearest expression we have of this in the scriptures is found in the book of Ezekiel, in the description of the millennial temple. Here all the aforementioned features come together:

> Then he [that is, the man who was guiding Ezekiel in his celestial visions on a high mountain] brought me back to the door of the temple; and behold, water was issuing from below the threshold of the temple toward the east. . . . And on the banks, on both sides of the river, there will grow all kinds of trees for food.

35 (referring to my study "What Is a Temple?"); Jonathan Klawans, *Purity, Sacrifice, and the Temple: Symbolism and Supersessionism in the Study of Ancient Judaism* (New York: Oxford University Press, 2006), 280 (referring to my studies "Common Temple Ideology" and "What Is a Temple?"); William Horbury, W. D. Davies, and John Sturdy, eds., *The Cambridge History of Judaism*, vol. 3, *The Early Roman Period* (Cambridge: Cambridge University Press, 2006), 300 (referring to my study "What Is a Temple?"); Brannon Wheeler, *Mecca and Eden: Ritual, Relics, and Territory in Islam* (Chicago: University of Chicago Press, 2006), 155 (referring to my study "Common Temple Ideology"); Steven W. Holloway, "What Ship Goes There: The Flood Narratives in the Gilgamesh Epic and Genesis Considered in Light of Ancient Near Eastern Temple Typology," *Zeitschrift für die Alttestamentliche Wissenschaft* 103/3 (1991): 328–55 (referring to my study "What Is a Temple?"); Raymond C. Van Leeuwen, "Cosmos, Temple, House: Building and Wisdom in Mesopotamia and Israel," in *Wisdom Literature in Mesopotamia and Israel*, ed. Richard J. Clifford (Atlanta: Society of Biblical Literature, 2007), 76 (referring to my study "What Is a Temple?"); Rachel Bowditch, "Temple of Tears: Revitalizing and Inventing Ritual in the Burning Man Community in Black Rock Desert, Nevada," *Journal of Religion and Theatre* 6/2 (Fall 2007): 140–54 (referring to my book *The Temple: Meeting Place of Heaven and Earth*), http://www.rtjournal.org/vol_6/no_2/bowditch.html (accessed August 18, 2010); and Winfried Vogel, *The Cultic Motif in the Book of Daniel* (New York: Peter Lang Publishing, 2010), 21 (referring to my studies *The Temple: Meeting Place of Heaven and Earth*, "What Is a Temple?" and *Studies on the Temple in the Ancient Near East* [PhD diss., University of Michigan, 1983]).

3. Lundquist, "Legitimizing Role of the Temple," 274.

4. Lundquist, "Legitimizing Role of the Temple," 274.

> Their leaves will not wither nor their fruit fail, but they will bear fresh fruit every month, because the water for them flows from the sanctuary. Their fruit will be for food, and their leaves for healing. (Ezekiel 47:1, 12 Revised Standard Version)

The tree of life is therefore an integral feature of the temple ideology, and it is there we can find it in its most developed form.

> The tree, like the water, is an integral part of the "primordial landscape," and as such plays a large role in the mythology and ritual of ancient Near Eastern temple symbolism. It is important to note that, in Mesopotamia at least, we are not dealing with "a specific botanical species nor . . . a single mythic or cultic entity." Many different species or parts of trees are mentioned in ancient Near Eastern texts within the context of what we may call the "sacred tree," or "tree of life." Generally speaking, the tree of life grows up out of the primordial waters of the abyss, and thus there is an intimate mythological and cultic connection between the tree and the waters of life. A characteristic expression of this relationship appears in the inscriptions of Gudea of Lagash, in Cylinder A, where the temple that he is building is compared to the *kiškanu* [a tree of unknown botanical derivation] of the abyss, whose top was raised over the lands. Another famous Sumerian incantation text states:
>
> In Eridu in a pure place the dark *kiškanu* grows;
> Its aspect is like lapis lazuli branching out from the *apsu*.
> In the place where Ea holds sway, in Eridu full of abundance
> His abode being in the Underworld,
> His chamber a recess of the goddess Engur
> In his pure house is a grove, shadow-extending, into whose midst no man has entered;
> There are Šamaš and Tammuz.[5]

5. Lundquist, "Common Temple Ideology," 67–68. Ellipsis and brackets in original.

It has been noted that the trees referred to in these ancient inscriptions were often artificial trees. Thus a distinction should be made between actual species of trees that grow in nature—such as the date palm, the birch, the fig tree, and the banyan, all of which figure as trees of life—and artificial trees of life, such as those depicted in Neo-Assyrian temple reliefs, where the king and a deity stand on either side of the sacred tree, watering it with the water of life.

> There is abundant evidence that ancient Near Eastern temples were conceived as fertile, green, well-watered paradises. . . . The source of this fertility was the sweet water of the abyss, and it is natural that a tree that has the power to bestow life would be seen as growing up out of the waters. There is extensive evidence in the inscriptions of Gudea [of Neo-Sumerian Lagash] and elsewhere that gardens were grown in the temple vicinity. One inscription calls a temple "the House of the Plant of Life."[6]

In this paper I will focus on five features of the tree of life in Asian art that seem most important to its role in ancient cosmology and in subsequent temple ritual, symbolism, and architecture. These five features are as follows: (1) The tree of life is cosmic; that is, it relates to ancient ideas of the center of the world, of the primary world or cosmic zones (usually three—the earth, the underworld, and heaven—but as many as nine or twelve), and forms the central world pillar uniting these zones. (2) The tree of life is a source of revelatory wisdom, of revelation from the divine sphere relating to knowledge of the future or to instructions to the people as to how they should live their lives. (3) The tree of life, in its role as the central pillar or axis of the three cosmic zones, provides the primary passageway into both the underworld and into heaven. (4) The tree of life is the locus, the place of initiation into the cosmic mysteries, and is thus the entryway to this knowledge. (5) The tree of life provides life-giving sustenance, health, and immortality through its fruit and leaves. I will first

6. Lundquist, "Common Temple Ideology," 68.

draw primarily on the evidence from central Asian shamanism, as presented by Eliade, to explicate these points. Then I will turn to the Indian religious traditions (primarily Hinduism and Buddhism) and discuss with the help of illustrations a number of Indian temples and other Asian works of art. In so doing I will attempt to place the tree of life in its ancient ritual and mythological setting.

The Tree in Central Asian Shamanism

"The Tree connects the three cosmic regions,"[7] Eliade observes. Furthermore, "it is, for example, clear that the birch symbolizes the Cosmic Tree or the Axis of the World, and that it is therefore conceived as occupying the Center of the World."[8] The branches of the tree reach into heaven while the roots sink into the underworld. "The 'microcosmic landscape'[9] gradually became reduced in time to but one of its constituents [the other two being primeval stone and the waters of life], to the most important: the tree or sacred pillar. The tree came to express the cosmos fully in itself."[10] This tree stands for the continual regeneration of cosmic life, of "absolute reality" and of immortal life. The Cosmic Tree is the "very reservoir of life and the master of destinies."[11]

In the shamanic traditions of central Asia, the tree of life is the locus of revelation. The shaman ascends the tree to enter into heaven to converse with the gods and returns to share the messages with the community. In a famous account published by Eliade, the complete

---

7. Eliade, *Shamanism*, 270. For more recent studies of shamanism, see Neil Price, ed., *The Archaeology of Shamanism* (London: Routledge, 2001), particularly the study therein by Peter Jordan, "The Materiality of Shamanism as a 'World-View,'" 87–104. On Eliade's positive influence on the study of shamanism, see pp. 5, 65, 124, 125, 129, 202 in the latter source as well as Nora K. Chadwick and Victor Zhirmunsky, *Oral Epics of Central Asia* (Cambridge: Cambridge University Press, 1969), 234–67. Eliade's work resonates over a wide range of disciplines, including architecture, as seen in C. B. Williams, "Dwelling at the Centre of the World," in *Sacred Architecture in the Traditions of India, China, Judaism and Islam*, ed. Emily Lyle (Edinburgh: Edinburgh University Press, 1992), 111–32.

8. Eliade, *Shamanism*, 120.

9. This is Eliade's term for what I call the "primordial landscape."

10. Eliade, *Patterns in Comparative Religion*, 271.

11. Eliade, *Shamanism*, 271.

process by which an Altaic shaman is prepared for his divine calling, ascends to heaven, receives messages, and returns is set out. The key method by which he ascends to the heavens is a birch tree growing inside the shaman's yurt (tent) as the center post, the *axis mundi*. The tree is stripped of its lower branches, and nine steps are notched into the trunk. The key instrument of the shaman is his drum, the hypnotic beating of which sends him into a trance. The shaman's drum is made from the wood of the birch tree, the shamanic tree of life. The birch tree standing at the center of his yurt is the World Tree, the Cosmic Tree, the site and origin of divine wisdom, the means of ascent into the heavens. The drum must be made from this same wood so that it partakes of the divine power of the tree. "By the fact that the shell of his drum is derived from the actual wood of the Cosmic Tree, the shaman, through his drumming, is magically projected into the vicinity of the Tree; he is projected to the 'Center of the World,' and thus can ascend to the sky."[12]

The shaman beats his drum vigorously and rhythmically, convulsing his body and reaching a state of exaltation, at which time he is ready for the ascent. He steps onto the first notch on the birch tree and "makes motions to indicate that he is mounting into the sky."[13] He gradually climbs up the tree via the notches, reaching the third heaven, where he mounts a goose for the continued ascent. As he ascends the tree, he reaches ever-higher celestial regions—the fifth, the sixth, the ninth, the twelfth heaven. In the fifth heaven he communicates with the Supreme Creator, "who reveals several secrets of the future to him."[14] Finally, he reaches the highest heaven and there is instructed by the highest divinity, Bai Ulgan. The shaman learns important information regarding the weather and the harvest and what sacrifices are expected; he also learns whether his own sacrifice has been accepted. Upon his return, he "collapses, exhausted." An official "approaches and takes the drum and stick from his hands. The

12. Eliade, *Shamanism*, 169; emphasis removed.

13. Mircea Eliade, *Essential Sacred Writings from around the World* (San Francisco: HarperSanFrancisco, 1967), 214.

14. Eliade, *Essential Sacred Writings*, 215.

shaman remains motionless and dumb. After a time he rubs his eyes, appears to wake from a deep sleep, and greets those present as if after a long absence."[15]

Another lengthy shamanic text republished by Eliade gives us insight into the role of the tree of life in the initiation of the novice shaman. It deals with a dream of initiation of a Samoyed shaman. The dream, of course, plays an enormous role in initiation processes all over the world. The shaman was deathly ill over a period of three days, to the point that he was almost buried. It was at this time that he experienced the dream, his calling as a shaman, and his initiation. In his dream, he was led by an ermine and a mouse through a series of ordeals and meetings with divine beings, beginning in the underworld. At one point he was led to an island, in the middle of which was a birch tree, the tree of the Lord of the Earth. Nine herbs grew near it, "the ancestors of all the plants on Earth." Voices told him that he would be given a drum from the wood of this tree. The drum from the branch of the tree of life is the symbol of his calling. Later, the ermine and the mouse "led him to a high, rounded mountain. He saw an opening before him and entered a bright cave, covered with mirrors, in the middle of which there was something like a fire."

Finally, he was brought to a desert with a distant mountain. Upon reaching it, he was chopped into pieces by a blacksmith, put into a cauldron, and boiled for three years. The initiate's head was forged on the best of three anvils, reserved for the best shamans. When the body and flesh were reunited, the blacksmith reformed the eyes so that the shaman could "not see with his bodily eyes but with these mystical eyes." His ears were reformed so that he could understand the language of plants. Finally, he "found himself on the summit of a mountain, and finally he woke in the yurt, among the family. Now he can sing and shamanize indefinitely, without ever growing tired."[16]

15. Eliade, *Essential Sacred Writings*, 216.
16. Eliade, *Essential Sacred Writings*, 434–37.

In these accounts we see that the tree of life does not stand alone, so to speak, but that the themes of mountain, cave, various world regions, descent into the underworld and ascent into the celestial regions, and many other associated symbols play major roles, giving us a total picture of the milieu in which these religious ideas flourished.

The tree of life is a source of life, of immortality, of life-giving plants and fruits; in fact, even its leaves are life-giving, as we saw in the passage from Ezekiel.

> Both the Tree of Life and the mountain are situated at the navel of the earth, a place which in many legends flows with mead or honey. The liquid sometimes flows from the tree itself; from the [Norse] ash Yggdrasil trickles honeydew, while from the Indian Jambu tree springs a yellow sap. In Brahman tradition the stream which flows around Mount Meru comes from the fruits of the Jambu tree. "These fruits are as big as the body of an elephant, and when they fall, they burst and from the juice arises the stream Jambunādi. Those who drink of it do not age, always retain the full power of their senses, do not sweat or have an unpleasant smell, and remain pure of heart. The Jambunādi flows round Meru and returns to the foot of the Jambu tree again."[17]
>
> Sometimes the sap is white and milk-like, but the liquid is found as often in the spring beneath the tree as in the tree itself. Sometimes it takes the form of a lake of milk. The Yakuts say it surrounds the throne of the god of heaven, and Altai tradition places it in the third heaven, where Paradise lies. In some stories from Central Asia the lake of milk is on a heaven-high mountain. A mighty Khan promised his daughter to the man who could get him a feather from the wing of the eagle Garuda. An expedition set out. A youth who had joined the hunting party of heroes asked where the bird

17. Butterworth, *Tree at the Navel of the Earth*, 7.

> dwelt. As the party reached the great mountain, they noticed that the sky above them had begun to turn white. The youth asked what lay behind the sky and was told that the Lake of Milk was there. "But what," he then asked, "is the dark patch in the middle?" "That," they answered, "is the wood in which the bird dwells." In this story the Lake of Milk lies on a heaven-high hill, which the heroes climb. The wood in the middle of the lake can hardly be other than the World Tree and Tree of Life, in the top of which, according to other legends, this great bird is to be found.[18]

In summarizing the survey of this theme as presented thus far in his book, Butterworth noted: "The beginning of all life and the power to regenerate is found in the Tree of Life or at its root; there lives a goddess who provides the life-giving drink, whether milk from her heavy breasts, or the honey-like sap of the Tree, the juice of its fruit or the water that gushes forth from beneath its roots or flows past it as a river, or again milk that lies at its foot as a lake, or the yet more mysterious nectar and ambrosia (*amṛta*) and *soma*."[19]

The tree can yield the richness and life-giving force of its fruit, but it can also destroy if it is misused. There is an Indian tale about a group of merchants who were wandering in a barren, waterless region when they suddenly came upon a lush banyan tree. The tree was dripping water from its eastern side, so they cut off the eastern branches and drank from and bathed in the water. They cut off the southern branches, which yielded all kinds of food. Cutting off the western branches caused beautifully clothed women to emerge and to entertain the merchants. The northern branches gave up fabulous jewels and rich silk and brocade garments and carpets. Finally, in their greed the merchants cut down the tree itself, after which the Naga king—that is, the cobra who rules the kingdom of the Nagas underneath the waters—destroyed the merchants.[20]

18. Butterworth, *Tree at the Navel of the Earth*, 11.
19. Butterworth, *Tree at the Navel of the Earth*, 11.
20. Butterworth, *Tree at the Navel of the Earth*, 79–80.

The Tree in Hindu and Buddhist Traditions

The central cosmic tradition of the areas in South and Southeast Asia under the influence of Hinduism is the mythic Mount Meru, the mountain and continent chain at the center of the earth. "According to Brahmanic doctrine, the world consists of a circular central continent, Jambūdvīpa, surrounded by seven annular oceans and seven annular continents. Beyond the last of the seven oceans the world is closed by an enormous mountain range. In the center of Jambūdvīpa, and thus in the center of the world, rises Mount Meru, the cosmic mountain around which sun, moon, and stars revolve. On its summit lies the city of the gods surrounded by the abodes of the eight Lokapālas or guardian gods of the world."[21]

In Buddhism this conception is somewhat different: Mount Meru stands at the center of the system and is surrounded by seven mountain ranges and seven ringlike seas. Beyond these mountain ranges and seas lies the ocean, in which stand four continents, one each at the four cardinal directions. The southernmost of these is Jambūdvīpa, the world in which we live.[22] Temples in South and Southeast Asia are assimilated to Mount Meru.[23] In the center of Mount Meru stands the World Tree, the tree of life. Thus Mount Meru, with the tree of life standing at its center, constitutes "the axis of the universe, representing the higher worlds that spread one above the other in innumerable planes beyond the summit of the sacred Meru like the branches of a gigantic tree."[24] "The spire of the *dāgoba*, *pagoda*, and *chorten* [the typical Buddhist temple structures] . . . represents this Tree of Life in its ideal form of the heavenly tree whose branches are the higher worlds spreading one above the other in innumerable planes beyond the summit of Mount Meru, the axis of the universe."[25]

21. Robert Heine-Geldern, "Conceptions of State and Kingship in Southeast Asia," *Far Eastern Quarterly* 2 (1942): 16–17.

22. Heine-Geldern, "Conceptions of State and Kingship," 17; and I. W. Mabbett, "The Symbolism of Mount Meru," *History of Religions* 23 (1983): 66–67.

23. Bosch, *Golden Germ*, 176.

24. Lama Anagarika Govinda, *Psycho-cosmic Symbolism of the Buddhist Stupa* (Berkeley, CA: Dharma, 1976), 14–15, 31–32.

25. Govinda, *Psycho-cosmic Symbolism*, 82–83; see Bosch, *Golden Germ*, 167–76.

Fig. 56. Mount Meru Temple banner.

Asian temples represent this concept in their architecture, symbolism, and ritual. As I have written elsewhere, "The temple is a visual representation of all the symbolism of the mountain, and thus the architecture reflects this symbolism in a thoroughgoing and repetitive way (for example, the pagoda structures of Indian, Chinese, Southeast Asian, and Japanese temple architecture, with the multi-level hipped roofs present on every building and gateway in the complex, or the *Prasada* of the Hindu temple), and is a constant visual reminder that the visitor/initiate is engaged on a journey up a mountain, to heaven."[26]

We now turn to Asian artwork and architecture to see how the tree of life functions in that culture. An image of the Mount Meru Temple banner was published some years ago by Alex Wayman[27] (see fig. 56). The banner shows the pyramidal Mount Meru with a base of five square platforms. Around the base are arrayed the continents, all resting in an ocean of milk. Two constellations are shown: Ursa Major on the left, associated with the sun; and the Pleiades on the right, associated with the moon. A three-tiered palace of Chinese design similar to the architectural type mentioned previously rises above Mount Meru, above the clouds, the palace of the primeval Buddhist deity,

26. Lundquist, *Temple: Meeting Place of Heaven and Earth*, 8.

27. Alex Wayman, *The Buddhist Tantras: Light on Indo-Tibetan Esotericism* (New York: Samuel Weise, 1973), 104–9; see John M. Lundquist, "Borobudur: The Top Plan and the Upper Terraces," *East and West* 45 (1995): 289–93.

the *Ādibuddha,* from whom "the multi-thousandfold emanations of primordial energy and . . . phenomena" derive.[28]

Wish-granting trees, along with the classic Buddhist symbols, surround Mount Meru and the heavenly palace. Protruding from the top of the heavenly palace is a tiny *stupa*, the classic form that Buddhist temple architecture assumes. Here the Indo-Tibetan-style *stupa* is functioning as the spire of the Chinese-style temple under it. The spire here represents the honorific umbrella or sunshade (*chattra* in Sanskrit). The sunshade is the uppermost extension of the Cosmic Tree, the pinnacle of the world mountain.[29] It arises from a lotus blossom, the mysterious water flower of the Indian tradition that symbolizes the very origins of life itself and functions as a species of the tree of life in the Indian tradition.[30]

The Temple of Borobudur

Perhaps the most famous temple in the world, Borobudur, on the island of Java (AD 700–800), is the most nearly perfect representation of the temple as the world mountain, Mount Meru (see fig. 57, also pl. 8).[31] As I wrote in my 1995 article on Borobudur:

Fig. 57. Borobudur, Java, Indonesia, eighth century AD. See plate 8.

> Borobudur is a magnificent temple of the Tantric (esoteric) Diamond Realm Mandala (*Vajradhatu*) type. . . . The temple represents the sacred mountain of the Hindu-Buddhist tradition, Mt. Meru, and the ascent of the mountain/temple

28. Blanche Christine Olschak and Geshe Thupten Wangyal, *Mystic Art of Ancient Tibet* (Boston: Shambhala Publications, 1973), 126. See Wayman, *Buddhist Tantras*, 53; Govinda, *Psycho-cosmic Symbolism*, 70; and Lundquist, *Temple: Meeting Place of Heaven and Earth*, 18.

29. Bosch, *Golden Germ*, 161, 169–71.

30. Bosch, *Golden Germ*, 81–83.

31. Lundquist, *Temple: Meeting Place of Heaven and Earth*, 40–41.

in a circumambulating fashion (*pradaksina*) takes the initiate through an elaborate process of learning the sacred doctrines by means of the reliefs carved into the square galleries of the first four levels. There are four hundred thirty-two Buddhas arranged along the four sides of the lower balustrades, giving the appearance, from a distance, of *Siddhas* meditating deep within caves on the sides of the sacred mountain. As the initiate would reach the platform on which the elliptical and circular levels were raised, he would have reached the summit of Mt. Meru, having left the world of appearances of the lower, gallery levels. His ultimate goal was the summit of Meru, represented at Borobudur by the central *stupa*, the summit of Mt. Meru and thus the center of the universe, within which it is thought that a statue of the primordial Ādibuddha was once placed. That level, formlessness and emptiness, must be reached, not all at once or directly by circumambulating three "circular" galleries, but must consist in a gradual, transitional process of circumambulation and instruction. The gradualness and transitional nature of the ritual is reflected in the gradualness of the architecture: square, with insets and projections (the shape of the lower terraces), elliptical (the first two upper terraces), and circular.[32]

The Temple of Sanchi

We come now to one of the greatest and earliest Buddhist temples: the Temple of Sanchi. Located in central India near Bhopal, this temple was built in several phases beginning in the reign of the third king of the Mauryan Dynasty, Ashoka (273–232 BC), and spanning the middle of the third century BC to the first century AD (see fig. 58).[33] Sanchi shows us the Buddhist *stupa* temple in its classic and well-developed form, with the square foundation, the hemispheric cupola (or dome,

32. Lundquist, "Borobudur," 288.

33. Sir John Marshall and Alfred Foucher, *The Monuments of Sanchi* (London: Probsthain, 1940), vol. 2, plate 6.

Fig. 58. Great Stupa of Sanchi, Central India, 3rd century BC.

called *anda* in Sanskrit and representing the primordial tumulus, or burial mound), and what in the West is called the *omphalos*, the symbol of the navel of the world.[34]

On top of the cupola stands the *harmika* (square altar), within which was placed a shrine for relics of the Buddha. Rising above the *harmika*, at the center, is the aforementioned *chattra*, which stands for the World Tree.[35] Here we see the classic confluence of circle and square that plays such a large role in Asian sacred architecture and is widely known as the *mandala*. The mandala has a distinct geometric aspect: "The mandala is a projection of the heavenly realm onto the earth, achieved by means of sacred geometry. It is thus the primary expression of sacred geometry in temple architecture, as well as the primary vehicle for meditation in esoteric (Tibetan and Japanese) Buddhism."[36]

34. Govinda, *Psycho-cosmic Symbolism*, 12–13, 78–79; and Butterworth, *Tree at the Navel of the Earth*, 26–51.

35. Govinda, *Psycho-cosmic Symbolism*, 79.

36. John M. Lundquist, "Fundamentals of Temple Ideology from Eastern Traditions," in *Revelation, Reason, and Faith: Essays in Honor of Truman G. Madsen*, ed. Donald W. Parry, Daniel C. Peterson, and Stephen D. Ricks (Provo, UT: FARMS, 2002), 667–68.

Fig. 59 (left). Gateway to the Great Stupa of Sanchi, Central India, 3rd century BC.

Fig. 60 (right). The reverse side of the eastern *torana*'s top lintel features the seven *Manushi*, or human Buddhas, the Buddhas of the world eras.

The Temple of Sanchi is entered through one of four monumental *toranas* (gates). One then circumambulates in a clockwise direction around the ground-level terrace, then mounts a staircase to the upper terrace's circumambulation path (see fig. 59).[37]

As we focus our view on the eastern *torana* and the reverse side of the top lintel, we see an arrangement of the seven *Manushi* (human) Buddhas of the world eras (see fig. 60).[38] Each of these Buddhas has his own *mudra* (sacred hand gesture) and his own species of sacred tree.[39] The Buddhas with their trees identified in Sanskrit are, from right to left, Sikhin (*Pundarika)*, Visvabhu (*Sala*), Krakucchanda (*Sirisa*), Kanakamuni (*Udumbara—Ficus glomerata*), Kasyapa (*Nyagrodha—Ficus indica*), Gautama Shakyamuni (*Asvattha—Ficus religiosa*), and Vipasyin (*Patali*).[40]

According to Buddhist doctrine, there have been countless worlds, each with its Buddha or many Buddhas and all having the same set

37. Marshall and Foucher, *Monuments of Sanchi*, vol. 2, plate 39.

38. Marshall and Foucher, *Monuments of Sanchi*, vol. 2, plate 45.

39. Marshall and Foucher, *Monuments of Sanchi*, vol. 1; and Olschak and Wangyal, *Mystic Art of Ancient Tibet*, 186–87.

40. Coomaraswamy, *Elements of Buddhist Iconography*, 46, 49–50, 52.

of symbols and functioning in the same manner in their respective worlds. "All the virtues, attained by maintaining the Highest Doctrine, have been ardently proclaimed by all the Buddhas through millions of aeons, but even today their number is not exhausted."[41]

The Bodhi and Other Sacred Trees

The most important Buddhas, for our purposes, are numbers six and seven. Number six is the Buddha Shakyamuni, the Buddha of our world. Number five is his immediate predecessor, Kasyapa (third from the left in fig. 60). The sacred tree of Kasyapa is the *Ficus indica*, or banyan tree. The sacred tree of the Buddha Shakyamuni (second from the left in fig. 60) is the *Ficus religiosa*, the *Pipal* or Bodhi tree. However, the tree at Bodh Gaya, in northeastern India, under which the Buddha attained his enlightenment was the banyan. There is thus somewhat of an art-historical discrepancy in the depiction of the Buddha, since he is always pictured alongside the *Ficus religiosa*, or Bodhi tree.[42] It is important to note that the primary role that the sacred tree plays in the mission of each Buddha is that it shelters him "at the moment of his *Sambodhi*," or enlightenment. "The importance of this symbol becomes clear from the Buddhist Scriptures, which describe the struggle of the Bodhisattva and Mara, the Evil One, for the place under the Bodhi tree, which was regarded as the holiest spot in the world, the incomparable diamond throne."[43] Thus it is a sign of revelatory wisdom,[44] as I suggested earlier. "Especially noteworthy is the designation of the 'Single Fig-tree' as the World-form of the 'One Awakener' . . . ; for just so also is the Buddha's Fig-tree . . . constantly spoken of as the 'Great Awakening' . . . ; being the chosen symbol of the Buddha's unseen essence, it is an enduring basis for the vision of Buddha."[45]

41. Olschak and Wangyal, *Mystic Art of Ancient Tibet*, 186–87.

42. Bosch, *Golden Germ*, 70.

43. Govinda, *Psycho-cosmic Symbolism*, 79; and Coomaraswamy, *Elements of Buddhist Iconography*, 41.

44. Marshall and Foucher, *Monuments of Sanchi*, 1:199. For the concept of the Buddha's enlightenment as revelation, see Bosch, *Golden Germ*, 68.

45. Coomaraswamy, *Elements of Buddhist Iconography*, 8–11, 40–41.

The Bodhi and the banyan trees are thus the most sacred of the Asian trees of life, and of these the Bodhi tree takes pride of place. It is worshipped in India today by many people:

> Up to the present time in various parts of India the aśvattha is still worshipped as the abode or symbol of a deity or is adored for its own sake. In the latter case the object is to secure the help of the magical power of the tree. Its branches drive away enemies, its leaves produce intelligence in the child, fulfil desires for wealth, male offspring, etc. It is worth noticing that this worship is attended with feelings of awe and fear. The tree is magically dangerous and should not be near a house. Its dedication has to be performed in silence, and its name remains unspoken, a taboo probably connected with the belief that the spirits of the ancestors dwell in the tree or are embodied in it.[46]

On the front side of the top lintel on the same *torana* in figure 61, we see on the left the Bodhi tree of the Buddha Shakyamuni and on the right the characteristic tree of the first of the Manushi Buddhas, Vipasyin (the *Sala—Shorea robusta*). Each tree is surmounted by the *chattra*, giving it the artistic or architectural ornament of the tree of life. Surrounding each tree are worshippers and garlanded *stupas* (or *omphaloi*), each one also topped by the *chattra*. So the actual botanical tree of life is surrounded by (and, so to speak, magnified, highlighted, or dramatized by) the architectural rendition of the tree of life that forms the top element of the *stupa* temple.[47]

The middle lintel depicts the "Great Departure"—that is, the Buddha leaving his palace at the city of Kapilavastu amidst a grand and solemn procession of followers, city dwellers, animals, musicians, and so on. On the left we can see the multistoried houses of the city dwellers. In the middle we see the Bodhi tree surrounded by worshippers and enclosed within a *vedica* rail, the rail that surrounds a *stupa*. On

46. Bosch, *Golden Germ*, 69.
47. Butterworth, *Tree at the Navel of the Earth*, 50–51.

Fig. 61. Front side of the top lintel of the eastern *torana*.

the far right we see the footprints of the Buddha, with a *chakra* (wheel) in the center, indicating that he is a universal sovereign.

On the bottom lintel we see King Ashoka, the third king of the Mauryan Dynasty, visiting the Bodhi tree. This time the tree is protruding from the top of a circular shrine surrounded by worshippers. The king is accompanied by his retinue, including the queen, musicians, a dwarf, and an elephant.[48] The point to emphasize here is that we see in these scenes the tree of life in the world, so to speak, along the roadside as the vast throngs of humankind pass by in all their variety. We see characteristic multistoried houses, animals, and various classes of people.

Of special interest are two Tibetan works of art, both with the theme of the sacred tree of the Buddhas. The first of these (see fig. 62)[49] is a late twelfth or early thirteenth-century wooden book or manuscript cover from Nepal. We see six scenes from the life of the Buddha Shakyamuni: from the left, the taming of a wild elephant, then his temptation by the demon Mara, the Buddha's protection by the serpent Mucalinda, then his first preaching, the miracle of Shravasti, and his *parinirvana* (death). In each of the four central scenes, particularly the two that show the Bodhi tree, we see the exquisite manner in which the leaves are represented. The trees extend above the Buddha's head in the manner of the *chattra* atop the *stupa*. In Buddhist doctrine the Buddha *is* the temple; the temple is his body. The typical Nepalese Buddhist *stupa* shows the Buddha's eyes looking out from

48. Madhukar K. Dhavalikar, *Sanchi* (New Delhi: Oxford University Press, 2003), 34–49.

49. Steven M. Kossak and Jane Casey Singer, *Sacred Visions: Early Paintings from Central Tibet* (New York: Metropolitan Museum of Art, 1998), 134–35.

Fig. 62. A late 12th- or early 13th-century wooden book or manuscript cover from Nepal.

the spire, as though he is seated in meditation, as we see in the illustration, "thus suggesting a human figure in the posture of meditation hidden in the stūpa, the crossed legs in the base, the body up to the shoulders in the hemisphere, the head in the harmikā."[50] "The body becomes a palace, the hallowed basis of all the Buddhas."[51]

The second Tibetan work of art brings us to the final point that I want to emphasize. This *thangka* (Tibetan silk painting with embroidery), coming from central Tibet in the thirteenth century AD (see fig. 63, also pl. 7),[52] shows the Buddha Maitreya, the future Buddha, counted as the eighth of the Manushi Buddhas.[53] We see him seated on a lotus throne[54] dressed in the simple *dhoti* pants, without elaborate jewelry. His hands form the *Dharmachakra mudra*, the sacred hand gesture representing the turning of the wheel of the law, or teaching. Important for our purposes are the two blossoms that extend above both of his shoulders from stems that are intertwined between his hands. The flower to his left is from the *Nagapushpa* (*Michelia champaka*), the alba tree, a highly fragrant type

50. Govinda, *Psycho-cosmic Symbolism*, 84–85. For the equivalence between temple and *stupa*, see Adrian Snodgrass, *The Symbolism of the Stupa* (Ithaca, NY: Southeast Asia Program, Cornell University, 1985). See also Lundquist, *Temple: Meeting Place of Heaven and Earth*; and Puay-Peng Ho, "The Symbolism of Central Pillars in Cave-Temples of Northwest China," in Lyle, *Sacred Architecture*, 59–70.

51. Wayman, *Buddhist Tantras*, 83. This quotation is taken from the Tibetan Tantric text *Guhyasamaja*. For the equivalence of the palace and temple within Buddhist texts, see Ferdinand Diederich Lessing, *Yung-Ho-Kung: An Iconography of the Lamaist Cathedral in Peking* (Stockholm, 1942), 141. See also, in general, Snodgrass, *Symbolism of the Stupa*.

52. Kossak and Singer, *Sacred Visions*, 109–11.

53. Marshall and Foucher, *Monuments of Sanchi*, 1:200.

54. Coomaraswamy, *Elements of Buddhist Iconography*, 39–59.

Fig. 63. *Thangka* of the Buddha Maitreya, central Tibet, 13th century. See plate 7.

of jasmine. This flower represents the tree of the future Buddha. In other words, what we see is not a fully formed tree but the blossom of that tree, a promise or affirmation that the next Buddha too, in his future incarnation, will experience *Mahasambodhi* (great awakening) under this tree. "For was it not when sitting under its branches that Sakyamuni had a vision of his former births? And was it not on that same spot that the highest wisdom was revealed to him, that he in truth became Buddha, 'the Awakened'?" We can therefore see the consistency and continuity of the tree of life motif in Buddhism, encompassing the Buddha of this world, as well as the future Buddha Maitreya.[55]

There is an exquisite, analogous painting from the Chinese realm that bears comparison with the Buddhas depicted in the two Tibetan works of art described above. This is an eighth-century (Tang Dynasty) ink-and-color painting on silk of the Buddha Shakyamuni preaching under the Bodhi tree, from Cave 17 at Dunhuang (Mogao), in western China. This image, stylistically Chinese, shows the Buddha seated under a lush canopy of Bodhi tree leaves with his right hand in *Vitarka mudra,* the *mudra* (sacred hand gesture) of preaching. Interestingly, the leaves are highly stylized rather than depicted with botanical accuracy as they are on the Tibetan book cover from the late twelfth or early thirteenth century shown in figure 62.[56]

Yet another example from China, again from the Dunhuang (Mogao) Buddhist cave temples of western China, is highlighted by Puay-Peng Ho. He presents the ubiquitous central pillar in these caves of the fifth and sixth centuries as "a representation of the *axis mundi,* the cosmic mountain and the link between the mundane and supramundane world, one aspect of *stupa* symbolism." He then refers us to Snodgrass's book *The Symbolism of the Stupa,* where we learn that the *axis mundi* of the Chinese *stupa* is the World Tree.[57]

Thus we see that in Asian art and religion the tree of life, the World Tree, represents and stands for the center of the world, the world axis, the temple in its highest manifestation as cosmic center, the place of

55. Bosch, *Golden Germ*, 68.

56. This image appears in Roderick Whitfield, *The Art of Central Asia: The Stein Collection in the British Museum*, vol. 1, *Paintings from Dunhuang* (Tokyo: Kodansha International Ltd., 1982), plate 7 (Stein Painting no. 6); and in Roderick Whitfield and Anne Farrer, *Caves of the Thousand Buddhas: Chinese Art from the Silk Route* (New York: George Braziller, 1990), plate 1. This image is also accessible at http://www.britishmuseum.org/research/search_the_collection_database/search_object_details.aspx?objectid=6551&partid=1&searchText=stein+painting+6&fromADBC=ad&toADBC=ad&numpages=10&orig=/research/search_the_collection_database.aspx¤tPage=11 (accessed August 19, 2010).

57. Puay-Peng Ho, "The Symbolism of the Central Pillars in Cave-Temples of Northwest China," in Lyle, *Sacred Architecture*, 65–69. See also Snodgrass, *Symbolism of the Stupa*, 177–84.

revelation, the tree of wisdom that stands along the road as an inspiration and guide to passersby, the passageway into heaven, and the place of initiation into the highest mysteries of heaven, indeed, the meeting place of heaven and earth.[58]

According to Coomaraswamy, "the Tree of Life, synonymous with all existence, all the worlds, all life, springs up, out, or down into space from its root in the navel centre of the Supreme Being. . . . The World-tree then, equally in and apart from its Buddhist application, is the procession of incessant life. Standing erect and midmost in the garden of life, extending from Earth to Heaven, branching throughout Space . . . is the one Wishing-tree . . . that yields the fruits of life, all that every creature calls 'good.'"[59]

John M. Lundquist earned a PhD in Near Eastern studies from the University of Michigan, Ann Arbor, and then worked as an assistant professor of anthropology and religious instruction at Brigham Young University from 1983 to 1985. He holds an MLS from Brigham Young University and recently retired as the Susan and Douglas Dillon Chief Librarian of the Asian and Middle Eastern Division of the New York Public Library, a position he held since 1985. He continues to work as an adjunct professor in the Department of Philosophy and Religious Studies at Pace University (since 2002) and as an instructor

---

58. Lundquist, *Temple: Meeting Place of Heaven and Earth.*

59. Coomaraswamy, *Elements of Buddhist Iconography,* 8, 11. The Sanskrit term corresponding to what Coomaraswamy means by the term *World Tree* is *asvattha* (*Ficus religiosa*), the Bodhi tree. The *asvattha* is attested in the Indus Valley tablets and in the Rig Veda, the Upanishads (Maitri Upanishad), and in the Bhagavad Gita. As has been pointed out above, from both early Buddhist textual sources as well as early Buddhist iconography, the *asvattha* is associated with the tree of the Buddha's enlightenment from the very beginning. As Bosch has written: "It is highly significant that this same Tree of Life and Wisdom has been chosen to play a predominant part in the legend of the Buddha. For, as Coomaraswamy has justly remarked, 'every traditional symbol necessarily carries with it its original values, even when used or intended to be used in a more restricted sense.' The bodhi-tree at Bodh Gaya, in fact, is strictly analogous to the 'One Awakener', the 'enduring basis of the vision of Brahman'. For was it not when sitting under its branches that Sakyamuni had a vision of his former births? And was it not on that same spot that the highest wisdom was revealed to him, that he in truth became Buddha 'the Awakened'?" Bosch, *Golden Germ,* 68 (*Sakyamuni* is an alternative spelling of *Shakyamuni*); see also pp. 69–70 and Coomaraswamy, *Elements of Buddhist Iconography,* 8–9, 11, 40–41.

for the C. G. Jung Foundation of New York (since 1993). His published work includes The Temple of Jerusalem: Past, Present, and Future *(2008);* The Temple: Meeting Place of Heaven and Earth *(1993); "Fundamentals of Temple Ideology from Eastern Traditions," in* Revelation, Reason, and Faith: Essays in Honor of Truman G. Madsen *(2002); and "New Light on the Temple Ideology,"* East and West *50 (2000).*

The Tree of Life: A Cross-Cultural Perspective in Mormon Art

Richard Oman

Mormonism is a rapidly expanding world faith. This expansion is most rapid in areas that are often quite different from mainline American culture.[1] How can this increasing cultural variety reinforce and sometimes expand our understanding of the tree of life? This paper is an attempt to deal with this question by looking at pieces of contemporary Mormon art from a wide variety of cultural regions.

Narrowing the list of art down to a manageable size was difficult. As curator of acquisitions at the Museum of Church History and Art in Salt Lake City, Utah, I began by focusing on the art that had been collected at that museum or that had been exhibited there over the last twenty-plus years. After making a list of Latter-day Saint artwork featuring the tree of life, I sorted each item geographically and culturally. Included were the following countries and cultures: Norway, Sweden, Portugal, France, Italy, Germany, Ukraine, Armenia, Russia, Lebanon, India, Nepal, China, Japan, New Zealand, Canada, Guatemala, Ecuador, Venezuela, Chile, Uruguay, Brazil, Peru, Mexico, Panama, Honduras, Sierra Leone, Kenya, the Navajos, the Santa Clara Pueblos, and many works of art from the United States.[2]

1. In 1950, 90 percent of Latter-day Saints lived in the United States. *Deseret News 1974 Church Almanac* (Salt Lake City: Deseret News, 1974), 197. By 2010, only 45 percent of Latter-day Saints lived in the United States and Canada combined. *Deseret News 2011 Church Almanac* (Salt Lake City: Deseret News, 2009), 191.

2. All of these works of art are part of the permanent collection of the Museum of Church History and Art, a division of the Family and Church History Department of the Church of Jesus Christ of Latter-day Saints. The museum is located directly west of Temple Square in Salt Lake City, Utah.

Thematically, this art springs from the shared Latter-day Saint faith of the artists. Interpretively, it often reflects the broader cultural framework from which the artists come. Aesthetically, this art is a mixture. Some seems to be fairly closely aligned with international artistic styles that are passed on primarily by university art departments. Other pieces were created by artists who are either self-taught or come from within the folk art traditions of their native lands. The museum's inclusion of Latter-day Saint folk art on the tree of life accomplishes three purposes: it increases the range of intellectual and spiritual interpretations of scriptural themes, it demonstrates the great aesthetic variety among Latter-day Saint artists worldwide, and it provides a broad-based sampling of Latter-day Saint art and thought. Historically, Mormonism tends to draw its converts from the lower and lower-middle classes. Because much of the art from this socioeconomic category is folk art, I have included several such works to better reflect the contemporary demographics of Mormonism.[3]

The theological foundation of the artistic and interpretive variety of this approach is based on this injunction found in the Book of Mormon: "I did liken all scriptures unto us, that it might be for our profit and learning" (1 Nephi 19:23). This is the same writer who recorded the story of the tree of life (1 Nephi 8:11–13).

The artwork to be reviewed here is from Sweden, Germany, the Navajos, South America, Mexico, Nepal, and Japan.

Sweden

A work of wooden sculpture by the Swedish artist and Mormon bishop Kurt William Sjokvist (see fig. 64) uses a traditional Swedish medium and style.[4] Sweden is one of the most heavily forested nations of Europe, and wood has been an important medium for Swedish sculptors going back to the age of the Vikings. Given its far northern

3. Most notably, the fact that more than half of the church membership lives outside the United States.

4. For an excellent discussion of the Swedish style of art and interior design, see *Carl and Karin Larsson: Creators of the Swedish Style*, ed. Michael Snodin and Elisabet Stavenow-Hidemark (Boston: Little, Brown, 1997).

location, Sweden has long, dark winters. In an attempt to alleviate the effects of this long winter gloom, Swedes tend to favor light-colored paint for the inside walls and furniture of their homes.

Fig. 64. *Lehi's Vision of the Tree of Life,* by Kurt William Sjokvist.

Because the Swedes are on the northern margins of European culture, borrowed high European styles have been modified and simplified. This is most apparent in Swedish decorative arts, particularly those based on eighteenth-century French styles. Sjokvist's work incorporates all of these elements: the medium of wood colored with soft, light colors and the simplified eighteenth-century French rococo design of the base.

While the style of this work is very Swedish, the thematic content is focused on Lehi's vision of the tree of life from the Book of Mormon. The core of Sjokvist's composition is a large, stylized, freestanding world globe. The artist's depiction of Lehi's vision hugs the shape of this globe. The appended sculpture section of the large and spacious building follows that curve, as does the tree of life. By compositionally linking the shape of the building, the tree, and the positioning of the figures to the curved surface of the globe, the artist reminds us of the universality of this story for all the people of the earth.

Germany

While Sjokvist's work stylistically looks back to the tradition of Swedish folk art, Johan Benthin's *The Iron Rod* (see fig. 65) uses the artistic vehicle of modern European academic abstraction and minimalism. Although he lived near Frankfurt, Germany, when he did this work, Benthin was born in Denmark, where he became the

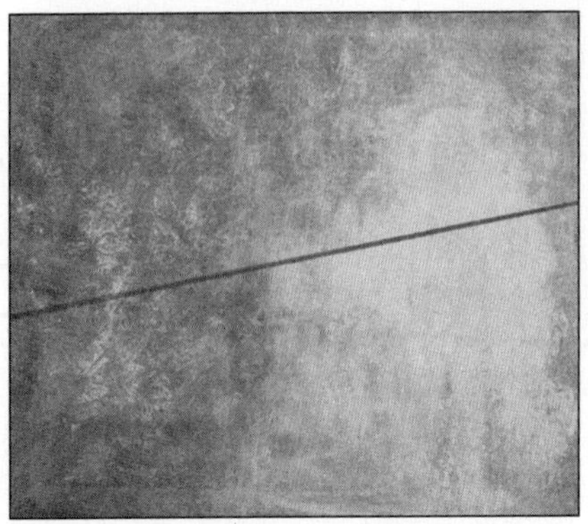

Fig. 65. *The Iron Rod,* by Johan Benthin. Oil on board.

first president of the Copenhagen Stake. In Frankfurt he served as the president of the Frankfurt Stake. The artist has lived in many places around the world, including North and South America, England, Spain, and Germany (he currently resides in the southern Indian city of Mysore). *The Iron Rod* mixes the early twentieth-century German *Bauhaus* design movement with European abstractionist painting. This style emphasizes extreme simplicity. Benthin's painting masterfully reaches out to the viewer while focusing on a central element of the story. This is accomplished with the minimum of visual forms. It is the simplicity of the painting that makes it so forceful and engaging for the viewer.

So how did he do it? Benthin shifts the focus from Lehi and his family to all mankind. He begins by leaving out many visual elements that are part of the story. There is no fruit. In fact, there is not even a tree of life. There is no Lehi. There are no crowds of people. There is no river. There is no "great and spacious building" (1 Nephi 8:26).

The artist very minimally depicts just two elements of the story: the iron rod and the angel who guides us along the journey. The angel is reduced to a faintly glowing figure of light in the background. Benthin's visual depiction of the angel is more of a reference and suggestion than a description. This has two effects on the viewer. First, discerning that the faintly depicted image is in fact an angel is a discovery process for the viewer, somewhat like the reality of how we make spiritual discoveries in the midst of a mundane world. Second, the iron rod is as bold as the angel is subtle. Benthin uses a broad, bold felt-tip marker and straightedge to create his iron rod. Physically, the smooth, hard surface of the iron rod is placed on the surface of the painting's soft impasto. This makes the iron rod by far the most forceful part of the composition.

What is the artist trying to accomplish? The answer is inherent in what he has not depicted; there are no pilgrims. The viewers of this painting are the missing pilgrims. All who view this work of art are invited to become part of the painting. By placing the iron rod so prominently on the surface of the composition, Benthin demands a choice: "Are you going to grasp the iron rod or not?"[5]

Involving the viewer in the creation of the art is a consistent aspect of Benthin's work. He has made the following statements about why and how he creates: "My desire [is] to invite viewers to become co-creators. . . . I want to give others the chance to step back, to reflect on their relationship with the world and with themselves. . . . I can show him [the viewer] the path, make it clear and inviting or hidden and mysterious, but the decision to walk the path is ultimately his. . . . By experiencing art, however, he is forced to . . . establish ever more firmly the concept of what he is."[6]

Navajo

Sjokvist and Benthin present their interpretation of the tree of life story as thematically universal but aesthetically culturally specific. Robert Yellowhair, a Navajo artist from Snowflake, Arizona, created a piece that reverses this approach. In his *Lehi's Vision of the Tree of Life* (see fig. 66, also pl. 9), he works in a widespread illustrative style, but his images are geographically and culturally specific.

Fig. 66. *Lehi's Vision of the Tree of Life*, by Robert Yellowhair. Oil on canvas. See plate 9.

5. Johan Benthin, LDS Artists Files, Museum of Church History and Art, Salt Lake City (hereafter "LDS Artists Files").

6. Johan H. Benthin, "Thoughts on Arts and Inspiration," in *Arts and Inspiration: Mormon Perspectives*, ed. Steven P. Sondrup (Provo, UT: Brigham Young University Press, 1980), 77.

Yellowhair creates a setting from the American Southwest that looks like the Navajo homeland of Arizona and New Mexico. His composition is filled with people, all of whom are Native Americans. Some are even specific historical or cultural figures. Knowledge of the cultures and flora of the Native American West, as well as the artist's personal history, is critical in understanding this work of art.[7]

Like Lehi's original vision, Yellowhair's interpretation contains specific family elements; the artist puts this family story into the broad context of Navajo history and culture in the Southwest. Over five hundred years ago, the Navajos migrated into this region from northwestern Canada. The Navajos forced their way into an area that was already occupied by the Pueblos and Paiutes. The more aggressive invading Navajos dislocated the more passive existing tribes of the area.[8]

But despite the resulting intertribal conflict, the Navajos soon began borrowing cultural elements from their more advanced and sedentary neighbors. They adopted many religious elements from the Hopi. Their borrowing of weaving from the Pueblos added to intertribal contention because the Navajos got both sheep and weavers by raiding the Pueblos.[9]

Embedded in Navajo clan names are records of some of these raids. At birth a Navajo child is assigned to the clan of the mother. If the mother was not born a Navajo (sometimes the result of her being captured on a raid of a neighboring tribe), the child is assigned to a clan that bears the name of the mother's birth tribe. The artist, Robert Yellowhair, for example, is a member of the Zuni clan of the Navajos, indicating that one of his distant grandmothers was a woman from the Zuni tribe who had been captured and made a wife by one of his distant Navajo grandfathers.

---

7. The interpretation of Yellowhair's painting is based upon my oral interviews with the artist. This information is in Robert Yellowhair, LDS Artists Files.

8. See Ruth M. Underhill, *The Navajos*, rev. ed. (Norman: University of Oklahoma Press, 1967); and Harry C. James, *Pages from Hopi History* (Tucson: University of Arizona Press, 1983).

9. Some Pueblos, bringing their sheep with them, also came to the Navajos to escape the wrath of the Spanish after the great Pueblo Rebellion of 1680. The Coyote Pass, or Jemez clan, for example, is specifically identified as being associated with these Pueblo refugees. Underhill, *The Navajos*, 41–48.

This pattern of raiding continued largely unchecked until the mid-nineteenth century, when the U.S. Army, under Col. Kit Carson, led a scorched-earth military action against the eastern Navajos, permanently ending Navajo raids into the Rio Grande Valley of New Mexico.[10] But the western Navajos continued to raid the Hopis and Mormon settlements to the west.[11] Today intertribal conflict is largely confined to the courts as the Navajos battle some of their neighbors over reservation boundaries. Occasionally this simmering hostility breaks out in fights and brawls.[12]

The artist was born into the middle of this intertribal conflict. But because of his father, a holy man and peacemaker among the Navajos, the artist's personal life took a different turn. Yellowhair's father spoke the languages of several of the surrounding tribes and held positions of religious responsibility in some of those tribes, particularly the Hopis. This is even more noteworthy when one considers that the epicenter of tribal conflict in the Southwest is between the Navajos and Hopis over reservation boundaries.

Yellowhair's family quest to foster peaceful respect among the various tribes of the Southwest permeates this painting. The central Lehi figure is depicted as a Hopi priest dressed in his most sacred religious robes. This "Hopi Lehi" offers the glowing fruit to his family, but his "family" turns out to be a collection of historical or cultural figures from the surrounding tribes. Each of these historical and mythological figures represents specific roles and values that match elements from Lehi's version of the story.[13]

Facing Lehi are three figures. On the right is Sam, the peacemaker of the family who is depicted as the Shoshone chief Washakie, shown holding a peace pipe and wrapped in a blanket. Washakie was one of

---

10. Underhill, *The Navajos*, 112–26.

11. Underhill, *The Navajos*, 119.

12. I have heard numerous accounts of physical conflict between Navajo aggressors and Hopi victims (mostly from Hopi sources) during fieldwork conducted in the Southwest between 1980 and 1990.

13. The artist explained the figures and their meaning to me. This information is on file in Yellowhair, LDS Artists Files.

the great intratribal and intracultural peacemakers of the nineteenth-century American West. The symbolism of the peace pipe is obvious. The blanket symbolizes the benefits that come from peaceful exchange between Indians and whites. Lehi's wife, Sariah, is depicted as "Crow Mother" of the Zunis. Most tribes in the Southwest claim Mother Earth as their mother, but the Zuni claim Crow Mother. Crow Mother is wearing the religious robes of a Zuni bride. Her role in feeding and serving her family is visually expressed through the basket she carries. To her left is a figure representing Nephi. He is depicted as Quanah Parker, the visionary Comanche chief. He wears a buffalo robe because buffalo are sacred to tribes from the Great Plains and Nephi was a holy man.

Behind these three figures are two more figures, representing Laman and Lemuel. Their background position reflects lack of commitment in living the gospel. They and their warlike descendants are meant to represent the Apache and Sioux people because they were great warriors.

Lehi stands before a tree of life that is depicted as a glorified piñon pine. The artist picked this tree because it is literally a "tree of life" for the people, animals, and birds of the Southwest, providing firewood for heat, construction material for shelter, and pine nuts for food. Next to the tree is a stone box with the gold plates in it. On the plates is written "Diyin Baahani," which means "the story of God" in Navajo.

The sacredness of the land is a recurring theme among most Native American cultures, as well as a recurring theme in the Book of Mormon. Yellowhair depicts northern Arizona's San Francisco Peaks in the upper left of this painting. These mountains are not only traditional tribal territorial markers for the Navajos, they are also sacred to the Navajos and Hopis—places where the "holy people" of both cultures dwell and where sacred things are believed to happen. In the painting these mountains recall the oft-quoted scriptural phrase for the temple: "mountain of the Lord's house" (Isaiah 2:2; Ezekiel 20:40; Doctrine and Covenants 133:13).

To the right of the mountains, the artist has created a composite of the "great and spacious building," representing the pride of the world.

This is depicted as a pan-Indian site: it is made up of a Pueblo village, Plains tepees, and even Navajo hogans. These dwellings are separated from the tree of life by a river representing the filthy waters of sin as described by Nephi in the Book of Mormon (1 Nephi 15:27). Interestingly, this scene also parallels a terrible division among the Navajo people in their own mythic history, which also includes a river.[14]

This Navajo Latter-day Saint artist has tried to localize Lehi's vision tribally, geographically, and culturally. He has also connected it to his own family history and values. Through his choice of figures and imagery, he has tried to use this story as a bridge of peace to surrounding Indian tribes.

Ecuador

Victor de la Torre grew up and received his early training in furniture making in the rural highlands of Ecuador. Later he studied wood carving near the colonial and capital city of Quito. Because of its availability and low cost, wood is the preferred sculptural medium for many of the traditional Andean peoples. After his training, de la Torre and his family moved to the sprawling, heavily populated modern city of Caracas, capital of Venezuela.[15]

Fig. 67. *Lehi's Vision of the Tree of Life*, by Victor de la Torre. Wood.

De la Torre's carved bas-relief titled *Lehi's Vision of the Tree of Life* (see fig. 67), created in the shape of a round tabletop, reflects his early training. The imagery is a commentary on the areas where the artist has lived. The composition's border draws on traditional Andean

14. Paul G. Zolbrod, *Diné bahane': The Navajo Creation Story* (Albuquerque: University of New Mexico Press, 1984), 55–70.

15. Victor de la Torre, LDS Artists Files. As of 2008, the population of Caracas exceeded 4.3 million (the population of Greater Caracas is approximately 6.2 million). "Caracas," http://en.wikipedia.org/wiki/caracas (accessed 6 March 2009).

Indian styles that predate the Spanish conquest. The river resembles the deep arroyos that, following torrential downpours falling on the steep hillsides of the Ecuadorian highlands, fill with water and carry large amounts of soil. Thus the arroyo-like river of de la Torre's bas-relief aptly recalls the filthy river in Lehi's vision.

But it is the "large and spacious building" (1 Nephi 11:35) that is perhaps the most poignant part of this composition. The building is depicted as a large modern luxury apartment building in Caracas. De la Torre's move to Caracas reflects a demographic reality in much of Latin America: the massive shift in population from rural areas to urban centers. Employment has driven much of this migration, which has been socially disruptive, with family ties and traditions strained and frequently broken. In de la Torre's case, he left his rural home as well as his country in an effort to make a better living.[16] In urban areas, where wealth is concentrated, the wealthy often live in high-rise apartment buildings that set them off from the rest of the population. The rich literally look down on the poor, who subsist in low, humble houses, sometimes assembled from discarded materials. De la Torre's rendering of this idea is a demographic statement of spiritual openness—that no one, including the poor and downtrodden, is excluded from seeking the full blessings of the gospel of Jesus Christ. In fact, converts to the Church of Jesus Christ mostly come from the lower and lower-middle classes, rather than from the wealthy. Unlike Yellowhair, de la Torre sees the spiritual and social "landmines" from competing tribes, but rather with respect to the forces of urbanism, modernism, and economic disparity.

Mexico

Another work of art from Latino culture is *Joseph Smith and the Tree of Life*, by Mexican artist Juan Escobedo (see fig. 68). The artist started life in the Mexican colonial city of San Luis Potosí. When

16. According to the World Bank, per capita yearly income in Venezuela is $7,320.00, compared to only $3,080.00 in Ecuador. The World Bank Group, "Doing Business: Measuring business regulations," http://www.doingbusiness.org/exploreeconomies/economycharacteristics.aspx (accessed 6 March 2009).

Fig. 68. *Joseph Smith and the Tree of Life*, by Juan Escobedo. Oil on canvas.

Juan was fourteen, his father found work as a migrant farmworker in Texas, where his family met the missionaries and eventually joined the Church of Jesus Christ of Latter-day Saints. Juan studied art at Brigham Young University, where he continued to cultivate an artistic style that remained rooted in the folk art of his native Mexico.[17]

Two elements that frequently appear in Mexican folk art are bright colors and compositions that include festive parades. In a physical environment colored primarily by earth tones, artwork done in bright, vibrant colors is associated with festivities and seen as buoyant, self-confident, and happy. For people living amid grinding poverty with its long hours of hard physical labor day after day, colorful festivals provide a brief respite.[18]

While the overall aesthetic of *Joseph Smith and the Tree of Life* is that of a festive parade, the bright colors are also a consistent metaphor for righteous joy. In fact, the specific features of the painting follow the

17. Juan Escobedo, LDS Artists Files.

18. For an excellent overview of the relationship of folk art to parades and festivals, see Henry Glassie, *The Spirit of Folk Art* (New York: Harry N. Abrams, 1989).

path of a new convert to the Church of Jesus Christ. The story begins on the left side of the composition, where a woman has plunged into the bright blue rolling waters of a pure stream issuing from the tree of life. On her back is a large, heavily laden, gray *rebozo*. Such shawls are used by Mexican peasant women to carry burdens. The heavy load represents sin, and the bright waters represent baptism. The woman next appears dressed in joyfully bright clothing. Her *rebozo* is now empty, and she is grasping the iron (golden) rod leading to the tree of life. She next appears dressed in even brighter clothing. Her previously gray *rebozo* has become a bright, festive shawl. She gestures to the viewer to join her on her new gospel journey.[19]

But then she begins to depart from the gospel path as she goes into spiritual regression. The bright, colorful costume is almost hidden by the heavily loaded *rebozo*. The weight of sin forces her down onto her hands and knees. Having let go of the iron rod, she moves away from the route of joy, spiritual safety, and progress. But, fortunately, golden tendrils emanating from the tree of life block her digression. Within these tendrils we discover names of the prophets of this dispensation. The most prominent figure is blue-clad Joseph Smith, who points her back to the path. Below him is the image of Brigham Young. It is the teachings and exhortations of modern prophets that help provide guidance to overcome sin and discouragement and get us back on the path to the tree of life.

Nearing the large white fruit of the tree is the young Joseph Smith, who was the first in this dispensation to proceed down the path toward the tree of life. He becomes the guide and model for the new convert.

Above the arm of Joseph in blue is the cosmos, worlds without end, symbolizing the eternal extension of the Lord's plan of exaltation. Swirling around the base of the tree, in a bright rainbow of color, are those who have successfully arrived.[20]

Escobedo has focused his painting on the multifaceted spiritual journey of a new convert. The visual blending of the tree of life with

19. Escobedo, LDS Artists Files.
20. Escobedo, LDS Artists Files.

the words of modern prophets is a rather unique addition. The artist gives encouragement to those on the path by celebrating the vast multitudes of spiritual pilgrims who have successfully arrived at the tree and are going around it in an eternal circle.[21] Through the rich, symbolic traditions and forms of Mexican folk art the artist is able to transcend time and space. Multiple stories are told, each with its spiritual commentary. Using the form of a Mexican fiesta procession visually and conceptually pulls the composition together. That all this can happen on the same canvas attests to the richness, flexibility, and versatility of traditional folk art to joyfully communicate complicated spiritual, narrative, and allegorical concepts.

Peru

The Peruvian artist Jerónimo Lozano uses the developing folk art form of *retablo* to express his interpretation of the tree of life (see fig. 69). Lozano, a Quechua Indian from the high mountain valleys near Ayucucho, Peru, grew up in the epicenter of this particular Peruvian folk art tradition. He was forced to flee from his ancestral village after the Shining Path guerilla movement killed his family and virtually everyone in his village. He currently lives in Salt Lake City, where he came for medical help and ended up becoming a Latter-day Saint.[22]

Fig. 69. *Lehi's Vision of the Tree of Life*, by Jerónimo Lozano. Wood, plaster, starch, and paint.

Retablo is a folk art form that goes back hundreds of years. Spanish priests first brought *retablos* to Peru in the sixteenth century. The

21. "The course of the Lord is one eternal round" (1 Nephi 10:19).

22. I learned this information in conversation with the artist.

priests used these small wooden boxes filled with little sculptural groupings to teach Christianity to the native populations. Thematic content usually revolved around such subjects as the nativity, the crucifixion, the last supper, and the lives of the saints. Priests also sometimes used small *retablos* as portable altars. Occasionally, traveling merchants carried them on their journeys for spiritual protection.[23]

Today, five hundred years after this art form arrived in the Americas, Peruvian folk artists have adapted it for their own uses. As *retablos* have moved into the world of popular folk art, gold leafing has been replaced by bright, colorful paint; the figurative forms have become more simplified; and the thematic content has become more linked with the lives of the common people. Today's *retablos* are made of common, readily available materials: scraps of thin, cheap plywood; bright paints; and a doughy mixture made of potato starch or gypsum powder. Most of the modeling is done with fingers and a sharpened stick. The overall form of contemporary *retablos* is that of a brightly painted wooden box reminiscent of a multistoried, many-roomed house, often including two-wing doors and a gable pediment.

The *retablo* is a dynamic and constantly evolving folk art among the native population of Peru, particularly in the area around Ayucucho. Today the narrative content often recounts local historical events, depicts fiestas and daily life, and tells religious stories.

Lozano depicts his interpretation of Lehi's vision of the tree of life by populating different shelves of his *retablo* with different aspects of the vision. The upper shelves, separated into small compartments, tell the story of Lehi and his family. Lozano's transition from the family story of Lehi on the upper shelves to the story of humanity on the lower ones is an Eden-like sequence that is one of the artist's most interesting commentaries on the story. Animals and children are joyfully proceeding toward the tree of life through a celebratory rainbow

23. Roger Hamilton, "Tradition and change in Peru's folk art," *IDB AMERICA* (online magazine of the Inter-American Development Bank), February 2004, http://www.iadb.org/idbamerica/index.cfm?thisid=2637 (accessed 9 March 2009).

arch.[24] Thus it is not the natural world of animals and children that is in conflict with the ways of God. This peaceful parade contrasts with Laman and Lemuel's rejection of the tree directly above and the chaos and conflict of the densely packed humanity below.

While the figures of humanity are dressed in vaguely antique dress, it is interesting that the "great and spacious building" resembles the terraced balconies of a contemporary Latin American urban high-rise luxury apartment building. This continues the theme of fear and distrust of urban modernism that we also saw in de la Torre's Latin American sculpture.

A great challenge of visually telling this complex story in a single work of art is that the narrative is actually composed of many smaller stories strung together. Traditional Western easel paintings are like a single snapshot, capable of depicting only a single moment in a particular place. That art form makes telling a sequential story, which sometimes takes place over widely differing times and places, rather difficult. An alternative approach is contemporary academic abstract art. While not limited by a single-snapshot form of presentation, abstract art has its own interpretive challenges. For instance, it usually loses narrative content and degenerates into opaque, idiosyncratic symbolism that fails to connect with most viewers.

Non-Western folk art is usually not under such compositional constraints. As in the scriptures, the values and worldviews of traditional cultures are usually embedded in stories. Over many generations, art forms have developed to tell those stories. It is interesting that Lozano's composition even reads like sentences in a book, moving from left to right and from top to bottom. With stories as complex as Lehi's vision, some seemingly naïve folk art traditions, with their highly flexible compositional systems, are actually quite sophisticated and functional aesthetic systems for telling complex narrative messages.

---

24. The rainbow symbolizes God's promise to mankind and the earth: "I do set my bow in the cloud, and it shall be for a token of a covenant between me and the earth" (Genesis 9:13).

Fig. 70. *Nephi's Vision of the Tree of Life*, by Gilbert Singh. Gouache on silk. See plate 10.

Nepal

By far the most narratively complex work of Mormon art depicting the story of the tree of life is *Nephi's Vision of the Tree of Life*, a Tibetan *thangka*-style painting[25] by Nepalese artist Gilbert Singh (see fig. 70, also pl. 10). A retired professional educator among Great Britain's famed Nepalese Gurkha regiments, Singh has developed his artistic talents by mastering one of the world's most complex art traditions. Nepal, located in the midst of the Himalayas, is wedged between India, Tibet, and China. The artistic traditions of these three incredibly rich cultures came together in Nepal. Singh's *thangka* painting is one of the results.[26]

---

25. In Nepal these types of paintings are called *paubha* paintings, while in Tibet they are called *thangka* paintings. However, even though this painting was created in Kathmandu, Nepal, by a Nepalese painter, the style is more Tibetan than Nepalese. See Pratapaditya Pal, *Art of the Himalayas: Treasures from Nepal and Tibet* (New York: Hudson Hills Press, 1992), 19, 101.

26. Michael Hutt, *Nepal: A Guide to the Art and Architecture of the Kathmandu Valley* (Gartmore, Stirling, Scotland: Kiscadale Publications, 1994), 64.

The basic purpose of many *thangka* paintings is to depict, through highly stylized forms, the religious universe. Not surprisingly, Singh's painting does not focus on just one or two aspects of Lehi's vision of the tree of life; rather, it takes on the task of visualizing the much more complex story of Nephi's related vision. Nephi's vision includes not only the tree of life but also a prophetic overview of what was to become Nephite history, much of the Savior's mortal life, and the second coming of Christ. However, communicating these themes with an art form typically used to describe the entire spiritual universe was, for Singh, a doable artistic task.

Singh uses local visual symbols to tell the stories. The whole composition is beautifully tied together with flowing water, landscape elements, and a consistent color palette. It also reflects the Oriental tradition of creation coming from a mound in the midst of water.

In traditional Buddhist paintings the Buddha, or perhaps a bodhisattva,[27] is usually the central figure. The surrounding figures or stories help define the teachings or life of the central figure. Singh has placed the second coming of Christ in the center of the composition. The surrounding vignettes follow the account in 1 Nephi 11 in describing the spiritual history of the world that will lead up to the second coming.

Japan

The final work of art treated here is also from Asia. Unlike Singh's narratively complex *thangka* painting of Nephi's vision of the tree of life, Japanese artist Kazuto Uoto's *Tree of Life* (see fig. 71) has an almost Zen-like sparseness. The simplicity of this painting is deceptive; embedded in it are allusions to Japanese culture that the artist uses to comment on the story of the tree of life.

Among the most structured and yet widespread rituals in Japan is the *cha-no-yu*, or tea ceremony. In a rigidly stratified society, this

---

27. Bodhisattvas are actual men who are believed to have gained spiritual perfection on this earth but who have chosen to serve as spiritual guides and saviors of mankind rather than going directly on to nirvana. See Mircea Eliade, *Essential Sacred Writings from Around the World* (New York: Harper & Row, 1977), 48–49.

Fig. 71. *The Tree of Life*, by Kazuto Uoto. Tempura on plaster and board.

ceremony emphasizes humility and classlessness.[28] Uoto uses elements of this ceremony as visual interpretive vehicles for his analysis of the tree of life vision. Formulated by Sen no Rikyū, the greatest of the early Japanese tea masters, the *wabi cha*, or "poverty tea," is the most austere, intimate, and influential form of this ceremony, stressing spiritual fulfillment through renunciation of material things. Within this ritual and its setting are embodied the Japanese expressions of humility, simplicity, aesthetics, and contemplation. Every aspect of the ceremony is carefully regulated.[29]

If you were participating in the *wabi cha*, the ritual would begin as you carefully walk through a small garden down a *roji*, or "dewy path." Before entering a small, rustic hut, you would stop to ritually wash your hands and mouth in a stone basin that was fed water through a bamboo pipe. You would remove your shoes as a sign of respect before entering the *chashitsu*, or tea hut, through a low doorway that would require you to crouch low as an expression of humility. The ritual journey, purification, and humility have parallels in Lehi's vision of commitment, humility, cooperation, and faith.[30]

The single room in the *chashitsu* is very simple, austere, and practically empty. In your presence the host, using very simple tools made of bamboo, would ritually prepare the tea as a symbol of humility.[31] Then he would ladle your tea into a *chawan*, or small tea bowl. In the

28. Liza Crihfield Dalby, *All-Japan: The Catalogue of Everything Japanese*, ed. Oliver Statler (New York: Quill, 1984), 93.

29. Dalby, *All-Japan*, 93.

30. Dalby, *All-Japan*, 96.

31. Dalby, *All-Japan*, 95.

wabi cha, a style of *chawan* called *raku* is used. It is a small, shallow, kiln-fired bowl with a rough-textured, earthen-colored glaze. As a guest, you would probably drink out of the same bowl as the other guests, though it would be ritually washed between uses. This shared use of the same *chawan* would emphasize the camaraderie among participants.

On one side of the room is a small, raised alcove called a *tokonoma*. Here is placed a very simple floral arrangement, frequently a small branch from a flowering tree or a branch with fruit on it. As a guest, you would be encouraged to quietly contemplate this floral arrangement and the benefits of instilling a similar simple peacefulness in your own life.

Uoto's painting incorporates many elements from the *wabi cha*. The background of the painting has a grid structure like the simple *shoji* panels that form the walls of the *chashitsu*.[32] The rough texture of the painting's surface also has meaning. The artist went to great lengths to apply a thin layer of rough plaster over the board to create a texture that simulates the most primitive style of *raku chawan*. He further enhanced this symbolism by using the same earthen colors as the consciously and symbolically simple and humble *raku chawan*.[33]

The simplicity of the painting—no human figures, iron rod, large building, stream, or mists, just a tree with glowing fruit—recalls the floral arrangement in the *tokonoma*.[34] The narrative part of Lehi's vision is expressed by the allusions to the *wabi cha* ceremony. While this painting visually presents a fairly complex message, the viewer must have some knowledge of Japanese culture in order to appreciate much of the spiritual commentary of the artist. The tree of life, with its glowing fruit, is an object for contemplation, reverence, inspiration, humility, and community. The artist is trying to inspire us with heavenly reward while alluding to the necessary values that must become part of our souls if we are to obtain that reward.

---

32. Dalby, *All-Japan*, 96.
33. Dalby, *All-Japan*, 94.
34. Dalby, *All-Japan*, 95.

Conclusion

Not only is more than half of the church's population now living outside the United States and Canada, but over 80 percent of church growth is also taking place outside that area.[35] Most of that growth is happening in countries that are most culturally different from the old western American core of Mormonism.[36] The contemporary demographics of Mormonism tend to outrun our cultural perceptions of what it means to be a worldwide church. Perhaps the shared religious focus of Latter-day Saint art can help bridge this gulf while also giving a rich interpretive and aesthetic reward for putting forth the effort.

Richard G. Oman earned a BA in history from Brigham Young University and did graduate work in art history at the University of Washington, where he specialized in non-Western art. He recently retired as senior curator of the Museum of Church History and Art, Salt Lake City, where he created a major repository of documentation on Latter-day Saint artists from early times to the present and acquired LDS artworks depicting the tree of life. The latter effort resulted in a large exhibition on the tree of life that he curated for the museum. In addition, he worked as art and artifact acquisitions curator for the Church History Department; and as a charter member of the Temple Art Committee (now the Church Art Committee), he advised on historical, iconographical, and artistic matters relating to temple construction, restoration, and maintenance. He has served as art advisor for temples in the United States, Canada, Europe, Latin America, Africa, Asia, and the Pacific Islands. He continues to serve on the Church Art Committee and to advise the acquisition committee of the Church History Department. He is a member of the editorial board of BYU Studies.

---

35. David G. Stewart, *Law of the Harvest: Practical Principles of Effective Missionary Work* (Henderson, NV: Cumorah Foundation, 2007), 16.

36. Compare the membership growth of the Church of Jesus Christ of Latter-day Saints from 1993 through 2007 in California (used here as an indicator of the church's overall growth in the United States) with that of selected regions throughout the world: California, 1993 = 774,000 and 2007 = 809,171 (4.54% increase); Europe, 1993 = 355,000 and 2007 = 469,839 (32.34% increase); Africa, 1993 = 77,000 and 2007 = 264,602 (243.63% increase); Brazil, 1993 = 474,000 and 2007 = 1,018,901 (114.95% increase); Asia (excluding Korea, Japan, and the Philippines), 1993 = 54,000 and 2007 = 133,593 (147.39% increase). The statistics are from the 1995–96 and 2009 editions of the *Church Almanac*.

Selected Bibliography

Latter-day Saint Sources

Bradshaw, Jeffrey M. *In God's Image and Likeness: Ancient and Modern Perspectives on the Book of Moses*, 163–68, 462, 591, 748–49. Salt Lake City: Eborn, 2010.

Brewer, Stewart W. "The History of an Idea: The Scene on Stela 5 from Izapa, Mexico, as a Representation of Lehi's Vision of the Tree of Life." *Journal of Book of Mormon Studies* 8, no. 1 (1999): 12–21.

Briggs, Irene M. "The Tree of Life Symbol: Its Significance in Ancient American Religion." Master's thesis, Brigham Young University, 1950.

Burgon, Glade L. "The Tree of Life as a World Symbol of Divine Origin." Paper for Scripture 651 course at Brigham Young University, 1959.

Christenson, Allen J. "The Sacred Tree and the Ancient Maya." *Journal of Book of Mormon Studies* 6, no. 1 (1997): 1–23.

Clark, John E. "A New Artistic Rendering of Izapa Stela 5: A Step Toward Improved Interpretation." *Journal of Book of Mormon Studies* 8, no. 1 (1999): 22–33.

Draper, Richard D. "Blessed Are They That Do His Commandments." In *Opening the Seven Seals: The Visions of John the Revelator*, 241–42. Salt Lake City: Deseret Book, 1991.

———, and Donald W. Parry. "Seven Promises to Those Who Overcome: Aspects of Genesis 2–3 in the Seven Letters." In *The Temple in Time and Eternity*, edited by Donald W. Parry and Stephen D. Ricks, 123–29. Provo, UT: FARMS, 1999.

Faulconer, James E. "The Olive Tree and the Work of God: Jacob 5 and Romans 11." In Ricks and Welch, *Allegory of the Olive Tree*, 347–66.

Griggs, C. Wilfred. "The Book of Mormon as an Ancient Book." In *Book of Mormon Authorship: New Light on Ancient Origins*, edited by Noel B. Reynolds, 75–101. Provo, UT: FARMS, 1982.

______. "The Tree of Life in Ancient Cultures." *Ensign*, June 1988, 26–31.

Harrop, James D. "Tree Imagery in Scriptures and the Writings of the Church Fathers: Symbols of the Character and Ministry of Jesus Christ." Master's thesis, Brigham Young University, 2008.

Hoskisson, Paul Y. "The Allegory of the Olive Tree in Jacob." In Ricks and Welch, *Allegory of the Olive Tree*, 70–104.

Jackson, Kent P. "The Tree of Life and the Ministry of Christ." In *Studies in Scripture: 1 Nephi to Alma 29*, 34–43. Salt Lake City: Deseret Book, 1987.

Jorgensen, Bruce W. "The Dark Way to the Tree: Typological Unity in the Book of Mormon." In *Literature of Belief: Sacred Scripture and Religious Experience*, edited by Neal E. Lambert, 217–31. Provo, UT: Religious Studies Center, Brigham Young University, 1981.

King, Arthur Henry. "Language Themes in Jacob 5: 'The vineyard of the Lord of hosts is the house of Israel' (Isaiah 5:7)." In Ricks and Welch, *Allegory of the Olive Tree*, 140–73.

Maddox, Julie Adams. "Lehi's Vision of the Tree of Life: An Anagogic Interpretation." Master's thesis, Brigham Young University, 1986.

Miller, Jeanette W. "The Tree of Life, a Personification of Christ." *Journal of Book of Mormon Studies* 2, no. 1 (Spring 1993): 93–106.

Nibley, Hugh. "Checking on Long-Forgotten Lore." In *Since Cumorah*, 189–92. Salt Lake City: Deseret Book and FARMS, 1988.

______. "Lehi's Dreams." In *An Approach to the Book of Mormon*, 253–64. Salt Lake City: Deseret Book and FARMS, 1988.

———. "The Tree of Life." In *Teachings of the Book of Mormon, Semester 1: Transcripts of Lectures Presented to an Honors Book of Mormon Class at Brigham Young University, 1988–90*, 137–49. Provo, UT: FARMS, 2004.

Norman, V. Garth. "The Tree of Life Symbol in Ancient Israel." In *Papers of the Fourteenth Annual Symposium on the Archaeology of the Scriptures*, edited by Forrest R. Hauck, 37–51. Provo, UT: Department of Extension Publications, Brigham Young University, 1963.

Parry, Donald W. "Garden of Eden: Prototype Sanctuary." In *Temples of the Ancient World: Ritual and Symbolism*, edited by Donald W. Parry, 126–29. Salt Lake City: Deseret Book and FARMS, 1994.

Peterson, Daniel C. "Nephi and His Asherah: A Note on 1 Nephi 11:8–23." In *Mormons, Scripture, and the Ancient World: Studies in Honor of John L. Sorenson*, edited by Davis Bitton, 191–243. Provo, UT: FARMS, 1998.

Raish, Martin. "Tree of Life." In *Encyclopedia of Mormonism*, edited by Daniel H. Ludlow, 1486–88. New York: Macmillan, 1992.

Reynolds, Noel B. "Nephite Uses and Interpretations of Zenos." In Ricks and Welch, *Allegory of the Olive Tree*, 21–49.

Richardson, Matthew O. "Vision, Voice, Path, and Rod: Coming to Partake of the Fulness." In *The Fulness of the Gospel: Foundational Teachings from the Book of Mormon: The 32nd Annual Sidney B. Sperry Symposium*, 26–38. Salt Lake City: Deseret Book and Religious Studies Center, Brigham Young University, 2003.

Ricks, Stephen D. "Converging Paths: Language and Cultural Notes on the Ancient Near Eastern Background of the Book of Mormon." In *Echoes and Evidences of the Book of Mormon*, edited by Donald W. Parry, Daniel C. Peterson, and John W. Welch, 397–98. Provo, UT: FARMS, 2002.

———. "Olive Culture in the Second Temple Era and Early Rabbinic Period." In Ricks and Welch, *Allegory of the Olive Tree*, 460–76.

———, and John W. Welch, eds. *The Allegory of the Olive Tree: The Olive, the Bible, and Jacob 5*. Salt Lake City: Deseret Book and FARMS, 1994.

Riddle, Chauncey C. "Code Language in the Book of Mormon," 8–11. FARMS Paper. Provo: UT: Foundation for Ancient Research and Mormon Studies, 1992.

Rust, Richard Dilworth. "'Not Cast Off Forever': Imagery." In *Feasting on the Word: The Literary Testimony of the Book of Mormon*, 179–80. Salt Lake City: Deseret Book and FARMS, 1997.

Seely, David Rolph. "The Allegory of the Olive Tree and the Use of Related Figurative Language in the Ancient Near East and the Old Testament." In Ricks and Welch, *Allegory of the Olive Tree*, 290–304.

Swift, Charles. "'I Have Dreamed a Dream': Typological Images of Teaching and Learning in the Vision of the Tree of Life." PhD diss., Brigham Young University, 2003.

———. "Lehi's Vision of the Tree of Life: Understanding the Dream as Visionary Literature." *Journal of Book of Mormon Studies* 14, no. 2 (2005): 52–63.

Thomas, M. Catherine. "Jacob's Allegory: The Mystery of Christ." In Ricks and Welch, *Allegory of the Olive Tree*, 11–20.

Tvedtnes, John A. "Borrowings from the Parable of Zenos." In Ricks and Welch, *Allegory of the Olive Tree*, 373–426.

———. "Vineyard or Olive Orchard?" In Ricks and Welch, *Allegory of the Olive Tree*, 477–83.

Underwood, Grant. "Jacob 5 in the Nineteenth Century." In Ricks and Welch, *Allegory of the Olive Tree*, 50–69.

Volluz, Corbin T. "Lehi's Dream of the Tree of Life: Springboard to Prophecy." *Journal of Book of Mormon Studies* 2, no. 2 (1993): 14–38.

Welch, John W. "The Narrative of Zosimus and the Book of Mormon." *BYU Studies* 22, no. 3 (Summer 1982): 18–23.

Woodford, Irene B. "The Tree of Life in Ancient America." *Bulletin of the University Archaeological Society*, March 1953.

Non–Latter-day Saint Sources

Altmann, Alexander. "The Gnostic Background of the Rabbinic Adam Legends." *Jewish Quarterly Review* 35 (1944–45): 371–91.

Ameisenowa, Zofja, and W. F. Mainland. "The Tree of Life in Jewish Iconography." *Journal of the Warburg Institute* 2, no. 4 (1939): 326–45.

Barker, Margaret. *The Gate of Heaven: The History and Symbolism of the Temple in Jerusalem.* London: SPCK, 1991.

———. *The Revelation of Jesus Christ*, 328–33. Edinburgh: T&T Clark, 2000.

Bodenstein, W., and O. F. Raum. "A Present Day Zulu Philosopher." *Africa: Journal of the International African Institute* 30, no. 2 (April 1960): 170–79.

Boudreau, Gordon V. *The Roots of Walden and the Tree of Life.* Nashville: Vanderbilt University Press, 1990.

Buhl, Marie-Louise. "The Goddess of the Egyptian Tree Cult." *Journal of Near Eastern Studies* 6 (1947): 80–97.

Buren, E. Douglas van. *Symbols of the Gods in Mesopotamian Art.* Rome: Pontifical Biblical Institute, 1945.

Butterworth, E. A. S. *The Tree at the Navel of the Earth.* Berlin: Walter de Gruyter, 1970.

Childs, Brevard S. "Tree of Knowledge, Tree of Life." In *The Interpreter's Dictionary of the Bible*, edited by George Arthur Buttrick, 4:695–97. New York: Abingdon Press, 1962.

Cleveland, R. L. "Cherubs and the 'Tree of Life' in Ancient South Arabia." *Bulletin of the American Schools of Oriental Research* 172 (December 1963): 55–60.

Clifford, Richard J. *The Cosmic Mountain in Canaan and the Old Testament.* Cambridge, MA: Harvard University, 1972.

Clines, D. J. A. "The Tree of Knowledge and the Law of Yahweh (Psalm XIX)." *Vetus Testamentum* 24 (1974): 8–14.

Cook, Roger C. *The Tree of Life: Image for the Cosmos.* New York: Avon, 1974.

Creach, Jerome F. D. "Like a Tree Planted by the Temple Stream: The Portrait of the Righteous in Psalm 1:3." *Catholic Biblical Quarterly* 61, no. 1 (January 1999): 34–46.

D'Alviella, Eugène. *The Migration of Symbols.* New York: University Books, 1956.

Daniélou, Jean. *Primitive Christian Symbols.* Baltimore: Helicon Press, 1964.

Dillistone, Frederick W. *Christianity and Symbolism.* London: Collins, 1955.

Francke, Sylvia. *The Tree of Life and the Holy Grail: Ancient and Modern Spiritual Paths and the Mystery of Rennes-le-Château.* Forest Row, England: Temple Lodge, 2007.

Freedman, David Noel. "Yahweh of Samaria and His Asherah." *Biblical Archaeologist* 50, no. 4 (December 1987): 241–49.

Freidel, David, Linda Schele, and Joy Parker. *Maya Cosmos: Three Thousand Years on the Shaman's Path.* New York: William Morrow, 1993.

Gaster, Theodor Herzl. *Myth, Legend, and Custom in the Old Testament.* New York: Harper and Row, 1969.

Gilhus, Saelid. "The Tree of Life and the Tree of Death." *Religion: Journal of Religion and Religions* 17 (October 1987): 337–53.

Guénon, René. *Symbolism of the Cross.* London: Luzac, 1958.

James, E. O. *The Tree of Life: An Archaeological Study.* Leiden: E. J. Brill, 1966.

______. "The Tree of Life and the Water of Life." In *Religion und Religionen: Festschrift für Gustav Mensching,* 118–30. Bonn, Germany: 1967.

Johnston, Caryl. *Consecrated Venom: The Serpent and the Tree of Knowledge.* Edinburgh: Floris Books, 2000.

Korsak, Mary Phil. "A Fresh Look at the Garden of Eden." *Semeia* 81 (1998): 131–45.

Kronholm, Tryggve. "The Trees of Paradise in the Hymns of Ephraem Syrus." *Annual of the Swedish Theological Institute* 11 (1977–78): 48–56.

Lecher, G. "The Tree of Life in Indo-European and Islamic Cultures." *Ars Islamica* 4 (1937): 369–416.

Lemaire, André. "Who or What Was Yahweh's Asherah?" *Biblical Archaeology Review* 10, no. 6 (1984): 42–51.

Levin, Arnold Gunnar. "The Tree of Life: Genesis 2:9 and 3:22–24 in Jewish, Gnostic and Early Christian Texts." PhD diss., Harvard University, 1966.

Magné, Jean. *From Christianity to Gnosis and from Gnosis to Christianity: An Itinerary through the Texts to and from the Tree of Paradise*. Translated by A. F. W. Armstrong. Atlanta: Scholars Press, 1993.

Marcus, Ralph. "The Tree of Life in Proverbs." *Journal of Biblical Literature* 62, no. 2 (1943): 117–20.

Meyer, Carol L. *The Tabernacle Menorah: A Synthetic Study of a Symbol from the Biblical Cult*, 95–122. Missoula, MT: Scholars Press, 1976.

Moore, Peter G. "Cross and Crucifixion in Christian Iconography." *Religion* 4 (1974): 104–13.

Mowry, Lucetta. "Revelation 4–5 and Early Christian Liturgical Usage." *Journal of Biblical Literature* 71 (1952): 75–84.

Murray, Robert. "The Vineyard, the Grape, and the Tree of Life." In *Symbols of Church and Kingdom: A Study in Early Syriac Tradition*, 95–130. Cambridge: Cambridge University Press, 1975.

Neumann, Erich. *The Great Mother: An Analysis of the Archetype*. Princeton, NJ: Princeton University Press, 1963.

Nielsen, Kirsten. "Old Testament Metaphors in the New Testament." In *New Directions in Biblical Theology*, edited by Sigfred Pedersen, 126–42. Leiden: E. J. Brill, 1994.

Obbink, H. Th. "The Tree of Life in Eden." *Zeitschrift für die Alttestamentliche Wissenschaft* 46 (1928): 105–12.

Olyan, Saul M. *Asherah and the Cult of Yahweh in Israel*. Atlanta: Scholars Press, 1988.

Parpola, Simo. "The Assyrian Tree of Life: Tracing the Origins of Jewish Monotheism and Greek Philosophy." *Journal of Near Eastern Studies* 52, no. 3 (1993): 161–208.

Porter, Barbara N. "Sacred Trees, Date Palms, and the Royal Persona of Ashurnasirpal II." *Journal of Near Eastern Studies* 52 (1993): 129–39.

Reicke, Bo. "The Knowledge Hidden in the Tree of Paradise." *Journal of Semitic Studies* 1, no. 3 (1956): 193–201.

Reno, Stephen J. *The Sacred Tree as an Early Christian Literary Symbol: A Phenomenological Study*. Saarbrücken, Germany: Alfred Rupp, 1978.

Robinson, B. P. "Symbolism in Exod. 15:22–27." *Revue Biblique* 94, no. 3 (July 1987): 376–88.

Seymour, William Wood. *The Cross in Tradition, History, and Art.* New York: G. P. Putnam's Sons, 1898.

Shimoff, S. R. "Gardens: From Eden to Jerusalem." *Journal for the Study of Judaism* 26 (June 1995): 145–55.

Sitchin, Zecharia. *The Lost Realms.* Santa Fe, NM: Bear, 1990.

Stordalen, Terje. "Man, Soil, Garden: Basic Plot in Genesis 2–3 Reconsidered." *Journal for the Study of the Old Testament* 17, no. 53 (1992): 3–25.

Taylor, Joan E. "The Asherah, the Menorah and the Sacred Tree." *Journal for the Study of the Old Testament* 20, no. 66 (June 1995): 29–54.

Vann, Gerald. *The Paradise Tree: On Living the Symbols of the Church.* New York: Sheed and Ward, 1959.

Weinfeld, Moshe. "Feminine Features in the Imagery of God in Israel: The Sacred Marriage and the Sacred Tree." *Vetus Testamentum* 46, no. 4 (1996): 515–29.

West, Edward N. *The History of the Cross.* New York: Macmillan, 1960.

Widengren, Geo. *The King and the Tree of Life in Ancient Near Eastern Religion.* Uppsala, Sweden: A.-B. Lundequistka Bokhandeln, 1951.

Wiggins, Steve A. *A Reassessment of "Asherah": A Study according to the Textual Sources of the First Two Millennia B.C.E.* Kevelaer, Germany: Butzon und Bercker, 1993.

Winzen, Damasus. *Symbols of Christ: The Old Testament, the New Testament.* New York: P. J. Kenedy, 1955.

Wright, G. R. H. "Joseph's Grave under the Tree by the Omphalos at Shechem." *Vetus Testamentum* 22, no. 4 (1972): 476–86.

Yarden, Leon. *The Tree of Life: A Study of the Menorah, the Seven-Branched Lampstand.* Ithaca, NY: Cornell University Press, 1971.

York, Anthony. "The Maturation Theme in the Adam and Eve Story." In *"Go to the Land I Will Show You": Studies in Honor of Dwight W. Young,* edited by Joseph Coleson and Victor Matthews, 393–410. Winona Lake, IN: Eisenbrauns, 1996.

Citation Index

Subject Index